Edinburgh

Also in the series

Edinburgh

A CULTURAL HISTORY

Donald Campbell

foreword by Allan Massie

Interlink Books

An imprint of Interlink Publishing Group, Inc.
Northampton, Massachusetts

This edition first published 2008 by

INTERLINK BOOKS
An imprint of Interlink Publishing Group, Inc.
46 Crosby Street, Northampton, Massachusetts 01060
www.interlinkbooks.com

Library of Congress Cataloging-in-Publication Data
Campbell, Donald, 1940–
Edinburgh : a cultural history / by Donald Campbell.—
1st American ed. p cm. —(The cities of the imagination)
Includes bibliographical references.
ISBN 978-1-56656-722-0
1. Edinburgh (Scotland)—History. 2. Edinburgh (Scotland)—Intellectual life. 3.
Literary landmarks—Scotland—Edinburgh. 4. Historic buildings—Scotland—
Edinburgh. 5. Authors, Scottish—Homes and haunts—Scotland—Edinburgh. 6.
Edinburgh (Scotland)—Buildings, structures, etc. 7. Edinburgh (Scotland)—In
literature.
I. Title II. Series
DA890.E2C24 2003 941.3'4—dc21
2003012255

Drawings by Wendy Skinner Smith
Cover Images: Baseline Arts; Still Moving Picture Company

Printed in the United States of America

Contents

CHAPTER NINE
ROYAL CITY: HOLYROOD

CHAPTER TEN
OPEN HORIZONS: MULTICULTURAL EDINBURGH

CHAPTER ELEVEN
A GREAT AND ANCIENT CITY: THE EDINBURGH FESTIVAL

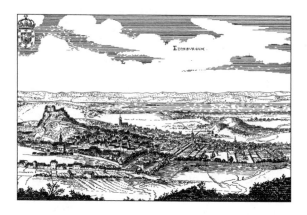

Foreword

There are few cities that have not been made the subject of books. Local piety ensures that someone will sometime write something. But there are not many that repeatedly invite the attention of authors. Edinburgh is one of those that do. In his suggested "Further Reading" Donald Campbell has listed more than thirty books, as well as ten novels set in the city. He might have multiplied both numbers by ten, and still have left many unmentioned.

This inevitably leads to the question: do we need another book about Edinburgh? Actually, it's a dull question which only reviewers ask. The answer anyway is obvious. If it's a good book, it will find its market, no matter how many others have been written on the same topic. Think, for example, of all those written about Mary Queen of Scots or Napoleon. If it isn't, it won't, but will expire quietly.

Campbell's is a good book, written with love and deep knowledge. His qualifications for writing about Edinburgh are excellent. He is a poet, and Edinburgh has inspired poetry for at least six hundred years. He is a dramatist who has written some of the best Scottish plays of the last half-century, and Edinburgh is a city of sharply dramatic contrasts. Finally, though his roots are in Caithness, he was brought up in Edinburgh, educated at Boroughmuir High School, and has lived for many years in the most thoroughly Edinburgh part of the city, the Southside, just by Bruntsfield Links and the Meadows. He knows Edinburgh in and out, its history and its present, the character of its different quarters, its literature and its legends. You couldn't wish for a better guide. Some years ago I myself wrote a book on Edinburgh which I thought well of; it's not half as good as this one.

"The first sight of Edinburgh after an absence is invariably exciting," wrote Edwin Muir in his *Scottish Journey*. This is true. The centre of the city is like a magnificent stage set—no wonder Edinburgh hosts the world's finest Festival. The contrast between the Old Town, which is still essentially the mediaeval city, even though few buildings are older than the seventeenth century and much has disappeared, and the calm classicism of the New Town, has been remarked upon by everyone who has ever written about the place. The opposites are almost trite: Romantic and Classical, darkness and light, mystery and reason, the two-faced city. Curiously, one never tires of them. Yet it is only when one has gone beyond them, and looked more closely, that the city yields to understanding. Edinburgh is a city of sharp divisions; and yet it has—indeed is—a unity. The delight is in the detail; and this Campbell reveals to us.

Despite the hills and the often purgatorial wind, it is a walker's city. (One of the best old books on Edinburgh, by James Bone, is appropriately entitled *The Pedestrian in Edinburgh*.) You can walk from the Castle to the palace of Holyroodhouse in an easy twenty minutes, but if you choose, as you should, to explore every court and close, it will take you the best part of a day.

Stevenson, whose *Picturesque Notes* give such a vivid portrait of nineteenth-century Edinburgh, thought the city's climate pestilential. Yet the violent and often abrupt changes in weather contribute to its character. Some days Edinburgh is grey, dour, forbidding, stern as Calvinism; the next morning may be sparkling and exuberant, putting a spring in your step. Then, everywhere you walk, you happen on unexpected and enticing vistas of the sea or the hills. History presses in on you. Yet everywhere there are glimpses of *rus in urbe*. Stevenson again remarked on this. In no other city, he wrote "does the sight of the country enter so far... The place is full of theatre tricks in the way of scenery. You peep under an arch, you descend stairs that look as if they would land you in a cellar, you turn to the back window of a grimy tenement in a lane:—and behold! you are face to face with distant and bright prospects. You turn a corner, and there is the sun going down into the Highland hills. You look down an alley and see ships tacking for the Baltic."

Campbell gives us the city in all its moods, all its rich variety. He gives us its great men and women too, and writes of them with warm appreciation. But he catches also, as few writers have done, the quiet unremarkable lives of citizens over the centuries. His is a city of lawyers, scholars, medical men and writers—but also a city where for more than a century now the fortunes of its two football teams, Hibs and Hearts, have mattered more to more people than the goings-on in Parliament House—mattered more, it may be, to some of the advocates and judges whose workplace that is.

He has given us the best sort of guide to Edinburgh, one that explores all the quarters of the city, some of which the casual tourist never thinks to visit. It is a true portrait of Edinburgh, that city where past and present co-exist. Many who think they know Edinburgh well will nevertheless find much here that is new to them. Those who come to Edinburgh for the first time will find in this book precisely what they need. It is a celebration of the city which will at the same time enrich the reader's understanding, stimulate his imagination, and inspire his curiosity. What more could you ask for?

—Allan Massie

Acknowledgements

Acknowledgements are due to the following individuals and organizations for assistance in the writing of this book: Kate Burwell, British Council Edinburgh, Jean Campbell, Edinburgh City Council, Edinburgh Room Central Library, Edinburgh Mela, French Institute, John Hamilton, Nicola Ireland, Italian Institute, National Galleries of Scotland, W. K. Ritchie, Terry Sandell, Scottish National Heritage, Dr. Donald Smith, and Visiting Arts.

For Jean, as always

Preface
The Surprising City

Apart from a few years in London—gaining what I am pleased to call my education—I have spent practically my entire life in Edinburgh. I am not, however, a native of the city, but was born in the little town of Wick, in the far north of Scotland. I first arrived in Edinburgh when I was just five years old.

In the beginning, I have to say that I absolutely loathed the place. In the Gorgie/Dalry district, where I grew up, I found myself surrounded by a dark, dirty, noisy, and smelly conglomeration of gray, canyon-like tenements, with thousands of people living in enclosed communities within them. Everything—the streets, shops, houses, faces and clothes of the people—appeared to be covered in a kind of grayish dust, the sound of traffic thundered in my ears all day long, and the smell of nearby factories, manufacturing yeast, glue, and rubber, almost made me physically sick. Accustomed as I was to the open fields and big sky of Caithness, at first I felt trapped, restricted and, I suppose, more than a little unhappy.

Then, one sunny Saturday morning, shortly after I had started school, I accompanied my mother on a shopping trip to Princes Street. As the tram (we still had trams then) emerged from Shandwick Place, the sight of the Castle, seeming to thrust itself up into the sky, suddenly confronted me. This cannot possibly have been the first time I had witnessed this sight—I was certainly aware of the Castle's existence before then—but it was the first of many surprises that the city was to hold in store for me.

Edinburgh seems to thrive on surprise. It is the only place that I know where you will find restaurateurs who promote their business by *refusing* to advertise. The New Town, in particular, is full of eating-houses that are hidden away from public view, presumably because the thrill of discovery is understood to add to the charm of the meal. This principle, moreover, is not restricted to restaurants but comes into play in all kinds of cultural contexts.

Often enough, during the course of writing this book, I would visit some familiar part of the city in order to confirm my knowledge, only to find that I had been completely wrong. When writing my chapter on the Old Town, for instance, I was absolutely convinced that the Magdalen Chapel, where the first act of the Scottish Reformation took place, was a shell of a building that had been allowed to deteriorate beyond repair. On going to the Cowgate to confirm this belief, I discovered that not only was this not the case, but that what I had thought to be the Magdalen Chapel was another building entirely!

The city that I have come to know is not now and never will be the city of popular legend. I simply cannot recognize the Edinburgh that Irvine Welsh defines in his novel, *Maribou Stork Nightmares*, as "a dirty, cold, wet, run-down slum; a city of dull, black tenements and crass, concrete housing schemes." The tenements in which I grew up were neither dull nor black—as a matter of fact, they were usually gray and sometimes red—and, mercifully, I have never had the misfortune to live on *any* housing scheme. In any case, I rather subscribe to Hugh MacDiarmid's dictum that "people do not live in slums, but the other way around." Although I would not, of course, deny the authenticity of Welsh's perception, I certainly do not share it.

Perceptions are one thing: stereotypes are quite another. For some reason that I have never been able to understand, there is a certain species of Scottish intellectual—in all other respects civilized, intelligent, reasonable and rational people—who tend to become positively batty when it comes to discussing Edinburgh. What on earth, for instance, could have persuaded Tom Nairn to write the following?

> *Edinburgh's soul is bible-black, pickled in boredom by centuries of sermons, swaddled in the shabby gentility of the Kirk—what difference could 21 years of Festival make to this? In Edinburgh the iron age of Calvinism has long since turned into rust, and it is this rust which chokes and corrodes the eye and the ear.*

Such a view is, of course, complete poppycock. Yet it does raise two important points. First, there might have been some validity in this criticism if it had been made in the 1920s, when church affairs still had some influence on the lifestyle of the city. Yet Nairn's essay appeared in *The New Statesman* in 1967. Secondly, even when these affairs *were* dominant, they could hardly be described as genteel. As I have tried to show here, the pre-occupations of the Scottish Church have always had more to do with social reform than with theology.

For me, the city that Nairn describes has always seemed a fiction, if not exactly a myth—and I have always felt obliged to question it. Over the past thirty years, my work as a dramatist has led to a creative exploration of some of the lesser known aspects of Edinburgh culture, including theater history, prostitution, and football, and has included successful stage adaptations of Edinburgh's most celebrated novelists: Sir Walter Scott and Robert Louis Stevenson. In addition to this, the three years that I spent as Writer-in-Residence to Edinburgh Schools (and, to a lesser extent, during my time as Resident Playwright at the Royal Lyceum Theatre and, much later, RLF Fellow at Napier University) involved visiting communities in every part of the city. In the process, I have discovered a cultural ambiance that would astonish the likes of Tom Nairn.

The people of Edinburgh can be extremely surprising in this respect. Visitors have often declared themselves agreeably overwhelmed by the extent of hospitality, generosity and sheer friendliness they receive in our city. In 1949, for instance, the poet T. S. Eliot visited Edinburgh for the opening performance of his play, *The Cocktail Party*, which premiered at the Festival that year. On arrival at his hotel, as he reached for his wallet to pay the fare, he was immediately told to put his money away. "I would never dream," the driver told him, "of accepting a fare from such a distinguished poet."

If the people of Edinburgh have anything in common, it is a certain sense of security in our civic identity. Although I have never heard any of my fellow citizens claim that Edinburgh is at the center of the universe, I do know that this is a proposition with which most of them would not necessarily disagree. At the very least, unlike their counterparts in other cities—Glasgow, for instance—they feel no need to seek the approval of others for anything that takes place here.

Edinburgh is a capital city. This simple fact is crucial to any real understanding of this place. Other cities may owe their status to industry or commerce or academia, but in the case of Edinburgh, the opposite is true. Although it has its share of industry, has an important financial sector, and boasts no fewer than four universities, the presence of such institutions in Edinburgh is entirely due to the fact that the city is the capital of Scotland.

This is not simply a matter of history—although it is certainly that in part. (In the chapters that follow, I have made an effort to concentrate on the modern city, but it is never really possible to get away from history in Edinburgh.) Capital status may have been conferred through historical accident, but the fact that it has been maintained through the centuries is a tribute to the dignity, sense of style and, above all, the continuously engaging personality of the city of Edinburgh.

—Donald Campbell
Edinburgh

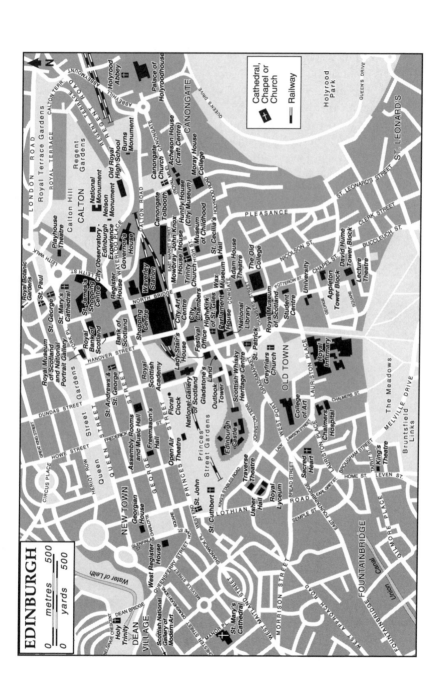

INTRODUCTION

The View from Arthur's Seat

"It seems like a city built on precipices, a perilous city. Great roads rush down hill like rivers in spate. Great buildings rush up like rockets."
G. K. Chesterton, *Illustrated London News,* 1905

Edinburgh resounds with history. As one of the city's most beloved poets, Robert Garioch, was fond of saying, it is a place where time does not pass but simply adds up. It is undoubtedly true that there are certain places in Edinburgh that tend to hold on to a particular function even when their origins are changed out of recognition. At the very heart of the city, for instance, there is an area of open ground, immediately adjacent to the Royal Scottish Academy, which used to be occupied by a wooden theater called the Victorian Temple. Although this building was demolished many decades ago, the site continues to be used, during the Festival and at other times, for the performance of street theater. History in Edinburgh, it seems, is not to be denied.

Yet even the most cursory study will quickly reveal that geography, too, has played no small part in the city's creation. This can best be appreciated by making a stiff climb to Edinburgh's highest point, the summit of Arthur's Seat.

Here, the whole city is laid out at one's feet and it is possible to take in at a glance the complete story of Edinburgh's development. On the high ground immediately opposite, the sight of the ancient castle, first established in the seventh century by a Northumbrian king, tells us immediately where the city had its genesis. Ever since the twelfth century, when it became established as a royal residence, Edinburgh Castle has functioned as an important symbol of Edinburgh and, indeed, of all Scotland. The sight of its proud eminence above the city—particularly when the sun is shining—makes it quite obvious how this function came about.

From this vantage-point, it is obvious, too, how the city began to develop on the ridge that forms the main approach to the Castle. The disposition of the Royal Mile, with its towering tenements and narrow closes, seems entirely logical from this point of view, as it tumbles down the hill to link the Castle with the equally ancient and picturesque suburb of Holyrood. This "great street" (as one distinguished visitor called it) simply grew outwards from the Castle, with buildings being added as they were required, and became the focal point of the rich cultural period known as the Scottish Enlightenment. This episode in Scottish history—running roughly from the Act of Union in 1707 until the death of Sir Walter Scott in 1832—was noted for its intellectual rigour and, for this reason, has largely been discredited by the modern Scottish consciousness. Yet there is absolutely no doubt of its continuing influence on the city of Edinburgh in terms of architecture, academia and, indeed, political discourse.

In the towering tenements of the Royal Mile, sometimes described as "the world's first skyscrapers", intellectual giants such as Adam Smith and David Hume lived cheek-by-jowl with aristocracy and common tradesmen, thereby initiating a certain democratic culture that is still quite noticeable in the city today. The march of history has removed most of the original tenements, replacing them with similar structures that date from the Georgian and Victorian periods, merging together in an outline of gray sandstone, but one quite distinctive feature has survived the centuries. The crown-shaped tower of the High Kirk of St. Giles has been a permanent feature of the Edinburgh landscape since the twelfth century, signifying the important part that religious affairs have played in the development of Edinburgh's culture.

On the lee of the ridge, the chaotic growth of the Old Town can be clearly identified. The wynds and closes, in a hotchpotch of building styles, can seem so confusing at ground level, yet take on a certain order, not to say personality, when viewed from above. This was where Sir Walter Scott was born, where Robert Burns enjoyed his first celebrity, where John Knox preached his most effective sermons, where Henry Cockburn practiced law, and where Sir Patrick Geddes conducted his first experiments in town planning. This is also where the Scottish Reformation was initiated, where Francis Jeffrey founded the *Edinburgh Review*, and where the world's largest arts festival, the Edinburgh Festival Fringe, first saw the light of day.

Yet it has a darker side, too. It was here that Lord Darnley, consort to Mary, Queen of Scots, was foully murdered, where Burke and Hare trapped their defenseless victims, and where the career of Deacon William Brodie provided the inspiration for Robert Louis Stevenson's *The Strange Case of Dr Jekyll and Mr Hyde.* It was here, too, that, in an act of quite astonishing civic vandalism, some fine old buildings in the vernacular classical style were demolished in the late twentieth century. While this has proved a severe loss to the character and appearance of the Old Town, as David Daiches points out, "enough remains for its history to be visible in its streets and buildings to a quite conspicuous degree."

Edinburgh's world-famous Medical School, where James Young Simpson discovered chloroform and Joseph Lister developed antiseptic surgery, has had, of course, an important part to play in this history and is still in business here, educating physicians. Although the Medical School itself cannot be seen from our viewpoint, there is a clear view of Old College, central institution of the University of Edinburgh, where figures as diverse as Charles Darwin, Edward Jenner, Thomas Carlyle and Sir Arthur Conan Doyle received an education. This historic building was planned by one great architect, Robert Adam, and completed by another, William Playfair.

The work of these architects can also be seen on the other side of the ridge, where the elegant design of the New Town stands in stark contrast to the urban confusion of the Old. Here, our view from Arthur's Seat demonstrates quite clearly the rationale behind the New Town's creation. The growth of the city's population during the eighteenth century meant that the Old Town was bursting at the seams, so that the expansion of the city was only ever possible in a northerly direction. The vision of Provost George Drummond for an extension that would "enlarge and beautify the town" lies before us in its scrupulously arranged implementation.

We can see how the drained basin of the Nor' Loch was transformed into the green luxuriance of Princes Street Gardens, with the Ross Bandstand sitting sedately at its center. The rocket-like structure of the Scott Monument is clearly visible, as are two great hotels: the Caledonian and the NB (formerly the North British, now the New Balmoral, but always known in Edinburgh by its initials), standing like sentinels at each end of the platform-like image of Princes Street itself.

Although the New Town is usually discussed in the singular (and will be here), we can see that its growth was just as organic as that of the Old Town, coming in a number of stages. This visual rendering of the ideals of the eighteenth century remains one of the most elegant urban areas in Europe, its neoclassical style as striking today as when it was first conceived. If, however, we can gain some appreciation of the extent to which James Craig's vision for the New Town was realized, we can also discern the logic of the spread eastward—to the community around the Calton Hill—and westward to the West End. The view of the Firth of Forth shows us why expansion to the coast became inevitable, while the distant view of the Pentland hills indicates a further restriction to the city's growth. All this is quite evident at the summit of Arthur's Seat.

Equally evident is the diversity of urban landscape. The Royal Palace of Holyrood is immediately beneath one's feet, as is the emerging modern building of the Scottish Parliament. Yet this diversity is not always so edifying, including as it does some of the disasters of modern town planning. If the sandstone solidity of the Southside tenements can be seen, so too can the tower blocks that have been established in less comfortable parts of the city.

Nevertheless, we are presented here with the opportunity of seeing Edinburgh as a unity. This is the context, for instance, in which Miss Jean Brodie received *her own* education, in which Inspector John Rebus continues to make his inquiries, the image of Edinburgh that Sir Henry Irving always remembered and Robert Louis Stevenson could never forget. It is also in this context, of course, that one of the world's greatest arts festivals has its being.

In order to explore the city thoroughly, it has been necessary to deconstruct this view, to unpack it, as it were, in order that the constituent parts of the city can be examined. Yet it should not be forgotten that these parts relate to each other as parts of a greater whole. Whatever the differences in lifestyle, income or cultural attitude, every Edinburgh citizen, in whatever neighborhood they live, is aware of belonging to that city that can be seen from the summit of Arthur's Seat.

CHAPTER ONE

The Citadel: Edinburgh Castle

> *"The castle on a lofty rock is so strongly grounded, bounded, and founded, that by force of man it can never be confounded; the foundation and walls are unpenetrable, the rampiers impregnable, the bulwarks invincible, no way but one to it is or can be possible to be made passable. In a word, I have seen many straights and fortresses in Germany, the Netherlands, Spain, and England, but they must all give place to this unconquered castle, both for strength and situation."*
>
> John Taylor, *The Pennyless Pilgrimage*, 1618

Castle Rock is where Edinburgh began. The very name of the city tells us that.

To understand these distant origins, we must go back to the seventh century, to a time when a large swathe of what is now southern Scotland formed part of the ancient kingdom of Northumbria. Edwin of Deira, who acceded to the Northumbrian throne in 616, seems to have been a rather devout monarch—an early Christian convert, he was canonized shortly after his death in 633—but he was also a warlike leader, an expansionist who extended his power as far west as Anglesey and Man and who, for a time, held sway over most of England. He established the first stronghold on Castle Rock, which was then known as "Lookout Hill", with a view no doubt to securing his northern border against the Picts. This fortress first became known by the name that survives in our Celtic languages, *Dun-Eideann*—literally Edwin's fort—later anglicized into Edwinesburch, of which the name we use today is simply a contraction.

Over the centuries, the Castle has fulfilled many functions: royal residence, state prison, and, not least, storehouse of Scotland's national treasures. Although it no longer possesses a garrison—the last was finally withdrawn in 1923—it is still guarded and retains a number of military connections. It is the headquarters of the Army's Scottish Division, houses a number of military museums, and accommodates the Scottish National War Memorial. It ceased to have any kind of military use many years ago, however, and today functions as one of the most popular tourist attractions in Europe.

When it was first established, the Castle bore little resemblance to the building or buildings that we know today, being simply a collection of huts enclosed within a wooden palisade. As the kingdom of Northumbria declined and the territory we now call Scotland began to emerge, centuries of war—between the Scots, the Picts, the Strathclyde Britons, the Vikings and, of course, the English—led to the stronghold changing hands many times, thereby increasing its fortification. Yet it did not begin to assume its present form until after 1314, when, as we shall see, the Castle was captured and almost completely destroyed by the Scottish army under Thomas Randolph.

The Castle's most accessible feature is the Esplanade, the open land that lies between the Castle gate and the Royal Mile. Roughly fourteen hundred square yards in area, ringed by walls and railings, the Esplanade was constructed in 1753 as a ceremonial parade ground. Prior to that date, as part of Castlehill, it was a place of execution, particularly of witches. As late as 1659, five women were "worryit at the stake" (i.e. strangled, then burned) for "renouncing their baptism and dancing with the devil." A small tablet fountain was installed at the foot of the Esplanade in 1894, in commemoration of the suffering of these women. This is just one of some half-dozen monuments which are to be found on the Esplanade's perimeter. These are mostly military, commemorating Scottish regiments and soldiers. The most striking is that of Field Marshal Earl Haig, depicting the First World War commander on horseback. This statue was created by the sculptor, G. E. Wade and presented (for some obscure reason) by a leading citizen of Bombay, Sir Dhunjibhoy Bomanji. The other monument of interest is the tomb of Ensign Ewart, an Edinburgh boy who won fame at the Battle of Waterloo by his single-handed capture of the Eagle of the French 45th Infantry.

Apart from providing access to the Castle, the Esplanade would appear to fulfill no function whatsoever and, indeed, it is used for most of the year as nothing more than a convenient parking space for those who have business in or near the Castle. Every August, however, the space is transformed into a temporary amphitheater for the staging of a spectacular event that is transmitted to television screens all over the world: the Edinburgh Military Tattoo.

The Military Tattoo

Although it runs alongside the Edinburgh International Festival, the Tattoo is not, and never has been, under the Festival's management. Yet there is a direct connection between the two events. The inaugural Festival of 1947, despite its success, found itself open to charges of elitism, with specific reference to the absence of Scottish content. These charges, which led directly to the establishment of the Edinburgh Fringe, the plethora of small and "alternative" events, also served to create the Military Tattoo. As a matter of fact, the Tattoo could claim, with justice, to be the oldest and grandest Fringe show of them all!

Its beginnings were modest enough. In 1948 and 1949, under the direction of Colonel George Malcolm of Poltalloch, displays of piping and highland dancing took place each evening on the Castle Esplanade. Then, as now, such displays were far from being uncommon in Edinburgh during the summer, and, initially at least, much of their appeal lay in their location. In 1950, however, Brigadier Alasdair Maclean CBE of the Queen's Own Cameron Highlanders took over from Colonel Malcolm and began to create the Tattoo as we know it today. For the next sixteen years, Brigadier Maclean traveled the world in search of participants, engaging contributions from places as far apart as Denmark and Singapore. With every passing year, the Tattoo became more and more of a spectacle.

The popularity of the event is tremendous, as the poet George Bruce describes in his *Festival in the North* (1975):

> *The appeal is world-wide—one elderly lady has made the pilgrimage annually from Pennsylvania for many years—and the devotion from many south of the Border, especially the North of England, is such that they make the journey to Edinburgh for the Tattoo alone but, all in all, it touches most deeply the Scots...The pipes and drums provide the most inspiriting music of all and the one piper who ends the Tattoo on the battlements brings a melancholy beauty that removes each Scot at least, and many others, to those places of the heart where listening is everything and speech nothing.*

By the time those words were written, more than twenty-five years ago, the spectacle had been witnessed on the Esplanade by more than five million people. Television coverage, of course, has since multiplied this figure a great many times over, but there is something particularly appealing about being part of the audience on the Esplanade. In order to take full advantage of the floodlighting, Tattoo performances necessarily take place late in the evening and, the Scottish climate being what it is, the temperature is not always at a comfortable level. People arrive by the busload from all over the country, well wrapped up and carrying rugs and thermos flasks. As they take their places on the temporary seating, a picnic atmosphere is created, making a substantial contribution to the overall experience. And performance here matches setting so perfectly that it is difficult to imagine the Tattoo taking place anywhere else. Within the Castle itself, history and romance come together in a conjunction that is no less ideal.

Statues and Heroes
At the Castle gate, as one takes the drawbridge across the ancient (and now redundant) moat, the first sight that catches the eye is that of two, life-size bronze statues, standing on each side of the portcullis. These were made by the modern Scottish sculptors, Alexander Carrick and T. J. Clapperton, and depict Scotland's two great heroes—Sir William Wallace (c. 1270-1305) and King Robert the Bruce (1274-1329)—in full battle attire.

These are the men who gave definition to the Scottish identity. They are both historical figures, of course, yet somehow they seem to be rather more than that. Wallace, in particular, has a mythical dimension, as demonstrated by the success of the recent film, *Braveheart*, which depicts him as a kind of Scottish Robin Hood. (There is something of an irony, therefore, in the fact that this film has been criticized in some parts of the Scottish media for what commentators are pleased to describe as "a lack of historical authenticity". Legends, by their very nature, do not require authentication.) It was Wallace who initiated the Wars of Independence, and although his victory over the English at Stirling Bridge in 1297 did not prove to be decisive, it earned him an unrivaled place in Scottish affections. On the six hundredth anniversary of his most famous victory, a former Prime Minister of the United Kingdom, Lord Roseberry summed up his appeal in the following words.

There are junctures in the affairs of men when what is wanted is a Man—not treasures, not fleets, not legions, but a Man—the man of the moment, the man of the occasion, the man of Destiny, whose spirit attracts and unites and inspires, whose capacity is congenial to the crisis, whose powers are equal to the convulsion—the child and the outcome of the storm... We recognize in Wallace one of these men—a man of Fate given to Scotland in the storms of the thirteenth century. It is that fact, the fact of his destiny and his fatefulness, that succeeding generations have instinctively recognized.

Robert the Bruce holds a rather different place in Scottish affections, being thought of as the man who, by his victory over Edward II at Bannockburn, put an end to English aggression for good. (This is not strictly accurate. The death of King Robert in 1329 was followed by a second, rather messier, War of Independence, which only ended when the English king decided that his troops were needed elsewhere.) It was on King Robert's behalf that the nobles and commons of Scotland wrote a letter to Pope John XXII that is now known as the Declaration of Arbroath. This is the document that, more than any other, embodies the sovereignty of the Scottish people, with its ringing notification that "for so long as a mere hundred of us live, we will never submit to the dominion of England."

Yet there is a mythical dimension present in Bruce also—that of the Scottish King Arthur—and, more than any other Scot who ever lived, he is regarded as the Father of the Nation. A distinguished Scottish historian of the twentieth century, Agnes Mure Mackenzie writes glowingly of him in her *The Kingdom of Scotland* (1940):

It was the secret of his power as leader that he had, magnificently, the human touch. The outcome of the controlled force in his nature was a noble courtesy that showed to the humblest—though it could, when occasion required, be a sharp-edged weapon. Men so treated know they are recognized as men, and when they are trusted to work in great affairs, feel responsible for them, and rise to that. Bruce not only trusted them but knew how to trust them, and (what was no less essential) he won their trust by a method that is simple if not easy: whatever he asked them to bear, hunger or weariness or long odds of danger, he would bear with

them, and better than the best, and keep them aware there was reason
for endurance, aware of what things alone are to be feared: and that
awareness is the heart of courage.

The positioning of these two figures on each side of the Castle gate has a certain ceremonial purpose, which makes an immediate impression on all visitors. Within these walls, it seems to say, is something so precious and vital that it requires the protection of heroes. As one passes the Guardhouse in order to begin the ascent that leads to the highest part of the Castle, known as the Citadel, the atmosphere is positively medieval. At the very least, one has a distinct feeling of stepping into another age.

The Citadel

At 440 feet above sea level, the Citadel is the highest point of Castle Rock and is where most of the Castle's most visited features are to be found. The highest point of all is occupied by the Scottish National War Memorial. Built on a site that was previously occupied by barrack buildings, there is an elegiac quality about this imposing building, which was designed by Sir Robert Lorimer. Inaugurated in 1927 in memory of the fallen of the First World War, it houses many regimental memorials and battle honors. The names of those who died during the conflict are listed by number and regiment in its Roll of Honour, and it contains a small chapel—the Shrine—where the act of remembrance takes a less specific, yet rather more public form. There are stained glass windows and other decorations, including the Royal Casket (given by George V and Queen Mary), that contains a hundred thousand names of the fallen. The most intriguing symbol of all, however, is to be found on the floor of the Shrine. Here, Castle Rock itself has been allowed to project, as if to indicate the sure foundation on which the Memorial is built.

The War Memorial overlooks Crown Square, once the mustering-point of the Castle's garrison. This was the setting for a rather curious ghost story, based on events which reportedly took place in 1651, shortly after Charles II's coronation at Scone and Cromwell's victory over the Scots at Dunbar, when a Colonel William Dundas commanded the Royalist garrison.

The great fear at that time was that Cromwell would march on Edinburgh. Late one night, the sentry on duty heard the sound of marching, accompanied by drumbeats, and sounded the alarm by firing his musket. Colonel Dundas was immediately informed, but by the time he arrived at the sentry-post, the sound had gone and there was no sign of any attack. The sentry was immediately put under arrest and replaced by another soldier. After a short time, the second sentry heard the same sound and, once again, the alarm was raised. Yet again, the Colonel was called and yet again there was no sign of Cromwell's army. This time, however, Colonel Dundas took personal charge of the sentry-post and, before too long, heard the same sounds as his sentries. As on the two previous occasions, no enemy appeared. In the event, Cromwell's army bypassed Edinburgh and pushed on to capture Perth.

Nowadays Crown Square is the location of a number of private homes, occupied exclusively by Army personnel, whose presence adds a human dimension to the Castle's historic atmosphere. Adjoining Crown Square is the Scottish Naval and Military Museum, where, among a unique array of relics, portraits, medals, colors, trophies, and uniforms of the Scottish fighting forces through the centuries, there is an extraordinary series of oak statuettes by Pilkington Jackson, representing the development of Scottish uniforms. On the southern side of the square stands one of the most historic of all Castle buildings, the Banqueting Hall, with its museum of armor. The exhibits on display here include the gun carriage on which the body of Queen Victoria was conveyed in 1901 from Osborne House on the Isle of Wight and the personal arms of many Scottish sovereigns.

For some reason, the Banqueting Hall is always associated with James IV, although it was certainly in existence at least a century before his reign (1488-1513). It was the site of the earliest meetings of the old Scots Estates (Parliament) and for this reason it is sometimes known as Parliament Hall. At one time, it functioned as the garrison hospital, but history mainly celebrates its use as a place for the holding of state banquets. It was here, in 1633, that a banquet was given in honor of Charles I, on the occasion of his first visit as king to Scotland. Exactly fifteen years later, a similar occasion was held in honor of Oliver Cromwell! The Banqueting Hall is still occasionally used for such a purpose, by either the Queen or Scotland's First Minister.

Beneath the Banqueting Hall are a number of stone-vaulted chambers of great antiquity. This part of the Castle is accessible to the public only under the direction of a guide and includes the reservoirs, which once supplied the fortress with water, and the dungeons, where French prisoners were held during the Napoleonic Wars. More than a century earlier, on July 27, 1689, a Jacobite prisoner, Lord Balcarres had a supernatural experience in these dungeons. One night, just as he was about to go to sleep, he was surprised by the arrival of an unexpected visitor whom Balcarres immediately recognized as his friend, Graham of Claverhouse, Viscount Dundee. Knowing that Dundee was in command of a Royalist army in the north, Balcarres must have been surprised to meet his friend in such circumstances. Before he could ask him how he came to be in prison, the figure of Dundee simply looked at Balcarres and slowly disappeared. It was not until much later that Balcarres learned that "Bonnie Dundee" (as he is described in the famous song) had that day been killed at the Battle of Killiecrankie.

It is from these dungeons that Robert Louis Stevenson's hero makes his thrilling escape in the unfinished novel *St. Ives* (1897):

The tunnel was cleared, the stake driven, the rope extended. As I moved forward to the place, many of my comrades caught me by the hand and wrung it, an attention I could well have done without...

The line was knotted at intervals of eighteen inches; and to the inexpert it may seem as if it should have been even easy to descend. The trouble was, this devil of a piece of rope appeared to be inspired, not with life alone, but with a personal malignity against myself. It turned to the one side, paused for a moment, and then spun me like a toasting-jack to the other; slipped like an eel from the clasp of my feet; kept me all the time in the most outrageous fury of exertion; and hashed me at intervals against the face of the rock. I had no eyes to see with; and I doubt if there was anything to see but darkness. I must occasionally have caught a gasp of breath, but it was quite unconscious. And the whole forces of my mind were so consumed with losing hold and getting it again, that I could scarce have told whether I was going up or coming down.

Of a sudden I knocked against the cliff with such a thump as almost bereft me of my sense; and, as reason twinkled back I was amazed to find that I was in a state of rest, that the face of the precipice here inclined outwards at an angle which relieved me almost wholly of the burthen of my own weight and that one of my feet was safely planted on a ledge. I drew one of the sweetest breaths in my experience, hugged myself against the rope, and closed my eyes in a kind of ecstasy of relief. It occurred to me next to see how far I was advanced on my unlucky journey, a point on which I had not a shadow of a guess. I looked up: there was nothing above me but the blackness of the night and the fog. I craned timidly forward and looked down. There, upon a floor of darkness, I beheld a certain pattern of hazy lights, some of them aligned as in thoroughfares, others standing apart as in solitary houses; and before I could well realise it, or had in the least estimated my distance, a wave of nausea and vertigo warned me to lie back and close my eyes. In this situation I had really but the one wish, and that was: something else to think of! Strange to say, I got it: a veil was torn from my mind, and I saw what a fool I was—what fools we had all been—and that I had no business to be thus dangling between earth and heaven by my arms. The only thing to have done was to have attached me to a rope and lowered me, and I had never the wit to see it till that moment!

I filled my lungs, got a good hold on my rope, and once more launched myself on the descent…

Sometime early in the nineteenth century, so the story goes, the entrance to a subterranean tunnel was discovered in the dungeons. The authorities were naturally interested (it might, after all, have been an escape route) and ordered an investigation. Since the entrance was too small for a full-grown man, they decided to use a ten-year-old boy and, for the purposes of the investigation, supplied him with a small drum. As the boy made his way down the tunnel, he continued to beat his drum and the investigators were able to follow his progress. This led them through the Castle and down the Royal Mile until, at a spot very near to where the visitors' center at the Tron stands today, the drumbeats came to an abrupt end. As for the boy, he was never seen again and, as a result, the investigation was abandoned and the entrance to the tunnel sealed up.

Among the many legends associated with the Castle, this is possibly the most persistent. While there are a number of variations in the telling—sometimes the leading figure in the story is a piper rather than a drummer—it seems to be widely believed. As Jan-Andrew Henderson suggests in his fascinating study of underground Edinburgh, *The Town Below the Ground*, it may simply be a folk-tale, invented as an object lesson for naughty children. On the other hand, there may very well be some truth in the existence of the tunnel. There must have been many times during the Castle's history when a secret route to the outside would have proved useful.

Crown Square is also where the Royal Apartments are situated. Here, once again, history and legend come together. In the southeast corner is the bedroom where, on June 10, 1566, Mary, Queen of Scots gave birth to James VI of Scotland and I of England. In 1830 the remains of a coffin, some infant bones and fragments of clothing were discovered hidden in the wall of this room. This gave rise to the legend that the boy who became "the wisest fool in Christendom" was, in fact, a changeling and not the true monarch at all. In addition, there is another tradition that states that the infant prince was taken from the Castle, to escape capture by the queen's enemies, by being lowered from a window in this room.

National Treasures

Adjoining the Royal Apartments is the Crown Room, where the Scottish regalia—otherwise known as "the Honours of Scotland"—are on display. These comprise the crown, the sceptre, the sword of state and the Lord Treasurer's rod of office. Although the crown is made of gold, the sceptre of silver and the workmanship of the other artifacts of the highest order, the decorative jewels are mostly of semi-precious stones: freshwater pearls, amethyst, imitation sapphire, etc. Yet although these Scottish crown jewels are by no means as opulent as their English counterparts, they are very ancient and are valued as such. In November 1996 they were joined by an artifact that is even plainer in appearance and of even greater antiquity: the *Lia Fail* or Stone of Destiny, also known as the Stone of Scone. This famous relic is simply a large block of sandstone, more than 400 lb in weight, with a metal ring attached to each end.

Seven centuries earlier, during the First War of Independence, Edward I, the so-called "Hammer of the Scots" ordered the Stone to be taken south to Westminster Abbey, where it was incorporated into the Coronation Chair. This of course was an attempt to weaken Scottish resolve, but its effect was to give the Stone potency as a symbol of Scottish nationhood. On Christmas Eve, 1950, four Glasgow University students, led by Iain Hamilton (who would later, somewhat ironically, follow a distinguished career at the Scottish Bar) caused a sensation when they managed to steal the Stone from Westminster Abbey and bring it back to Scotland. In the face of a somewhat hysterical reaction from the English authorities, involving roadblocks, border patrols, and the dispatch north of senior Scotland Yard detectives, the Stone was eventually returned.

This created a legend to the effect that those involved in the event had a copy made, which was returned in place of the genuine Stone. If this is true—and Hamilton, who really ought to know, has strenuously repudiated the story—then the Stone that was returned from Westminster in 1996 is a counterfeit.

It may be, however, that the Stone that Hamilton and Co. repatriated was itself a counterfeit, for there is another legend to the effect that the original theft, by Edward I, was of a copy and that the true Stone has never left Scotland. According to this version of events, the genuine Stone of Scone can be seen today in a church building in Dundee.

Whatever the truth of these tales, the fact remains that the Stone that is currently held in Edinburgh Castle is recognized as the genuine article, and was the seat upon which the ancient kings of Scotland received their coronation.

St. Margaret's Chapel

One of the strongest and ablest of these monarchs was Malcolm III (c. 1031-93), who was crowned at Scone in 1058. This is Shakespeare's Malcolm, the son of Duncan I, who escaped into exile, at the court of Edward the Confessor, after the death of his father at the hands of Maelbeatha (Macbeth), in 1040. After an absence of seventeen years, Malcolm returned to Scotland and took his revenge on the usurper at Lumphanan on Deeside in 1057. Known to history as Malcolm

Canmore after his Gaelic byname, *Ceann Mor* (literally "great head", although whether this refers to his anatomy, his intellect or, indeed, his personality, is unclear), his memory and that of his queen survives in the oldest part of Edinburgh Castle: St. Margaret's Chapel.

The story of the marriage of Malcolm Canmore and Queen Margaret (1045-93) is an exceptionally romantic one. In 1066, following the victory at Hastings of William of Normandy, the remains of the Saxon royal family, Edgar Atheling and his sisters Margaret and Christina, fled for refuge into Scotland. They arrived, so tradition has it, at a spot on the Firth of Forth that later became known as St. Margaret's Hope, and were entertained at Dunfermline by King Malcolm, who very quickly fell in love with Margaret. The following passage from the *Anglo-Saxon Chronicle* describes Malcolm's courtship.

> *Then the King Malcolm began to yearn for (Edgar's) sister Margaret as his wife, but (Edgar) and all his men long refused; and she herself long opposed it; and said she would have neither him nor any one, if the sublime mercy would grant to her that she might please the mighty Lord in maidenhood with bodily heart in this short life, in pure continence.*
>
> *The King eagerly urged her brother until he said "yea" to it, and indeed he dared not do otherwise, because they had come into his power.*

If this seems to suggest a somewhat rough wooing, the tradition is that the marriage itself was, or at least became, a genuine love-match. After Margaret's death, an account of her life as Queen of Scots was written by her confessor, Father Turgot, Prior of Durham and Bishop of St. Andrews. A copy of this text survives today in the British Museum and contains many stories of the mutual devotion between Malcolm and his queen. Turgot also records that, after the death of Malcolm at Alnwick in 1093, Margaret prayed for her own death, a request that was fulfilled just three days later.

The true significance of the marriage (one ought to say partnership) of Malcolm and Margaret lies in the extent to which they brought Scotland in touch with new ideas which were beginning to emerge in Europe as the Dark Ages came to an end. Margaret, for instance, seems to have been particularly keen on a new style of architecture that we now describe as Norman. According to Turgot, she initiated a number of substantial new church buildings in this style. (Another writer, Ordericus Vitalis, tells us that, in addition, she was responsible for the restoration of the monastery at Iona, which had fallen to ruin since the time of St. Columba.) Since the chapel that commemorates her name is the oldest specimen of Norman architecture in Scotland, it seems reasonable to assume that this was another of her projects, although there are at least two other theories. One is that Malcolm built it for Margaret's personal use. This also seems reasonable, as does the second, that her son, David I (1084-1153), built the chapel in her memory.

The chapel is very small, its interior measuring little more than 27 feet from east to west and nine feet in height. The walls are unadorned, and it is only the presence of a small altar, upon which rests an open bible, that makes one aware that this is a place intended for worship. Even so, within this plain and limited space there is an atmosphere of peace and sanctity so palpable that, even today, it is impossible to enter it without being immediately aware that this is a shrine to the memory of someone who was deeply loved. Although, as we shall see, the chapel has not always been treated with such reverence, it is certainly true that, for the first five hundred years of its existence, it was regarded as one of the holiest places in Scotland. Margaret herself was elevated to sainthood in 1250 and, like many saints, has often been credited with mystical and, indeed, magical powers.

One of the most thrilling episodes in Scottish history provides us with an example of this tradition of sanctity. In March 1314, during the First War of Independence, the Castle was captured by storm for the first time in its history. Thomas Randolph, nephew of Robert the Bruce, led a party of men up Castle Rock and, surprising the sleeping garrison, reclaimed the Castle for the Scottish king. A local shepherd (or a renegade English soldier, there are a number of versions of the story) by the name of William Francis, guided Randolph and his men in their ascent and made this audacious action possible. John Barbour (1316-95) tells the story in some detail in his epic poem, *The Brus*. In another passage in the same poem—of which the following is an English prose translation by Tom Scott of Barbour's Scots verse—Queen Margaret's part in the affair is also mentioned.

An interesting fact about this capture is that Malcolm Canmore's sainted Queen Margaret had foreseen it all, back in the eleventh century. For she caused to be engraved on the wall of her chapel, which can still be seen in Edinburgh Castle, a picture of the castle with a ladder standing against the wall, with a man climbing up it: and under the picture she had engraved in French "Gardez vous de Francois". And men thought that it meant that the French would so take the castle—but it was Francis, not the French, who took it, and the real meaning there was "beware of Francis."

Having taken the Castle, Randolph was under orders to demolish all the buildings on the Rock and it was at this time that the wooden ramparts finally disappeared. But by 1335 the Castle was once more in English hands, and it was Edward III of England who began the fortifications in locally quarried stone. Even then, it was not until the conclusion of the Wars of Independence that the Castle as we know it today began to take shape, when Bruce's son and successor, David II (1324-71), ordered extensive fortifications in 1356. By this time, the only remaining building of the previous Castle was the tiny St. Margaret's Chapel, which had been spared by Randolph, at the command of the king.

Robert the Bruce, in fact, would appear to have had a special devotion to St. Margaret. As he lay dying from leprosy in 1329, practically his last action as king was to give instructions regarding the maintenance of the chapel. He also appointed a royal chaplain, Sir John Jordan, to ensure that his orders were carried out.

Sir John was the first of a succession of appointees, the last of whom was one Sir Andrew Drysdale, whose duties were abruptly terminated on August 24, 1560, when the Roman Catholic religion was formally abolished by Act of Parliament. For the best part of the next three centuries, the chapel was neglected to such an extent that its very existence was all but forgotten. Although the building survived, its function was changed to that of a powder magazine, as described by Sir Daniel Wilson in a paper to the Society of Antiquaries in 1887.

> When pursuing the searches in the Castle in 1845, with a view to the Memorials of Edinburgh in the Olden Time, which I had then in hand, I learned of what was described to me by the garrison chaplain as a small baptismal font, existing in one of the vaults. With some difficulty I obtained access to a powder magazine on the Argyll battery, where the gunpowder used in firing salutes on special occasions was stored. The only light was derived from a small window in the west wall; and, in the obscurity of the little chamber, I was able to identify not a font, but what proved to be one of the sockets for the pillars of the chancel arch of a small Norman chapel. A wooden floor, which divided the nave into two stories, was on a level with a spring of the arch, and so effectually concealed the ecclesiastical character of the building. The gunpowder was stored in the apse; the little round-beaded window on its south side was built up; and the garrison chapel, a plain unsightly modern building, which then stood immediately to the east, effectually blocked up the central window.

Sir Daniel immediately set out to restore the chapel and, in doing so, obtained the aid and encouragement of Queen Victoria, to whom one of the chapel's five stained glass windows is dedicated. The work was completed in 1853 and, since then, the chapel has become one of the most visited parts of Edinburgh Castle.

Pets and Guns

Scarcely less popular is the pets' cemetery that stands nearby, next to the giant gun, Mons Meg. Among the many pets and regimental mascots buried here, two dogs are of particular interest. The first is "Pat" of the 72nd Highlanders, who in 1921 received the Dickin Medal (the so-called "animal's VC") for saving his master, a color sergeant, during the Afghan War. The second, "Bob" of the Scots Fusilier Guards served in the Crimea where he apparently "chased the cannonballs and often burned his nose on a hot one." He was also decorated, but unfortunately was run over outside Buckingham Palace shortly after receiving his medal. There is also a story about a young elephant, the regimental pet of the 78th Highlanders, being buried here, but given the respective sizes of the plot and even a small elephant, this scarcely seems likely.

The famous artillery piece that casts its shadow over this cemetery is also a popular sight. According to an inscription on its carriage, it was manufactured in Mons in 1486—although there appears to be some doubt about this information. There is another tradition, that a Galloway blacksmith with the name (or nickname) of Mon, was responsible for the gun's construction. There is absolutely no doubt, however, about its size; it is twelve feet in length, with a bore that has a diameter of twenty inches, and this has given rise to a peculiar rumor

about its use among the soldiers of the garrison. John Taylor, the London waterboatman poet, who visited the city in 1618, and whose view of the Castle is quoted at the head of this chapter, was told that a child had once been conceived inside the gun. In order to put this story to the test, Taylor crawled up the barrel and found so much room that he had to agree that such a thing was certainly possible!

As for the employment for which it was actually designed, Mons Meg seems to have been seriously under-used. Apart from a couple of actions, both sieges, which took place in the sixteenth century, the gun has never been fired in anger. In 1682 an attempt was made to fire a salvo for the visiting Duke of York, but the barrel burst and Mons Meg has never been fired since. In the summer of 2001, however, repairs were carried out and a discharge was simulated on Hogmanay to bring in the New Year. In 1754, for some obscure reason, Mons Meg was removed to the Tower of London, where it remained until 1829. In that year it was returned to the Castle by George IV, at the suggestion of his friend, Sir Walter Scott. Since then, Scots have regarded this ancient cannon as a national relic.

It is not, despite its great age, the most famous gun that sits on Castle Rock. This distinction belongs to the Time Gun, or as it is more usually known, the "One O'clock Gun", located in the Half-Moon Battery on the eastern front of the Citadel behind the Scottish National War Memorial. Every day of the week except Sunday, a firing party of the Castle guard fires this cannon at 1 p.m. precisely, the time determined by an electronically controlled clock connected to the Royal Observatory on nearby Blackford Hill. To the people of Edinburgh, there is no more familiar sound. The One O'clock Gun, in fact, is emblematic of the relationship the Castle enjoys with the city and its people. As the most representative image of Edinburgh's identity, Edinburgh Castle features on the municipal crest and becomes the focal point at all times of civic rejoicing, be it the Hogmanay Festival at New Year or the fireworks concert which traditionally brings the annual Festival to a conclusion. Being visible from all parts of Edinburgh—even at night, when floodlighting can make it look as if it is hanging in the air—it is an inescapable feature, not only of the Edinburgh landscape, but also of the Edinburgh experience.

CHAPTER TWO

"The Great Street":
The Royal Mile

"A city that possesses a boldness and grandeur of situation beyond any that I have ever seen. It is built on the edges and sides of a vast sloping rock, of a great and precipitous height at the upper extremity, and the sides declining very quick and steep into the plain. The view of the houses at a distance strikes the traveller with wonder; their own loftiness, improved by their almost aerial situation, gives them a look of magnificence not to be found in any other part of Great Britain. All these conspicuous buildings form the upper part of the great street, are of stone, and make a handsome appearance: they are generally six or seven stories high in front; but, by reason of the declivity of the hill, much higher backward; one in particular, called Babel, has about twelve or thirteen stories. Every house has a common staircase, and every story is the habitation of a separate family."

Thomas Pennant, *A Tour in Scotland,* 1769

The heart of Edinburgh lies in the "great street" that Thomas Pennant describes above. Yet this is not one street but four: Castlehill, Lawnmarket, High Street, and Canongate, which lead in to each other, extending from Castle Rock in the west to Holyrood Palace in the east. Known collectively as The Royal Mile, these streets, together with their adjoining courts and closes, constitute the main thoroughfare of Edinburgh's Old Town.

These streets received their "Royal" epithet during the reign of James IV (1473-1513). Next to Robert the Bruce, James is the most popular and charismatic monarch in Scottish history and his reign has long been regarded as something of a Golden Age. According to the historian Robert Lindsay of Pitscottie (c.1532-c.1580), he was "gritumly given to bigging of palaces" and established his home at Holyrood. The Castle, of course, remained the center of military power and there was much traffic between the two establishments, with the result that the "great street" became known as the *Via Regis*, of which "Royal Mile" is simply the modern equivalent. Following the king's example, the Scottish aristocracy began to establish town houses along the street and they and their retinues required the services of tradesmen and merchants. The proximity of the Court made the area attractive to purveyors of luxury goods, such as jewelers, goldsmiths, and furriers. These people, too, encouraged further businesses, with the result that the Royal Mile became a hive of activity. By the time that James' granddaughter, Mary, acceded to the throne in 1542, there was, in the Royal Mile alone, a wealthy community of 300 merchants and 400 craftsmen, serving a population of approximately 12,500.

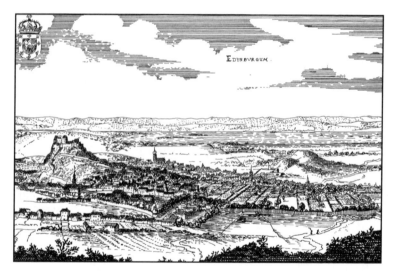

At the heart of all this activity lay the Mercat Cross, where decisions of state and public information were dispensed on a daily basis. Wars were declared, armies were raised, estates became forfeit, traitors were denounced and, on occasion, executions were carried out at this place. As Charles McKean has written, "the day-to-day reality of sixteenth century Scotland was such that nowhere else in the world was the effect of the Wheel of Fortune so apparent as at the Edinburgh Mercat Cross."

There is a timeless quality about the Royal Mile. In medieval times, the entire city of Edinburgh was contained within this thoroughfare, and even today it is regarded by most Edinburgh people as the true heart of the city. At regular intervals, as one passes down the hill, stone well-heads act as reminders of antiquity, yet the overall impression is one that has a curiously contemporary feel, as if all the centuries of development had conspired to create the present moment—and this has probably been the case for at least three hundred years.

Since the thoroughfare has been established since at least the twelfth century, one would expect to see a great deal of history reflected in its architecture. Although this is certainly possible, it takes the eye of an expert to do so properly. In 1995 contemporary architects David Page and Brian Park were invited by the City of Edinburgh Council to make some proposals for the Royal Mile. In 1998 their reflections were published by the Scottish Sculpture Trust.

Seen as a whole, one delights in the richness and complexity of the scene as it swirls in the mind. But looking more closely, one finds the individual, the singular, the very simple. Were it possible to freeze-frame this scene—to petrify the city evolving from the rock—the individual forms revealed would, indeed, be simple.

Behind its classical facade, the City Chambers is of almost stark, ten-storied simplicity. It is part of an ensemble. And the typical tenement buildings that flank the Mile and occupy the wall of stone are simple, with little elaboration. They, too, form part of the ensemble. Like players in an orchestra, the majority of the buildings are ordinary; working simply together to achieve a richness, a sense of history and a special place. Each plays its necessary part but with reserve and dignity. There is a calmness in these individual forms—nothing much to be excited about.

But release the freeze-frame and, trapped inside, a world-wide nostalgia for this great line becomes apparent—a wealth of cosmopolitan activity—a stage for the Edinburgh International Festival.

St. Giles

The most dominant building on the Royal Mile is the High Kirk of St. Giles, sometimes called (quite erroneously) St. Giles Cathedral. Apart from a period of some forty years—during the time when an attempt was made to impose episcopacy on Scotland—St. Giles has *never* been a cathedral, not even in the pre-Reformation period. But perhaps this is a permissible error, given the appearance of the church.

St. Giles is a quite magnificent Gothic edifice, 206 feet long and 129 feet in breadth. Major renovations in 1832 and 1871 may have detracted from its medieval character, but the spire has remained unaltered since the fourteenth century. This, the most visible part of the building, is 161 feet high, terminating in the representation of an imperial crown. One of Edinburgh's most recognizable landmarks, it can be seen with fine effect from most parts of the city.

Only a fragment of masonry now survives of the original church, which was destroyed by fire during an English invasion in 1385. It was built on the instructions of David I, the saintly son of Queen Margaret and King Malcolm Canmore, who gave charge of it to the Lazarites, a religious order devoted to the care of lepers. There is also a legend that St. Giles, the patron saint of cripples, had a particular interest in lepers, so this may be the origin of the church's name.

The parish of St. Giles covers a small area in the middle of the Royal Mile, which includes Parliament Square, the site of the old Scottish Parliament which came to an end with the Union of 1707. (After the departure of this legislature, the law expropriated the building for courts and, today Parliament Hall is no more than a promenade area, where lawyers are to be seen walking up and down as they discuss business with their clients.) Another vanished institution is the Tolbooth prison, which features so prominently in Sir Walter Scott's novel, *The Heart of Midlothian* (1818). Although the prison itself had been demolished a year before that novel appeared, a detailed description of the building survives in Robert Chambers' *Traditions of Edinburgh* (1868), which also quotes the lines that appeared on the door of the prison chapel:

> *A prison is a house of care,*
> *a place where none can thrive,*
> *a touchstone true to try a friend,*
> *a grave for men alive.*
>
> *Sometimes a place of right,*
> *sometimes a place of wrong,*
> *sometimes a place for jades and thieves,*
> *and honest men among.*

All that remains of this unpopular building is a marker, in the shape of a heart, built into the paving stones outside the High Kirk. This, according to local tradition, is where the only entrance to the prison was located and it was apparently a custom in former days for the people of Edinburgh to spit on the door as they passed by. Even today, this marker is often covered in spittle. Directly across the road from St. Giles is a building now used as the City Chambers, but which was originally built, in 1763, as the Royal Exchange, in order to provide a home for the merchants of Edinburgh who, until then, had been obliged to carry out their business in the street.

In the beginning, St. Giles was simply Edinburgh's parish church, under the patronage of the Abbot of Scone. But over the years a number of altars and special chapels—known as "aisles"—were bequeathed by wealthier citizens, and the number of priests conducting services consequently increased. By 1466 there seem to have been no fewer than forty altars and aisles founded and supported in the church, and it was at this time that St. Giles became a collegiate church. The chapter consisted of a provost, curate, sixteen prebendaries, a minister of the choir, four choristers, a sacristan, and a beadle. Among the most celebrated of these clerics was the Scottish poet and translator of Virgil, Gavin Douglas (c. 1474-1521), who was for some time Provost of St. Giles. But the most celebrated cleric of all, without any doubt, was John Knox (1517-72), minister of St. Giles from 1559 until his death. One of the most iconic and influential figures in the entire history of Scotland, Knox is remembered on the Royal Mile in a somewhat unusual, one might almost say mysterious, manner.

John Knox

At the foot of the High Street, almost at the point where it leads into the Canongate, is an ancient tenement that has become known as John Knox House, encouraging the widespread belief that this is where the great Protestant reformer lived. This house has long been the property of the Church of Scotland, whose establishment of a museum there has rather encouraged this conviction. Standing close to the site of the Netherbow Port—one of the ancient gates to the city—and next door to the Netherbow Arts Centre, which the Church also owns, it is, in fact, the oldest museum in the Royal Mile.

In 1990, at the instigation of Dr. Donald Smith, the Netherbow's director, John Knox House was renovated and a great deal of research carried out regarding its history. This revealed no evidence of John Knox's ownership or tenancy of the house, and much evidence to the contrary. The true owner of the house, it transpired, had been James Mossman, a goldsmith, Roman Catholic, and supporter of Mary, Queen of Scots!

At the time of Knox's death in August 1572, Scotland was in the grip of civil war. The supporters of Mary, known as the Queen's Men, lay under siege in Edinburgh Castle. Mossman was among them and, as a result, all his property, including the house, was confiscated. According to Donald Smith, it is just possible that it may have been used as the St. Giles manse at this time. This, if true, would explain the

connection with Knox, for which there is otherwise little substance. It certainly seems something of an irony that this most rigorous of Protestants should be associated so closely with the home of one of his enemies, not to mention the fact that the building now holds an art gallery and a theater. Yet this is by no means the only irony to be discovered in Edinburgh's recollection of the founder of the Church of Scotland.

On June 29, 1559, shortly before the Roman Catholic religion in Scotland was formally abolished by Act of Parliament, John Knox preached an important sermon in St. Giles. As with all Knox's sermons, not a single word of what he actually said on that occasion has come down to us. Curiously enough, this most garrulous of Scottish Reformers is today remembered chiefly in terms of images, of which he would have almost certainly disapproved and which, in any case, probably fail to do him justice. There are two of these in St. Giles: a stained glass window made by Ballantine and Son in 1881, depicting Knox preaching at the funeral of Regent Moray; and a statue cast by Pittendrigh MacGillivray in 1904, which attempts to reflect the putative energy of the preaching. Apart from these, there is another memorial in St. Giles with which Knox's memory is connected, albeit indirectly. This is a brass plate in one of the aisles that bears the following inscription: "Constant tradition affirms that near this spot a brave Scotswoman, Janet Geddes, on the 23rd July 1637, struck the first blow in the great struggle for the freedom of Conscience which, after a conflict of half a century, ended in the establishment of civil and religious liberty."

This is a reference to the riot of 1637, when an attempt was made to substitute John Knox's *Book of Common Order* for a new liturgy that had been devised by Archbishop Laud, Charles I's Archbishop of Canterbury. When the Dean of Edinburgh, James Hannay, attempted to read from the new prayer-book, a stool was flung at his head and a riot ensued. This riot is known as the Stony Sabbath because after the magistrates had used soldiers to clear the church, the congregation tore cobbles from the High Street with which to smash the windows of St. Giles.

It is interesting that the plate that commemorates this event uses the expression "constant tradition". As far as can be established from the historical record, there was no one of the name of Janet Geddes in the church that day. Even so, the story of Jenny Geddes remains a firm favorite in the realms of Edinburgh folklore.

Other memorials which feature in the church interior include a low-relief portrait of Robert Louis Stevenson by the American sculptor Augustus St. Gaudens, a monument in memory of the medical pioneer, suffragette and First World War heroine, Elsie Inglis, and a quite magnificent stained glass window commemorating Robert Burns. This was designed by the Icelandic artist, Leifur Breidfjord and installed in 1985. It depicts a group of figures gathered around the Cross, of which only one is identified, standing at the foot of the Cross, with the caption "R. Burns".

The Thistle Chapel

Possibly the most interesting part of St. Giles is the Thistle Chapel, meeting place of the Knights of the Thistle. This order, sometimes called the Order of St. Andrew, is the Scottish order of chivalry, ranking second only to the Order of the Garter. It consists of sixteen knights (besides royalty), and its officers are the Dean, the secretary, the Lyon King of Arms, and the Gentleman Usher of the Green Rod. According to legend, the order is very old, dating back to the eighth century. Although present-day historians generally dispute this, there is no doubt that it was in existence prior to the Glorious Revolution of 1688, after which it fell into abeyance. Queen Anne revived the order in 1703, but for two hundred years the knights had no chapel of their own. In 1906, the 11th Earl of Leven and Melville left funds to be used in building a chapel at St. Giles and Sir Robert Lorimer was the architect who received the commission. The work was carried out between 1909 and 1911.

Lorimer managed to achieve an astonishing richness of effect within a comparatively small space—the area of the chapel measures only 37 feet by 18—and to create an impression of antiquity that is entirely appropriate to the order. The official St. Giles guidebook describes the chapel as follows:

> *Entered through a low-vaulted vestibule, the chapel is a rectangle of three bays, with a polygonal eastern apse and a stone vault encrusted with a rich pattern of rib and carved bosses. There is hardly any exposed stone or timber that is not carved or molded and the effect is greatly enhanced by the heraldic and figurative stained glass in the windows.*
>
> *Down the sides of the chapel are the knights' stalls, which are capped by lavishly carved canopies with the helms and crests of the knights rising above. The richest effect of all, however, is reserved for the sovereign's stall at the west end of the chapel.*

The presence of such a creation within the precincts of St. Giles, together with the various monuments and memorials, not to mention the fact that the building is usually open to the general public, might give the visitor the impression that the High Kirk is no more than a vast ecclesiastical museum. This would be to miss the point. The true function of St. Giles is that of a Christian church, its main business being the services that are held there on a regular basis. Although the parish of St. Giles is very small, a congregation of just under 800 communicants, drawn from all over Edinburgh, attends such services. The form of worship is Presbyterian, as is the government of the congregation, the business of which is managed by the minister, Gilleasbuig Macmillan and a Kirk Session of some fifty elders. This simple truth need not detract from the appeal that St. Giles holds for the interested visitor and, indeed, may even add to it. There is something particularly fascinating about the fact that a place with historical associations *is still being used* for its original purpose.

Museums and Writers

The events of the past can be fascinating, particularly when they have the kind of romantic association that one finds in the Royal Mile. Romantic or not, moreover, the past is remembered here with a degree of humanity. Far from being a shrine to history, the Royal Mile remains a commonplace community, whose citizens lead the same kind of workaday existence as their counterparts elsewhere. The fact that this existence is carried out in a location that once knew Mary, Queen of Scots, Bonnie Prince Charlie, and Robert Burns may add considerably to the attraction.

In any event, it is certainly the case that in recent years the Royal Mile has become a magnet for tourists. Even this role, it should be said, is performed with a measure of dignity. Although it has its fair share of the negative aspects of the tourist industry—there are plenty of tawdry knick-knacks on sale and the cost of a cup of coffee has an alarming tendency to rise in the Royal Mile—it is still clear that the experience on offer has its own, distinctive quality.

At the top of Castlehill, for instance, two of Scotland's most famous exports are promoted in a civilized manner. On one side of the street, in a building that once housed the city's water supply, is the Edinburgh Old Town Weaving Co., a fully operational weaving mill, together with a permanent exhibition of Scottish tartan. This exhibition fills five stories of the building, covering every aspect of tartan making. There is also a gift shop, dealing in all kinds of tartan goods, kilt-making, Scottish knitwear, jewelry and crystal. On the other side of the road stands the Scottish Whisky Heritage Centre, doing much the same job for Scotland's national drink. There is a working distillery, a bar and bistro, films and lectures, and a virtual tour that takes the visitor through three hundred years of the history of whisky making. There is also, inevitably, a gift shop, selling a wide selection of Scotch whiskies and liqueurs.

Places such as these, not to mention the large number of quality bars, bistros and restaurants, help to invest the Royal Mile with an eminently social atmosphere. At the same time, it can hardly be denied that there is a sense in which the "living museum" aspect of the place is fully justified. Apart from John Knox House, there are, in fact, no fewer than five more museums to be found along the Royal Mile

The Museum of Edinburgh is based in Huntly House in the Canongate and traces the history of the city from prehistoric times until the present day. There are displays illustrating life in the Old Town from the seventeenth century onwards, together with extensive collections of silver, glass, pottery, and other decorative objects created by Edinburgh craftsmen. The National Covenant, Scotland's great petition for religious freedom, signed by so many in 1638, can be seen here, as can the collar and feeding bowl the civic authorities presented to the famous Greyfriars Bobby, whose story will be told later. But perhaps the most fascinating exhibit of all is a watercolor depicting a number of Victorian street entertainers. This was painted by one of the most mercurial characters the Royal Mile has ever known, the actor and artist Edmund Holt.

Ned Holt (1836-92) began his working life as an apprentice to an Edinburgh baker called Wilkinson, but very soon became bored by this conventional lifestyle. For most of his life he was a market trader and in his later years ran a corner shop at the Netherbow, almost next door to John Knox House. Although he seems to have no training as a painter, he was successful enough to sell his sketches to a number of public houses in the Royal Mile. In September 1892 Holt was found dead at the side of the road after returning from a race meeting.

His work survives in various collections that are held by the Royal Scottish Academy and the City Art Centre, and there is also a fascinating book of crayon drawings among the holdings of the Edinburgh Room of the Central Public Library. The aforementioned watercolor illustrates perfectly the faintly grotesque theatrical world in which Holt lived and its location is most appropriate. Ned Holt's home for many years was in White Horse Close, practically next door to the Museum of Edinburgh. Among the figures in the Huntly House painting is "Old Malabar", whose spectacular juggling displays, in which he would juggle his balls beyond the height of the buildings, were frequently seen in the Royal Mile. Also present are two of Holt's particular friends, Davie Arkley and Jamie Main, two blind street singers who someow managed to guide each other to wherever they wished to go.

During his lifetime, Ned Holt was best known in Edinburgh as an actor, particularly in the role of Hamlet. His performances were given in a little theater called Connor's in Blackfriars Wynd, off the High Street. This was a species of playhouse known as a "penny gaff" (presumably because admission cost no more than a penny), and one can hardly believe that any production of *Hamlet* (or any other play) would be given there in any great detail. In all likelihood, Ned Holt's playing of the role was restricted to a recitation of one or two of the soliloquies.

Another popular Edinburgh character whose work was regularly featured at Connor's was the poet and storyteller James Smith (1824-87). Born in a crumbling tenement in St. Mary's Wynd (now St. Mary's Street) at the head of the Canongate, Smith was a true poet of the Edinburgh streets. He served his time as a printer and worked for a number of years as a proofreader on *The Scotsman* newspaper, in which his first poems appeared. In 1869, however, he became librarian of the Mechanics Library and held this post for the remainder of his life. This library was based in Riddle's Court off the Lawnmarket, in premises now occupied by the Workers' Educational Association. While never more than a minor poet, Smith was certainly very popular in his own day. He wrote in the medium of Metropolitan Scots, the dialect of the Old Town that was the main speech of all classes in Edinburgh for centuries. His *Poems, Songs and Ballads* (originally set up and printed by his own hand and later reprinted by Blackwood) went through four editions and his dramatic poem *The Merry Bridal o Firthmains* was scarcely less popular. Yet perhaps his most lasting piece is the song-lyric *The Cries of Edinburgh*, a marvelous evocation of the life of the Old

Town over the course of a year, with the cries of street traders built into the chorus.

July comes—the queen o' beauty—
Simmer's sonsy, smiling dame.
Aa the rich are at the country,
Puirtith's hard an' fast at hame;
Through the toun, baith wat an' dry
Hark yon sturdy hizzie's cry—

Wha'll buy my bonnie water-cresses,
aa the road frae Loudon Burn!

August reigns in aa her glory,
Rizzarts red in clusters shine;
Heavy-laden berry-bushes,
Sugar ploums sae sweet an' fine
Through the toun, baith wat an' dry,
Hark yon bonnie lassie's cry—

Fine ripe berries, the big pint a hap'ny—
the big pint a hap'ny—sell them off!

Such was Smith's reputation that in May 1875 he was presented with a silver salver and a purse of 200 sovereigns, raised by public subscription, in recognition of "his genius and character". Furthermore, twelve years later, when Smith died from an acute attack of asthma, the citizens of Edinburgh felt constrained to dip into their pockets once more, in order to provide a suitable memorial. Commissioned from a leading Edinburgh sculptor, Charles MacBride, this takes the form of a spectacular headstone in sandstone and bronze, which is still to be seen today on Smith's grave in the Grange Cemetery in the Southside.

Although he was very much a man of his own time and place, Smith's work has a curiously lasting quality. While he is recognizably a Victorian writer, the best of his work simply does not date. His best-known lyric is the children's song "Clap, clap, handies", which Scottish mothers still sing to their babies, even if they are completely ignorant of its authorship. There again, as recently as 1994, a modern adaptation of one of Smith's stories, *Nancy Sleekit,* scored a huge popular success when it was performed at the Netherbow during the Edinburgh Festival of that year.

Characters such as Ned Holt and James Smith represent a strand of popular culture that has all too often been overlooked in an Edinburgh context. In the Canongate is a museum that seeks to correct this deficiency. The People's Story, originally instituted as an archive of labour and trade union history, uses sound and videotape in a profusion of displays that celebrate the life, work, and leisure of the ordinary people of Edinburgh through the ages. There are reconstructions of pubs, tearooms, wash houses and workshops, along with more formal displays of old photographs, everyday objects from the past and rare artifacts such as trade union banners.

The most popular museum of all, however, is to be found in the High Street. This is the Museum of Childhood, founded by Councillor Patrick Murray in 1955. In the five galleries of this museum, the happiness and adversity of childhood are celebrated in all forms, with toys and games from all over the world, school items, films of street games, and sound recordings of classroom exercises from earlier decades. The Museum of Childhood is especially popular with children and has been described as "the noisiest museum in the world". On the other side of the High Street stands the rather more esoteric Brass Rubbing Centre. This museum contains a collection of rare brasses and replicas molded from ancient Pictish stones. The staff assist and advise visitors in making rubbings of their own and there are, in addition, high-quality completed rubbings and brass rubbing kits on sale.

The last of the six museums is to be found in the Lawnmarket, in Lady Stairs Close. The Writers' Museum celebrates the life and work of Scotland's best-known writers, Robert Burns, Sir Walter Scott and Robert Louis Stevenson. All three have strong associations with the Royal Mile, although Scott probably knew it best. He was born nearby, in College Wynd and as a practicing advocate probably spent a great deal of his time there.

Burns, too, was familiar with the Royal Mile. His first lodgings, during his Edinburgh sojourn from 1786 until 1788, were in the

Lawnmarket, quite close to Lady Stair's Close, and his publisher, William Creech, had a bookshop opposite St. Giles. It was also during this time that Burns fathered one of his numerous illegitimate children, to a prostitute called Jenny Clow, who lived in the Canongate. An important product of this period in the poet's life is his *Merry Muses of Caledonia*, which was unpublished in this lifetime, suppressed after his death, and did not appear in its entirety until 1959. These bawdy verses were dedicated to the members of The Crochallan Fencibles, a notorious drinking club that held its meetings at Dawney Douglas's tavern in Anchor Close in the High Street. Burns became a member of the Crochallan Fencibles through his friendship with the club's founder, William Smellie. Although he worked as a humble printer, Smellie had something of the all-round ability of a Renaissance man, contributing many articles to scientific and literary journals. His main claim to fame, however, lies in the fact that he was the founder and first editor of the *Encyclopaedia Britannica*, for which he wrote most of the original entries in 1768. Burns would later celebrate his old friend in a verse that reads as follows:

> *Crochallan came:*
> *The old cock'd hat, the brown surtout the same;*
> *His grisly beard just bristling in its might*
> *(Twas four long nights and days to shaving night);*
> *His uncomb'd hoary locks, wild-staring, thach'd*
> *A head for thought profound and clear unmatch'd;*
> *Yet, tho' his caustic wit was biting rude,*
> *His heart was warm, benevolent, and good.*

The Crochallan Fencibles, for all its notoriety, was just one of a number of similar clubs that flourished in Edinburgh in the late eighteenth century. Although all were devoted to conviviality, some of them were rather eccentric. There was the Dirty Club, whose members were forbidden to wear clean linen; the Odd Fellows, who were required to sign their names upside-down; and the Pious Club, a rather irreligious body whose name was based on a pun—the members met in a pie-house.

A great deal of drunken conviviality took place—as indeed there still does today—in the many taverns that throng the Royal Mile. One of the most celebrated of these was the Star and Garter in Writers' Court, next to the City Chambers, directly opposite St. Giles. This was once owned by a publican called Clerihugh and it is as Clerihugh's that it makes an appearance in Scott's *Guy Mannering* (1815), where Mannering first meets the lawyer Pleydell. Although that episode is too long and unwieldy to lend itself to quotation here, there is another anecdote in the same novel that illustrates the drinking customs of the time. This passage involves not only the most celebrated publican of all, Johnnie Dowie, but also a leading Edinburgh financier, Sir William Forbes, banker to the royal family.

> *A gentleman one night stepped into Johnnie Dowie's, and, looking into a room, saw a heap of snoring drunks upon the floor, while the gleam of an expiring candle illumined the wreck and debris of a perfect pitched battle of Bacchus.*
>
> *"Wha may thae be, Mr. Dowie?" inquired the visitor.*
>
> *"Oh," answered Johnnie, in his usual quiet imperturbable way, "just twa-three o' Sir William's drucken clerks!"*

As for Stevenson, he was a familiar figure in the Royal Mile during his student days in the early 1870s, when he was known as "Velvetcoat" after the jacket he habitually wore. (That jacket can still be seen in the Writers' Museum, as can Burns' writing desk and Sir Walter Scott's chessboard.) In 1881, during a short visit home (he was by this time living in Bournemouth) Stevenson spent a day in the company of local historian, J. Wilson McLaren. It was an experience that McLaren never forgot and, forty-five years later, recounted it in his *Edinburgh Memories* (1926):

> *One of the events of my life was my meeting with Robert Louis Stevenson in Writers' Court in 1881. I had published a small book of verse in Braid Scots, and was credited with knowing something of the old houses and the old closes of the Royal Mile. Stevenson had heard of me, and, although only on a hurried visit to the city of his birth, he sought me out that summer afternoon in Writers' Court, High Street. I showed him through the quaint panelled apartment once occupied by the 'Star and Garter.' Together we made the round of once-familiar resorts. R. L. S. was*

particularly interested in Advocates' Close, with its scriptural texts cut out on the stone lintels of the doorways, and its dark turnpike stairs.

Recently an interesting correspondence appeared in the Scotsman regarding the place of meeting of the 'L. J. R.'—the interpretation of which is supposed to be Liberty, Justice, and Reverence. It was a mysterious society, and Stevenson was one of the six members. According to Sir Graham Balfour, 'its meetings, of which only five took place, were held in a public-house situated, I believe, in Advocates' Close, which had apparently been visited by Burns.'

I can give no information concerning the abortive Essay Club, but with regard to the assertion that a public house existed in Advocates' Close, which R. L. S., with other young bloods, frequented, I am of the opinion that there is no justification for this statement.

Even in the early days of Stevenson, Advocates' Close, with its steep declivity, was far from an inviting quarter for a 'howff' to be situated that might attract his brother Bohemians with a political or a literary turn of mind. The tall tenements on either side of the close were densely packed with poor artisans and their families, and remained so until they were demolished some years ago.

Some misconception must have arisen when the biographers of R. L. S. were compiling their books. If it had been said that the public house was situated near Advocates' Close, this would have been much nearer the mark. When I visited Advocates' Close along with Stevenson, although on that occasion very communicative on things pertaining to Old Edinburgh, he never hinted that in previous years he had frequented a public house there to discuss liberty, justice, and reverence.

John's Coffee House, in Writers' Court (not more than a stone-throw away), was visited by us. The famous 'howff' at that time was a favourite rendezvous not only for magistrates and town councillors, but also for budding advocates from the Parliament House, and a toothsome sandwich and a glass of ale could always be procured. Although this happened forty-five years ago, I have a clear recollection of what took place. Stevenson seemed to remember several of the rooms. Interrupting me, with a smile, he said, 'Not much alteration. I've been here before, and enjoyed the splores.' It is just possible that it was in John's Coffee House, at the

> *Royal Exchange, with its historic associations, and not in Advocates'*
> *Close, that the members of the Essay Club met.*

Ghostly Tales

Stevenson always had a strong affection for the Royal Mile. When one considers how much history, legend and folklore is to be found here, this is hardly surprising. H. V. Morton captured the almost eerie quality of the district in the 1920s:

> *Here are the ghosts of Edinburgh, here in these old stone courtyards, in*
> *these dim wynds and closes where pale, insignificant lamps hang above*
> *flights of grey stairs, the mighty history of this city stirs a little in its sleep.*
> *It is grey, sinister, mediaeval.*

While there are great many stories to be found in every nook and cranny of the Royal Mile, the available space allows the inclusion of just two.

One consequence of Edinburgh's growth as Scotland's capital during the sixteenth and seventeenth centuries, was the problem of overcrowding. While this had the effect of creating a rather democratic spirit—with all classes living cheek-by-jowl, a definite community spirit prevailed—there were more negative repercussions, too. In order to provide living space for a growing population, houses were piled on top of each other, creating towering tenements or "lands", as they were called. These buildings, described by Moray Maclaren as "the world's first skyscrapers", were not subject to the kind of building regulation that would be in force today and, as a result, were not always secure structures. Sometimes they collapsed.

One of the most famous collapses took place in 1861, when a tenement in Chalmers Close (today the location of the aforementioned Brass Rubbing Centre) fell with a terrifying crash, killing 37 people. As one would expect, a rescue squad was on the site very quickly and a search for survivors was undertaken. After toiling for some time without success, the rescuers were on the very point of giving up when a voice called out to them from beneath the debris: "Heave awa, lads! I'm no deid yet!" Thus encouraged, the rescuers resumed the work and rescued the boy, an incident that is commemorated by the building that

replaced the collapsed tenement. This has been known ever since as the "Heave Awa House".

Further up the High Street, almost directly opposite St. Giles, is the scene of the most famous Edinburgh folk-tale of them all. In 1645 Mary King's Close was home to 27 families, drawn from every rank in society: there was a representative of the landed gentry, three lawyers, two merchants, and a half-dozen tradesman. The arrival of plague in that year led to the death of all of them. As was the custom in those days, the close was sealed up, even as the inhabitants lay dying, and remained so for many years. It must have been during this period that Mary King's Close gained a reputation as a ghostly place. Bearing in mind the problem of overcrowding, it should have been a simple matter to find tenants for the empty houses, but nobody wanted to live there. Eventually the Council began to offer to let the houses rent-free, yet even this was unsuccessful.

Finally, in 1752, the problem of occupation was solved when the Royal Exchange was built over the top of Mary King's Close. Nonetheless, the spooky reputation remains to this day and holds a certain fascination for the general public. It features as the murder scene at the beginning of what is perhaps the most ambitious of Ian Rankin's Rebus novels, *Mortal Causes*, but is by no means as accessible as artistic license allows Rankin to suggest. Guided tours, however, do take place regularly and a number of visitors claim to have received supernatural experiences in the close. The most common of these appears to be the sighting of the ghost of a little girl called Sarah, who apparently haunts the old Royal Exchange coffee house. Sarah has been seen by a number of people and it has become the custom for visitors to Mary King's Close to bring a doll as a gift for the little ghost-girl.

The Enlightenment: Squalor and Genius

Such stories help to explain the abiding appeal of the Royal Mile, which enjoyed its most famous period in the eighteenth century. This was the time of the Enlightenment, of Adam Smith and David Hume, of Robert Burns and Alexander Nasmyth, all of whom were Edinburgh residents for at least part of this period. The Enlightenment was brought about as a direct consequence of the Treaty of Union in 1707. With the abolition of the Scottish Parliament and the removal of political leadership to London, Scottish identity found expression in other forms. From the eighteenth century on, these included the Church, Law and the universities, which provided Scotland's aristocratic elite with the kind of leadership it was unable to provide for itself. This meant that during the Enlightenment period science and philosophy dominated Scottish culture.

But it was also a time of great urban squalor, as described by the poet and polymath Douglas Young in *Edinburgh* (1965).

> *Tall chimneys belched smoke from coal, burned at the rate of about 500 tons a day, in the 1790s, costing half a guinea for 23 hundredweight. The nickname of the city was "Auld Reekie" ("Old Smoky"). But coal smoke was less offensive than the pervasive odor of human excreta from the tall, overcrowded buildings. At 10:00 P.M. drums gave warning, after which the day's slops were thrown onto the streets, with the cry*

"Gardyloo" (from French, "Prenez garde de l'eau"). These so-called flouers o Embro lay until 7:00 A.M., when scavengers collected them to sell. But there was no collection on Sunday, and no water carriers worked that day either. In spite of near success in the 1770's and 1780's Old Edinburgh never really beat its problems of sewage disposal and water supply; but people got used to them, like the courtiers of Versailles with its countless chaises percées. An odd feature of the Edinburgh scene was the Wha wants me? Man, who perambulated the main thoroughfare carrying a chaise percée and wearing an outsize cloak, to give privacy to the user of his itinerant convenience. There was much of the farmyard about the old city, with pigs running in the streets, kestrels nesting on the Castle rock, and corncrakes sounding in the meadows.

Curiously enough, it was in such an unpromising context that the novelist Tobias Smollett (1721-71) famously described Edinburgh as a "hotbed of genius". It was also against the same background that an English tourist, Mr. Amyat, made his much-quoted remark in 1750 to William Creech, bookseller, publisher of Burns, and future Lord Provost of Edinburgh: "Here I stand at what is called the Cross of Edinburgh, and can, in a few minutes, take 50 men of genius and learning by the hand." The cross in question is the Mercat Cross, still to be seen in Parliament Square, next to St. Giles. As for the men of genius, many of them were captured by the pencil of a clever artist, John Kay, barber and miniaturist, who had a shop in Parliament Close.

Kay (1742-1826) was a contemporary of the pioneer English cartoonists Thomas Rowlandson and James Gillray, and perhaps because of this is often described as a caricaturist. According to Robert Chambers, however, this is not quite correct.

To speak of his portraits as caricatures is doing them signal injustice. They were the most exact and faithful likenesses that could have been reproduced by any mode of art. He drew the man as he walked the street every day; his gait, his costume, every peculiarity of his appearance, done to a point, and no defect perceptible except the stiffness of the figures.

During his lifetime, Kay made more than 900 etchings, slightly more than a third of which have ever been published. They include representations of such notable Edinburgh citizens and visitors as the economist Adam Smith, the actress Sarah Siddons, the pioneering balloonist Vincent Lunardi, the politician Henry Dundas, and the literary critic, Francis Jeffrey. His work also includes a number of pieces that are not completely original. His portraits of figures such as John Knox, Mary Queen of Scots, Tom Paine and Paul I, Czar of Russia, were all made from originals that he had received from customers. Yet another category includes Edinburgh street scenes and every kind of local character, from advocates to oyster lasses.

One of the most interesting of his etchings is one of William Brodie, the respectable Deacon of the Incorporation of Wrights and Masons, who practiced burglary in his spare time and was eventually hanged on a gallows that he had himself constructed in 1787. Brodie was a familiar figure in the Royal Mile at that time and Kay, a near neighbor, would have known him well. Kay's depiction of Brodie's first meeting with his accomplice George Smith is, in any case, the only likeness we have of the man who, in the opinion of many, was the inspiration for Stevenson's Jekyll and Hyde.

The connection between Deacon Brodie and Dr. Jekyll is, in truth, rather tenuous, one of the many misconceptions about Stevenson's story to have entered the popular imagination. It is widely believed, for instance that *The Strange Case of Dr. Jekyll and Mr. Hyde* (1886) is a novel with an Edinburgh setting, whereas it is, in fact, a long short story that takes place in London. As far as Deacon Brodie is concerned, Stevenson was certainly interested in the man—he would later write an unsuccessful stage play about the case—but there are other characters, from both fact and fiction, who might just as easily have provided the inspiration. And there is one huge difference between Brodie and Jekyll. Dr. Jekyll is essentially a virtuous man who loses control of the dark side of his nature. Brodie, on the other hand, was a criminal who used respectability as a front for his felonious activities.

Allan Ramsay
Unfortunately, the most engaging of Royal Mile residents in the eighteenth century died before Kay's work began and was never drawn by him.

Adjoining Castlehill is Ramsay Garden, once the home of the poet Allan Ramsay (1684-1758), arguably the most influential figure in the entire history of Scottish literature. Born in the mining village of Leadhills, Dumfriesshire, Ramsay arrived in Edinburgh in the early years of the eighteenth century to be apprenticed to a wig-maker. He quickly excelled in that trade, which was his main means of support until 1718, when he opened a bookshop. Interested in literature from an early age, Ramsay began writing poetry in his late twenties, his first collection appearing in 1715. From then until his death in 1758, Ramsay's activities were almost entirely those of a cultural revivalist. Apart from his own work—the best example of which is his ballad opera, *The Gentle Shepherd* (1725)—he edited two anthologies that were to play a pivotal role in the history of Scottish literature. *The Ever Green* (1724) ensured the survival of great poets of the fifteenth and sixteenth centuries, William Dunbar and Robert Henryson among others, while *A Teatable Miscellany* (published in the same year) preserved many traditional ballads that might otherwise have perished. These two books, besides conserving the best poetry of the past, provided an example and a stimulus for the Scots poets of the future.

In addition to this literary production, Ramsay established the first circulating library in Scotland and even succeeded in creating Edinburgh's first regular theater. His activities, moreover, were not confined to literature. He also established a school of painting and gave much encouragement to his son, also named Allan (1713-84), who became the greatest portrait painter of his time.

Throughout his life, Allan Ramsay maintained his position as one of the best-known and most influential Edinburgh citizens of the day; a man of energy and versatility, whose zealous public spirit was matched by the unflinching courage with which he carried through his schemes. His artistic integrity, together with his generous nature and a certain flair for plain speaking, earned him the nickname "Honest Allan". It was in Ramsay Garden that Honest Allan built a house of somewhat unconventional design, which became known as "Goosepie Lodge". Although little remains of the original house today, another Edinburgh citizen of great vision and energy was to develop the site in the late nineteenth century.

Sir Patrick Geddes: Urban Reformer

Like Allan Ramsay, Sir Patrick Geddes (1854-1932) was a cultural revivalist whose activities were informed by a zealous public spirit. Indeed, its seems to be no coincidence that when, in 1895, Geddes created a journal to promote his ideas, he gave it the name of *Evergreen*. To no lesser extent than Ramsay, Geddes wanted to preserve, in his own words, Edinburgh's heritage of "beauty, of intellectual and practical endeavour, and of moral and spiritual intensity—however temporarily forgotten or depressed."

Often described as "Edinburgh's greatest all-round citizen", Geddes was in fact born in Ballater and brought up in Perth where he began his working life as a bank apprentice. Banking did not suit him, and he had soon decided to turn to the study of botany. Like so many gifted individuals, Geddes was something of a maverick; he quit the Department of Botany in Edinburgh after only a week's study. He then went to London, where he enrolled at the School of Mines, to study with the biologist T. H. Huxley. Always an extremely impatient man, he made a bet (which he subsequently won) that he could pass both elementary and advanced courses after only a week's study. Following five years with Huxley, Geddes continued his studies in Brittany and at the Sorbonne in Paris, before being appointed demonstrator and lecturer in Zoology at Edinburgh University.

This was the period of the Old Town's greatest decline. After the building of the New Town (a process that took almost a hundred years to complete and which will be discussed later) there was something of a revolution in the city's social structure. The most prosperous families lost little time in abandoning the Old Town for the New, with the result that the former gradually declined. Within a very short time, the entire district was a suppurating slum.

Geddes set out to reverse this process. He bought Goosepie Lodge, extended it, proceeding to build a number of other Ramsay Garden flats as residences for university lecturers and professors. In 1892 he took over the nearby Short's Observatory and transformed it into an Outlook Tower, which became what he called a "training ground for citizens". The Outlook Tower was arranged as an "index-museum" of the universe as seen from Edinburgh. Below the camera obscura was a hollow planetarium; in the Scotland Room below was a large floor-map of the country, and below it again the Edinburgh Room, followed by surveys of Britain as a whole, Europe and the other continents, and finally the World Room with two great globes, one geological and one showing vegetation. What Geddes attempted to demonstrate were the improvements that needed to be made in the environment and how to carry them out.

The idea was to practice what Geddes called "civic revivance", the aim being to reclaim the Old Town on behalf of the people of Edinburgh—*all* the people of Edinburgh. Geddes castigated the upper and middle classes for maintaining a "practical indifference to deplorable conditions" and pledged that the slums of the Old Town would be "renewed as gardens for the people." Geddes was no mere theorist, however, and was not content to suggest solutions and expect others to carry them out. After his marriage to Anna Morton in 1886, the couple moved from a comfortable New Town flat into a tenement block in James Court, off the Lawnmarket. In better days, this had been the former lodgings of James Boswell and was once the home of Scotland's greatest philosopher, David Hume. By 1886, however, it had suffered, like so much of the Old Town, from serious neglect. The newly married couple soon found that, while one or two of their neighbors struggled to maintain standards, most of them seemed content to live in squalor.

Geddes immediately set to work to improve matters. He personally repainted the exterior walls of the tenement, organized refuse disposal, and installed a common urinal in the court. At the same time, Anna Geddes began home-making classes for the women of the tenement, the start of an educational program that would later include singing, gymnastics, experimental science, and gardening.

Not content with these improvements, Geddes and his wife took over the tenement next door to the one in which they were living and converted it into a student hostel. University Hall, as it was called, became the first self-governing student residence in Britain. Over the next fifteen years, the Edinburgh Social Union, which Geddes had founded in 1884, carried out similar work in no fewer than 37 courts and closes along the Royal Mile. This led to the creation of four university residences housing 120 students, and 85 flats or apartments reconditioned or built in slum areas for working families.

As the nineteenth century drew to a close, Geddes gradually grew disillusioned with the lack of sympathy that the Edinburgh authorities showed towards his ideas. As his vision broadened, he turned to other projects, becoming involved with town-planning matters in France and India, developing the layout of the University of Jerusalem and finally moving to Montpellier in the South of France where he established a Scots College, complete with an Outlook Tower.

Although Edinburgh owes a great deal to Patrick Geddes, the debt might so easily have been much greater. As Charles McKean has written in *Edinburgh: Portrait of a City* (1991): "Although the Outlook Tower and Camera Obscura survive to this day, it is but a whisper of what Geddes imagined."

Renewal and Power

At the same time, it must be said that this imagination has continued to exert an influence in the Royal Mile. After the departure of Geddes, the Edinburgh Social Union rather faded away, but the aspirations of the organization have never really died. Throughout the twentieth century, there has been much activity in the field of restoration and renewal. In 1937, for instance, the Marquis of Bute commissioned the architect Robert Hurd to restore Acheson House in the Canongate. This had once been the residence of the Secretary of State for Scotland, but had degenerated into a slum tenement, housing thirteen families. Hurd's work so impressed the Marquis that he immediately provided funds for the restoration of other properties.

In the same year, the Saltire Society was founded, with the aim of preserving and enriching Scottish culture. One of the first actions of the new organization was to introduce a Housing Design Award. Although the Saltire Society is concerned with Scotland in its entirety—while having its headquarters in Edinburgh, the Society was actually founded in Glasgow—the success of this annual award has clearly had an influence on standards.

There has also been the matter of commercial development. The slum clearance program that took place after the Second World War had the effect of transferring the working-class population from the Old Town to new housing schemes on the fringes of Edinburgh. This created an opportunity for the vacated properties to be taken over, renovated and placed on the market as city-center flats. As a result of such development, a residence on the Royal Mile has become desirable once more.

One consequence of this urban transformation is that, in future, the Royal Mile—which was named as a World Heritage site in 1995—is unlikely to suffer depredation without energetic objection. In 2002, for instance, two leading Edinburgh citizens, the architect Charles McKean and the cultural entrepreneur Richard Demarco, made a public protest concerning the decaying state of the Royal Mile. Their opinions were reported on the front page of *The Scotsman,* which also included a generously illustrated feature in the daily *S2* supplement.

> *Demarco believes the Old Town will be saved only by a huge international effort, similar to the conference and support system which has formed around Venice. McKean agrees. "People will leap about and say: 'It's occupied, it's working, what more do you want?' But the argument is that it's not as good as it should be, within a European state."*

Such passionate protests illustrate the extent to which the Royal Mile occupies a place at the heart of Edinburgh's, and indeed Scotland's, consciousness. This is not simply because of the many symbols of Scottish identity that are to be found on the Royal Mile. While these are certainly important, the charm of history that pervades these streets has a tendency to obscure the fact that the whole area resonates with power.

At the top of the Royal Mile is the entrance to the debating chamber of the Scottish Parliament, temporarily housed in the Church of Scotland's Assembly Hall. For more than one hundred and fifty years, this impressive building, whose origins will be discussed presently, has been the center of ecclesiastical power. In Parliament Square, next door to St. Giles (itself a power center of sorts) is the Scottish Supreme Court, focus of legal power. At the foot of the Royal Mile, off the Canongate, the new Scottish Parliament building is currently under construction. Just to complete the picture, the Castle (representing the power of the armed forces) is situated at one end of the Royal Mile, while the power of the throne, in the form of the Palace of Holyrood House, is to be found at the other.

Yet, it should not be forgotten that, for all its importance and fascination, the Royal Mile is only a part of Edinburgh's Old Town. The streets and closes—particularly those on the south side of the street—lead into a part of the city that has a completely different atmosphere.

CHAPTER THREE

Dark Deeds: The Old Town

"You go under dark arches and down dark stairs and alleys. The way is so narrow that you can lay a hand on either wall; so steep that, in greasy winter weather, the pavement is almost as treacherous as ice. Washing dangles above washing from the windows; the houses bulge outwards upon flimsy brackets; you see a bit of sculpture in a dark corner; at the top of all, a gable and a few crowsteps are printed on the sky. Here, you come into a court where the children are at play and the grown people sit upon their doorsteps, and perhaps a church spire shows itself above the roofs. Here, in the narrowest of the entry, you find a great old mansion still erect, with some insignia of its former state—some scutcheon, some holy or courageous motto, on the lintel. The local antiquary points out where famous and well-born people had their lodging; and as you look up, out pops the head of a slatternly woman from the countess's window."

Robert Louis Stevenson, *Edinburgh: Picturesque Notes*, 1879

Edinburgh grew outwards from the Royal Mile. In the first five centuries of the second millennium, the presence of the court at Holyrood and burgeoning European trade via the port of Leith ensured that the city would become a magnet for courtiers and merchants. The creation of both royal and commercial communities, together with the servants and tradesmen that they required, led to a steady increase in population. By the end of the sixteenth century, civic expansion became inevitable.

The first movement was directed southwards. A key development took place in 1582, when the council arranged for a building to be prepared for the reception of students in a stretch of open country called High Riggs. The University of Edinburgh is still largely based in this location and, as a matter of fact, nearly all of Edinburgh's educational institutions are either to be found in this part of the city or have their roots here. The University's central establishment, Old College, stands on land that was once occupied by the Collegiate Church of St. Mary in the Fields. Founded by Alexander II in 1275, this church had been established in High Riggs for more than three hundred years, but was soon to become a casualty of the Reformation.

Among its associated domestic buildings was the Prebendaries Chamber, better known to history as Kirk o'Field. It was here, on February 9, 1567, that Henry, Lord Darnley, consort of Mary, Queen of Scots, was assassinated. The motives for this murder, which has fascinated historians for centuries, are somewhat complicated, involving the failure of the queen's marriage, her adulterous relationship with the Earl of Bothwell and, by no means least, Darnley's own ambition to seize power as sole monarch.

Like many other episodes of Edinburgh history, this is a story that has become distorted in the telling. Oral tradition has fostered the belief that the murder was committed by means of an explosion—and it is certainly true that on the day in question Kirk o'Field was blown up by substantial quantity of gunpowder that had been stored for this purpose within the house. (There is a degree of circumstantial evidence that Mary's lover, the Earl of Bothwell was responsible for this act, although whether or not the queen herself had any hand in the deed has never been established.) Darnley, however, did not die as a result of this explosion. Somehow or other, he became aware of the danger and managed to escape from the house. It was during the course of this escape that he was caught by a number of Bothwell's men and strangled to death. As Antonia Fraser put it in her biography of Mary, Darnley "died, a boy of not yet twenty-one, as pathetically and unheroically as he had lived."

Old College stands on the place where this murder took place. The present building was built between 1789 and 1834 to replace a previous building that, after some two hundred years, was deemed to have reached the end of its active life. The great Scottish architect Robert Adam originally created the plans for its construction, but did not, unfortunately, live to see their completion. William Playfair later modified Adam's design.

South Bridge and George VI Bridge

There is no feeling of "town and gown" in Edinburgh, mainly because the University, being spread over a number of locations, has a profile that is not so easily identified as is the case elsewhere. There is no single building (not even Old College) that Edinburgh citizens can point out, when asked directions for "the university". But there is a distinct university quarter, lying between the two bridges that connect the Royal Mile with the area that was formerly known as High Riggs.

The oldest of these is South Bridge, at the foot of the High Street. Today, this is mainly a shopping thoroughfare, but it does contain a number of buildings that are of more than ordinary interest. The Tron Church, at the High Street end, has always played an important part in Edinburgh life. Until it was superseded by the fireworks concert in Princes Street, it was the traditional spot for revelers to gather when welcoming the New Year on Hogmanay. Although it has been redundant as a place of worship since 1952, it still has a function as a visitors' center. The original spire, wrote George Scott-Moncrieff in *Edinburgh* (1947), "was a charming piece of seventeenth-century work, replaced by the present monstrosity, which dwarfs and makes inconspicuous the abbreviated little church behind it so that it looks like a grubby little boy skulking behind the skirts of an over-dressed and unpleasant mamma."

On the other side of South Bridge is Surgeon's Hall, headquarters of the Royal College of Surgeons. Like so many other prominent Edinburgh buildings, this was designed by William Playfair (1790-1857), an architect whose work formed part of what was known as the neoclassical or Greek revival. Surgeon's Hall, with its impressively columned façade, is a typical Playfair building, which today houses a museum collection, founded in the sixteenth century, and a library that was first established in 1696. It was built between 1828 and 1832, on the site of a former riding-school.

Almost directly across the road from this building is the Festival Theatre, Edinburgh's second largest venue for live performance, with a capacity of approximately 2,000 seats. This is a rather interesting theater, since it was built on the remains of what was, for many years, Edinburgh's premier music hall, the Empire. The Empire itself, however, was simply one episode in a long tradition, which began some time in the 1820s, when Andrew Ducrow, a celebrated horseman, opened a circus there. At various times over the next hundred years, it was known as Ducrow's, the Royal Amphitheatre, the Queen's Theatre, the Southminster, and eventually the Empire. Until the collapse of commercial theater at the end of the 1950s, the Empire was graded in the top echelon as a receiving house for variety shows. Unlike its predecessor, which was a typical Victorian playhouse, the Festival Theatre is a glass-fronted modern building, its extensive front-of-house, restaurant and five seating levels being visible from the street.

South Bridge was opened in 1788. George VI Bridge, leading from the foot of the Lawnmarket, was not completed until 1836, creating a street that is full of important and influential buildings. On the northwest corner, for instance, stands an office block housing the administrative headquarters of the Scottish Parliament, while further to the south is Edinburgh's main lending library. Directly across the road from this is the National Library of Scotland, one of the UK's five copyright libraries. This library is in direct descent from the Advocates' Library, founded in 1682 and still located in Parliament Square, which received its copyright status—an entitlement to receive a copy of every book published in the UK—in 1710. Although the Advocates' Library, with the exception of its legal section, was transferred to the National Library in 1925, it would take another thirty years to create the new institution, which first opened its doors to the public in 1956. When one considers the National Library today, one cannot help but wonder why it took so long to construct. It is one of the ugliest buildings in Edinburgh, a boring block of sandstone that resembles nothing so much as a public swimming bath.

Edinburgh's earliest literary tavern was to be found where the National Library now stands. This was Johnnie Dowie's, said to be the favored watering hole of, successively, Allan Ramsay; Edinburgh's boy genius, Robert Fergusson; and his most famous adherent, Robert Burns. Other literary luminaries who frequented this pub included the journalist and academic, Christopher North, the poet Thomas Campbell and the leading collector of Scottish songs, David Herd. As described by Robert Chambers in his *Traditions of Edinburgh*, it does not appear to have been so very different from many of the pubs one would find in the locality today.

Johnnie Dowie's *was chiefly celebrated for ale*—Younger's Edinburgh ale—*a potent fluid which almost glued the lips of the drinker together, and of which few, therefore, could dispatch more than a bottle. John, a sleek, quiet-looking man, in a last-century style of attire, always brought in the liquor himself, decanted it carefully, drank a glass to the health of the company, and then retired.*

The road that connects South Bridge and George VI Bridge was built in 1871 and named after one of Edinburgh's most dynamic lord provosts, William Chambers, whose life and career will be discussed presently. Chambers Street contains a whole clutch of university buildings, including the Dental Hospital, the Faculty of Arts at Minto House, the University Staff Club, and, of course, Old College itself. This was also the location of Heriot-Watt University until 1974, when its operations were removed to the campus at Riccarton, on the western edge of the city. The original building, however, is still in use, located directly opposite Old College at the South Bridge end of Chambers Street. At the other end—the George VI Bridge end—is the Museum of Scotland, displaying a collection of documents and artifacts from every part of Scottish history, from earliest times until the end of the twentieth century.

This stunning building of reddish-gold sandstone was designed by Edinburgh architects Benson & Forsyth and opened to the public in 1998. Its six levels take the visitor through every period in Scottish history, from prehistory (Level 0) to the twentieth century (Level 6). These collections are complemented by interactive screen presentations throughout the museum, and on Level 1 is a resource room where visitors can gain access to multimedia programs, CD-ROMs and selected websites. Perhaps the most popular facility is the Tower Restaurant on Level 5, which has already become a fashionable rendezvous. Here, lunch and dinner are accompanied by spectacular views of the Castle and the city skyline.

A recent addition to the Museum of Scotland is the Scottish Sports Hall of Fame, which was inaugurated on St. Andrew's Day, 2002. This honors Scottish sporting heroes with exhibits celebrating their achievements. The first fifty inductees include such names as Kenny Dalglish and Denis Law (football), Gavin Hastings (rugby union),

Mike Denness (cricket), Willie Carson (horse racing), James Braid and Tommy Armour (golf), Ian Stewart and Allan Wells (athletics), Ken Buchanan and Benny Lynch (boxing) and Jim Clark and Jackie Stewart (motor racing).

The Cowgate

Both bridges have become so absorbed into the city landscape that one tends to forget, while walking on them, that one is crossing a valley. The road that runs between High Riggs and the Royal Mile is known as the Cowgate, the name deriving from the fact that this was a route that farmers took when driving their cattle to pasture. In a bygone era, it was known as "thief's row" and is a place that appears to have maintained its atmosphere over the centuries. It is a long, narrow tunnel of a street, with buildings rising like cliffs on both sides, which runs exactly parallel with the Royal Mile. Its narrowness, in fact, has often created problems, never more so than in December 2002, when a fire broke out in the vicinity. The Edinburgh fire brigade, assisted by other units, had to struggle to prevent this conflagration from getting out of control; had the flames crossed the Cowgate, the blaze might have engulfed the historic buildings of the Royal Mile. As things turned out, there was less damage than had, at first, been feared. The most significant building to suffer was a popular nightspot called The Gilded Balloon—a celebrated venue for stand-up comedy—which was completely gutted. Mercifully, there were no fatalities.

Here, we are truly in Jekyll-and-Hyde territory. As a matter of fact, Deacon William Brodie, the reputed model for Stevenson's story, lived close by, as did an equally appropriate model, Major Thomas Weir, who was strangled and burnt for the crime of witchcraft in 1670.

Major Weir, an officer in the Town Guard, lived in the West Bow (now Victoria Street), a long sloping street that connects the Lawnmarket to the Grassmarket, at the western end of the Cowgate. In Major Weir's day, the inhabitants of the West Bow, the so-called "Bowhead Saints", were noted for their piety, and the Major was no exception. According to Robert Chambers, he "was thought more angel than man and was termed by some of the holy sisters *Angelical Thomas*." Perhaps he became so obsessed with religion that he lost his reason, for there is little doubt that the man was completely mad. It is difficult to identify the precise crime that Major Weir is supposed to have committed. (This was true even at the time of his arrest. As a matter of fact, Sir Andrew Ramsay, who was provost at the time, was so unconvinced of Major Weir's guilt that he initially refused to take him into custody.) There seems to have been no real evidence to corroborate Weir's own confession to the crime of witchcraft. Indeed, the only criminal act for which there was any evidence whatsoever was incest. Both the Major and his sister Grizel (who was executed at the same time as her brother) confessed to living together in a sexual relationship. Even here, however, there is some room for doubt. Grizel seems to have been as crazy as Thomas; at the time of her execution, she had to be restrained from stripping off all her clothes in order "to die with as much shame as possible". She also made a number of confessions that later proved to be untrue.

The Grassmarket

The execution of the Weirs took place in the Grassmarket, the great square that lies on the south side of Castle Rock. The Grassmarket today has a certain continental atmosphere, home to a number of smart restaurants and hotels, with a residential population that is distinctly up-market. As its name suggests, though, this was originally the site of Edinburgh's main agricultural market place. A weekly market was held here for almost 450 years until 1911, when it was moved to Saughton in west Edinburgh. The square was also an important terminus in the days of stage-coach travel and, indeed, the original coaching inn, The White Hart, is still in business here.

After the departure of the market, the area went into a steady decline, becoming notorious as a meeting-place for the down-and-out. By 1974 Norman MacCaig was able to describe the Grassmarket as a place "where dragons' breaths are methylated/and social workers trap the unwary."

In 1989 the Grassmarket began to acquire a different reputation. Two young theater directors, Jeremy Weller and Jean Findlay, founded the Grassmarket Project, a theater company with a policy (to quote their publicity) of seeking "to portray real-life experiences of representatives of a specific social group, which find themselves, for one reason or another, at the margins of mainstream society." One of their

first shows, *GLAD*, featuring the homeless down-and-outs of the Grassmarket, made a considerable impact internationally, touring extensively throughout Europe and North America. The Grassmarket Project, or GMP as it is now known, has since produced plays that are concerned with young offenders, the mentally ill, striptease dancers, prostitutes, soldiers, vulnerable young people and those who belong to the underclass. Disdaining the employment of trained, professional actors, GMP's normal practice is to cast its plays from whatever milieu it happens to be examining. What it does, in fact, is the ultimate form of community theater, from which the participants gain as much benefit as the audience. Although the company retains its Edinburgh base, it has recently been working as far afield as Northern Ireland, Poland, Austria, Kosovo and Brazil. It has also been branching out into other media, with the production of a radio play and two films.

In former times, we have seen, the Grassmarket was Edinburgh's chief place of public executions. It was here, for instance, that the martyrs of the Covenanting struggle of the seventeenth century were put to death—the place today is marked with a stone in their memory. The Stony Sabbath riot that followed the attempt of the Dean of Edinburgh to introduce Archbishop Laud's new liturgy (see p.XX) was the beginning of a fight for civil and religious liberty that was to be carried on for the next fifty years. The document that lay at the heart of this struggle was known as the National Covenant, and the following description of it appears in Ratcliffe Barnett's *The Story of the Covenant* (1928):

> *This Magna Charta of Scots religious liberty consisted of three parts. The first part was a reproduction of an older Covenant of 1581, called the King's Confession, which asserted that the Pope's "worldlie monarchie, and wicked hierarchie" was abhorred and detested; the second part, which consisted of a detailed list of Acts of Parliament condemning Popery and confirming Presbyterianism, was naturally the work of Sir Archibald Johnston of Warriston, the lawyer of the Covenant. The third part, which was a solemn protest against those innovations of worship that had caused the nation to revolt, was the work of the Rev. Alexander Henderson, the parish minister of Leuchars in Fife.*
>
> *These two men had been requested to draw up a Covenant, which would be satisfactory to the suppliants. They finished the draft after an all-night sitting on 27th February 1638.*

The ensuing document was revealed the following day, when it was read aloud from the pulpit of Greyfriars Church and signed by thousands of adherents. The copy of the National Covenant that is on display at Huntly House shows quite clearly that many of the men and women who signed did so in their own blood. Copies of what became known as "the Fair Parchment" were dispatched to every part of Scotland, attracting many thousands more signatures.

The National Covenant, although perfectly legal in every respect, constituted an act of defiance to the authority of the throne. The response of Charles I—a monarch with a very low level of tolerance for acts of defiance—was predictable and immediate. He initiated a period of persecution that would continue, under different regimes, until the Glorious Revolution of 1688. Many of the Covenanting martyrs were put to death in the Grassmarket.

It was here, too, that the greatest of all Edinburgh riots took place in 1737. The story of the Porteous Riot, which forms the background to Scott's greatest novel *The Heart of Midlothian*, is quickly told. In March of 1736, a convicted smuggler called Andrew Wilson was hanged in the Grassmarket. Wilson had been a popular figure, partly because smuggling was not really considered a crime—duty on spirits was one consequence of the Act of Union which proved highly unpopular in Scotland—and partly because of his heroic part in the escape of his fellow-accused, a young man called George Robertson, on the Sunday previous to the execution. After Wilson had been dispatched on the gallows, some boys in the crowd began to pelt the City Guard with dirt and stones, prompting the commander of the Guard, Captain John Porteous, to order his men to open fire. As a result of this order, nine people were killed. Porteous was charged with murder, tried and found guilty. He was due to hang on September 7, 1737. At the last moment—prompted, it is said, by some judges with whom Porteous habitually played golf—Queen Caroline, then acting as regent in George II's absence, canceled the execution with the issue of a pardon. The population of Edinburgh, incensed by this injustice, ran riot, broke into the Tolbooth prison (where the prisoner was still being held) dragged Porteous out and carried out the hanging themselves. Scott's character, Reuben Butler, is a witness to the last moments of the unfortunate Porteous.

> *A loud shout proclaimed the stern delight with which the agents of this deed regarded its completion. Butler, then, at the opening into the low street called the Cowgate, cast back a terrified glance, and, by the red and dusky light of the torches, he could discern a figure wavering and struggling as it hung suspended above the heads of the multitude, and could even observe men striking at it with their Lochaber-axes and partisans. The sight was of a nature to double his horror, and to add wings to his flight.*

Queen Caroline, when she heard of this lynching, was furious and threatened that this event would have dire consequences for the city of Edinburgh. She summoned the provost, Alexander Wilson, to London, stripped him of his office and flung him in jail. She proposed pulling down the city walls and abolishing the Edinburgh City Guard, saying that she would turn all Scotland into "a hunting field".

Mercifully for Edinburgh, the Queen Regent died before her threats could be carried out and, as a result, the penalties were substantially watered down. Alexander Wilson, although released, was banned for life from holding public office, and the city was ordered to pay a substantial pension to the widow of John Porteous. It had, however, been a near thing; if Queen Caroline had had her way, Edinburgh would, at the very least, have lost many of its ancient privileges.

Mob Rule

At the time of the Porteous Riot, the Edinburgh mob had, in the words of Robert Chambers, "a part in the state" and was something of an institution that could, with some justification, argue that it had the sanction of the Crown. Two hundred and fifty years earlier, when the nobles of Scotland had attempted to depose James III, the Edinburgh Trades had risen in the King's support and as a result had been rewarded with the gift of their own standard. This flag, known as the Blue Blanket, was for many decades a traditional rallying point at times of disaffection.

By the time of the Porteous Riot, the potency of the Blue Blanket had long been swept away—yet another casualty of the Reformation—but would shortly be replaced by a symbol of even greater potency. One of the most colorful characters of the Cowgate at this time was a cobbler called Joseph Smith. Owing to a physical deformity, he had a pronounced and permanent stoop, accounting for his nickname "Bowed Joseph". His charismatic leadership of popular protest also earned him another nickname: "General" Joe Smith. His influence became so great that the Town Council would often seek his advice before embarking on any measure that was likely to prove unpopular. His practice of beating on a drum, it is said, could summon a mob of ten thousand people within a single hour. The power of Joe's Drum is illustrated by an anecdote that Robert Chambers tells in his *Traditions of Edinburgh*.

A poor man in the Pleasance having been a little deficient in his rent, and in the country on business, his landlord seized and rouped his household furniture, turning out the family to the street. On the poor man's return, finding the house desolate and his family in misery, he went to a neighbouring stable and hanged himself. Bowed Joseph did not long remain ignorant of the case; and as soon as it was generally known in the city, he shouldered on his drum, and after beating it through the streets for half-an-hour, found himself followed by several thousand persons, inflamed with resentment at the landlord's cruelty. With his army he marched to an open space of ground named Thomson's Park, where, mounted upon the shoulders of six of his lieutenant generals, he proceeded to harangue them concerning the flagrant oppression that they were about to revenge. He concluded by directing his men to sack the premises of the cruel landlord, who by this time had wisely made his escape; and this order was instantly obeyed. Every article which the house contained was brought out to the street, where, being piled up in a heap, the general set fire to them with his own hand, while the crowd rent the air with their acclamations.

St. Cecilia's Hall

The Cowgate, where Bowed Joseph lived, has not always been on the dark side of Edinburgh. Lord Cockburn, in *Memorials of His Time* (1856), recalls the Cowgate as a resort of the most fashionable elements of Edinburgh society:

Saint Cecilia's Hall was the only public resort of the musical, and besides being our most selectly fashionable place of amusement, was the best and the most beautiful concert room I have ever yet seen. And there have I myself seen most of our literary and fashionable gentlemen, predominating with their side curls, and frills, and ruffles, and silver buckles; and our stately matrons stiffened in hoops, and gorgeous satin; and our beauties with high-heeled shoes, powdered and pomatumed hair, and lofty and composite head dresses. All this was in the Cowgate! The last retreat now a days of destitution and disease.

Since 1960, when it was restored for use as the University of Edinburgh's School of Music, St. Cecilia's Hall has become well known as a Festival venue. Originally built by William Mylne for the Musical Society of Edinburgh in 1762, its design was based on the Opera House at Parma and its oval hall had—and still has—a capacity of 500. Although this building has, in its time, been put to many uses, including Baptist church, Freemasons' meeting house, school and dance hall, it has successfully survived the centuries.

Across the road, its spire clearly visible from the South Bridge, is another historic building. This is the Magdalen Chapel, where the Scottish Reformation had its origins. It is at least possible that the very first General Assembly of the Church of Scotland met here in May 1560, and it is certainly true that the Assembly that decided that the Reformed Church would have a Presbyterian government made this decision here in 1578. Robert Chambers has left a precise account of its history prior to this date.

> It was erected immediately before the Reformation by a pious citizen, Michael Macquhan, and Janet Rhynd, his widow, whose tomb is shown in the floor. The windows towards the south were anciently filled with stained glass; and there still remain some specimens of that kind of ornament, which, by some strange chance, had survived the Reformation. In a large department at the top of one window are the arms of Mary of Guise, who was queen-regent at the time the chapel was built. The arms of Macquhan and his wife are also to be seen. In the lower panes, which have been filled with small figures of saints, only one remains—a St Bartholomew—who, by a rare chance, has survived the general massacre. The whole is now very carefully preserved.

Although it has performed absolutely no function for a great many years, the Magdalen Chapel remains intact and was recently taken over by the Scottish Reformation Society. At the time of writing, a degree of restoration is taking place and it will shortly be open to the public.

Underground City

One is bound to ask, nonetheless, what occurred to make this historic church building, and the thoroughfare on which it is situated, fall into decline in the first place. Social history, as is so often the case, provides the answer. The Industrial Revolution affected Edinburgh as crucially as any other British city, a significant event taking place in 1818, when work began on the Union Canal, linking Edinburgh with Glasgow. This was a very labor-intensive enterprise, providing work for many thousands of men. Many of these workers were Irish immigrants and, since the Edinburgh end of the waterway was originally planned to be in the suburb of Portsburgh, slightly to the west of the Grassmarket, a large number of them found accommodation in the Cowgate, lowering the social tone of the area. Buildings like the Magdalen Chapel, once emblematic of the area's distinction, duly fell into decline.

The arrival of so many new citizens would, in time, provide the basis for one of Edinburgh's most persistent legends: the idea that there is another city existing beneath the ground. This may seem preposterous, but when one examines the evidence, it is easy to understand how such a story originated. Overcrowding, as mentioned earlier, was a continual problem in the Old Town, leading to the creation of the towering "lands" of the Royal Mile. By the early nineteenth century, it simply was not possible to build these tenements any higher, and the only option left was to increase accommodation by developing cellars and opening up underground chambers at the very base of the Royal Mile.

The remains of this development are to be seen in the Cowgate, immediately below the South Bridge. Apart from the fact that a number of these chambers were built next to the foundations of the Bridge, the most dramatic evidence of the "underground city" is a large complex of subterranean chambers known as the South Bridge Vaults. In 1994 these vaults were open to the public for the first time and now house several bars, nightclubs and performance areas. Only part of the complex has been developed in this way, however, and there are still many tunnels and chambers that exist in their original form. Several ghost stories have become associated with these chambers and, for those who are interested in such matters, it is possible to visit them with an informed tour guide. It seems strange to think that these catacombs—constituting as they do, if not an underground city, at least an underground neighborhood—once provided living space for literally hundreds of families.

McGonagall: King of Doggerel

Sometime in the 1820s, a man called McGonagall brought his family to the Cowgate. Originally from Northern Ireland, he had recently been working in Ayr and would, after a number of years in the Cowgate, move on to Glasgow, Orkney and, finally, Dundee. Although McGonagall does not appear to have found the settled life for which he was looking, his son was to earn a peculiar sort of fame. William Topaz McGonagall, poet and tragedian, was born in the Cowgate in March 1825.

The amazing thing about McGonagall is that his verse (one can scarcely call it poetry) continues to attract attention. Since his death in 1902, his *Poetic Gems* (1890) have gone through edition after edition and his work has enjoyed a popularity that many more distinguished poets might envy. A contemporary critic, Owen Dudley Edwards, has explained this strange celebrity by contending that MacGonagall appeals to people who despise *all* poetry. The matter is complicated by the fact that his work has often been subjected to parody, to such an extent that many of the parodies have become accepted, through oral transmission, as genuine McGonagall pieces. For instance, when asked to quote McGonagall, many people will reply with the following verse:

When the moon is fair and roond
The fishes swim frae Ayr tae Troon
But when the moon is roond and fair,
The fishes swim frae Troon tae Ayr.

Now, that verse could not possibly have been written by McGonagall; it is much too clever. Apart from that, there is a giveaway in the Scots usage. McGonagall's exemplar was Shakespeare, not Burns, and he rather disdained the use of the Scots tongue. Additionally, there is an attempt at humor in that verse, immediately identifying it as a parody. McGonagall was only ever *unconsciously* funny. The following lines, coming from a poem McGonagall addressed to his native city, are typical of his grotesque style:

Beautiful city of Edinburgh!
Where the tourist can drown his sorrow

By viewing your monuments and statues fine
During the lovely summer-time.
I'm sure it will his spirits cheer
As Sir Walter Scott's monument draws near,
That stands in East Princes Street
Amongst flowery gardens, fine and neat.
And Edinburgh castle is magnificent to be seen
With its beautiful walks and trees so green.

For most of his life, MacGonagall lived in Dundee and it is from that city that the most detailed description of him comes. Lowden Macartney, a Dundee bookseller, remembered McGonagall well and wrote a commentary on him for a pamphlet edition of his verses.

He was a strange, weird, drab figure, and suggested more than anything else a broken-down actor. He wore his hair long, and sheltered it with a wide-rimmed hat. His clothes were always shabby, and even in summer he refused to discard his overcoat. Dignity and long skirts are considered inseparable, and a poet is ruined if he is not dignified. He had a solemn, sallow face, with heavy features and eyes of the sort termed fish-like (I don't know why). Slow of movement, with a slight stoop acquired at the hand-loom formerly, but latterly at the desk, when he left off weaving cloth to take up the more congenial task of weaving dreams, leaning as he walked on a stout stick, he moved about the street, from shop to shop, from office to office, and from house to house in the residential parts of the town, vending his broadsides.

McGonagall's life ended where it began, in the Cowgate. He returned to the city of his birth at some point in the 1890s and spent his final years in the Cowgate, prior to his death in 1902.

St. Patrick's: Irish Edinburgh

By 1865, the poet and novelist Alexander Smith was writing the following description of the Cowgate:

The Cowgate is the Irish portion of the city. They keep to their own quarters, and seldom come up to the light of day. Many an Edinburgh man

has never set his foot in the street: the condition of the inhabitants is as
little known to respectable Edinburgh as are the habits of moles, earth
worms and the mining population. The people of the Cowgate seldom
visit the upper streets.

The Irish contribution to Edinburgh culture is by no means insignificant, as evidenced by the existence in the city of a number of beautiful Catholic churches, one of which is to be found in the Cowgate itself.

This is St. Patrick's, perhaps the most beautiful of all Edinburgh churches, with its dome-shaped tower, graceful portico, and interior decorations by Alexander Runciman. It is also a church with a curious history. Although it is probably the best-known Catholic chapel in Edinburgh, it was originally built to house an Episcopalian congregation. These were the so-called "qualified" Episcopalians, who adopted the rituals of the Church of England and supported the Hanoverian cause, as opposed to the Episcopalians who supported the Stuart kings. Their numbers grew steadily after the failure of the Jacobite Rebellion, (which had been supported by all "non-qualified Episcopalians"), and by 1771 their existing chapels became too small to contain them. Since this congregation included some of the most wealthy and influential figures in Edinburgh society, they had little difficulty in raising the £8,000 that was required to build their new church, which opened on Sunday, October 9, 1774.

Over the next 44 years, the building flourished as a fashionable place of worship. By 1818, however, most of the congregation had moved to the New Town and attended services there, so the vacant church was sold to an evangelical congregation that had seceded from the Church of Scotland. For the next 38 years, therefore, an extremely strict form of Presbyterianism was the order of the day in this church. It was not until 1856, by which time the Irish Catholic population in Edinburgh had grown to considerable proportions, that the Roman Catholic Church bought St. Patrick's.

The arrival of such a large Catholic population in the center of the city of John Knox may seem like a recipe for disorder but, as a matter of fact, both Catholic and Presbyterian communities in Edinburgh have coexisted, on the whole, quite happily. There has certainly always been a sense of competition—expressed mainly through the rivalry of the football teams, Hibernian and Heart of Midlothian—but the occasions on which this has resulted in sectarian violence have been few. The most serious outbreaks took place during the course of the summer of 1935 and were orchestrated by a political party and its charismatic leader, John Cormack.

Cormack (1894-1978) is possibly the most intriguing figure in the entire history of Edinburgh politics. As a young man, during service as a soldier in Ireland, he had become convinced that Catholic priests were organizing the entire Irish struggle against the British. This made him a bitter and uncompromising enemy of the Church of Rome and, for more than thirty years, he fought a political campaign that was dedicated to this belief. He was an extremely eloquent and persuasive public speaker, and the party that he founded, Protestant Action, achieved a degree of political success because of this charisma, inviting comparisons with Hitler and the Nazis. But Cormack was no Hitler. As he grew older, he modified his beliefs quite considerably and, at the time of his death, had become something of an institution.

In 1935, however, John Cormack was still very much the demagogue. In April of that year, the Catholic Young Men's Society (an organization that had been created in imitation of the YMCA) was holding its Scottish conference in Edinburgh and, as was usual in such cases, was to be given a civic reception. Cormack angrily objected, calling on all Protestants to come out on the streets "ready for action if needs be". That week's *Edinburgh Evening Dispatch* described the response to this injunction:

> *The scene at St Patrick's Church was a remarkable one. From an early hour in the evening, parties of young men were to be seen about the grounds of the church. They formed an unofficial guard, and as the evening advanced, their numbers swelled by several hundreds of other young men of the parish. While the crowds were shouting at the High Street and at the Tron Church, they stood around the church in quiet groups.*
>
> *At one time there seemed to be as many as 300 of them present at the church. As the police moved the crowd down the High Street, the anti-Catholic cries of the demonstrators could be heard distinctly at the*

*church, and with the appearance at the entrance of the close leading to
the church of a group of men and women shouting "Down with the
papists", the Catholics feared an attack on the church itself.*

This was just the beginning of a campaign which raged through
Edinburgh that summer, culminating in a series of street battles that
took place during the Eucharistic Conference held in the city in the
same year. These were so bad that Andrew Joseph McDonald,
Archbishop of St. Andrews and Edinburgh, felt obliged to issue a
statement of protest, part of which reads as follows:

*Priests were savagely assaulted, elderly women attacked and kicked, bus-
loads of children mercilessly stoned and inoffensive citizens abused and
assailed in a manner that is almost unbelievable in any civilized community of today.*

*During all this campaign of attack and persecution, the self-restraint
of the Catholic body has been beyond all praise. In particular at the
concluding service of the Congress, had that forbearance not been hero-
ically sustained, bloodshed would undoubtedly have ensued.*

*There are limits to human endurance and, if the continuance of
these conditions leads to dangerous public order, then the disastrous consequences cannot be laid at the door of the Catholic body.*

*The disgraceful scenes to which I have referred have become known
in every quarter of the globe, and have sullied the fair name of a city,
which was justly regarded as a leader in all culture, thought and civilization.*

*It seems to me that the public of the capital of Scotland cannot regard
such a result with equanimity. I am certain that the bulk of the citizens,
fair-minded and enlightened as I know them to be, must, when the facts
are brought to their knowledge, regard with abhorrence the actions of
what, after all, is a mob of the lowest elements of the city, supported by
importees of a similar class from other parts of the country.*

*But the question which faces all who have the interests of the city at
heart is—can this mob-rule be allowed to continue?*

It is to the credit of the people of Edinburgh that they were able to
make a positive response to this appeal. After the summer of 1935,

electoral support for Protestant Action began to melt away and although he was to remain a city councilor for another 27 years, Cormack was never so influential again. While it would be erroneous to claim that sectarianism no longer exists in Edinburgh, it is certainly the case that a number of factors, in particular the decline in church adherence that has affected all denominations over the past half-century, have combined to rob it of any focus.

Today, the Cowgate no longer houses an Irish Catholic population or, indeed, much of a population of any kind. Cowgate residents are few in numbers compared with the 1930s. Nowadays, the street is full of clubs and late night drinking dens, giving it a reputation for excess and occasional violence. According to Ian Rankin's fictional Inspector Rebus, one of the nicknames the police have for the Cowgate is "Little Saigon". As recently as 2002, the television presenter Daisy Donovan mentioned this in an interview she gave to *The Scotsman* about her student days in the 1970s. Apparently, Ms. Donovan, who lived in a flat off the Royal Mile, recalled the sight of "pools of blood in the Cowgate" as her most enduring Edinburgh memory. When Irvine Welsh's character Renton, played by Ewan MacGregor, is seen running along the same street in the opening shot of Danny Boyle's film of *Trainspotting*, the location seems particularly appropriate.

The ambiance of the Cowgate is so different from that of the University quarter that they might be located in two different cities—and indeed, for all their geographical proximity, correspondence between them is something that occurs but rarely. In the early part of the nineteenth century, however, an occurrence took place that involved both districts in a dramatic, not to say sensational, manner.

Burke and Hare

Until the passing of the Anatomy Act in 1832, there were very few legal ways that dead bodies could be procured for medical research, which meant that, inevitably, the source of supply was both limited and unreliable. Anatomists such as Dr. Robert Knox, who lectured in anatomy at Edinburgh University, were therefore obliged to deal with so-called "resurrection men" who would, for a consideration, rob graves on their behalf. In December 1827, Knox paid an Irishman called William Burke eight pounds for the corpse of an old man. Over the course of the next year, Knox would have further dealings with Burke and his accomplice, William Hare. Quite clearly, he seems to have assumed that the two Irishmen had been robbing graves. This, of course, is what they encouraged him to think.

Burke and Hare, in fact, *never* robbed graves and would never have thought of doing so. As Owen Dudley Evans has pointed out, they "cut out the middleman." They were serial killers, pure and simple, who sought to profit from the heartless nature of the society in which they lived. Their victims were invariably people without any relatives who would notice that they had gone missing. It was only when they murdered a popular local character, a mentally retarded young man known as Daft Jamie, that their neighbors began to grow suspicious. When Burke was seen in the company of an old Irishwoman who later disappeared, these same neighbors sent for the police. After investigations had taken place, Hare agreed to give testimony against Burke in exchange for immunity from prosecution. Accordingly, Burke and his mistress Helen McDougal were charged with murder and their trial began on Wednesday, December 24, 1828. Burke was found guilty, condemned to death and hanged a month later. Helen McDougal was found "not proven" and released. Hare, of course, was not even charged.

During the course of the trial, it was revealed that there had been no fewer than fifteen victims and that Hare, irrespective of his testimony, was just as guilty as Burke. Guiltiest of all, however—at least in the eyes of the Edinburgh public—was the receiver of Burke and Hare's grisly acquisitions. Dr. Robert Knox was charged with no crime, did not figure in the trial (not even as a witness), and there is little reason to suppose that he knew anything at all about the murders. Nevertheless, there was a public outcry against the anatomist, his effigy was hanged outside his front door, the windows of his house were smashed, and he was eventually forced out of his place at the University. Even Sir Walter Scott was to write that the action of Knox was "a horrid example of how men may stumble and fall in the full march of intellect."

Later writers seem equally convinced of his guilt. The story has provided the inspiration for a number of pieces of imaginative fiction, including Stevenson's story *The Body Snatchers* (1884), James Bridie's play *The Anatomist* (1930) and Dylan Thomas' screenplay *The Doctor and the Devils* (published in 1953, never filmed). In every case, the character of Knox is given little sympathy.

The story has a final, ironic twist, which seems to have eluded most of these writers. After the execution of Burke on the January 28, 1829, the body was immediately taken to the Medical School to be dissected. This was to be William Burke's final contribution to medical research in Edinburgh.

Literary Connections

The Medical School itself stands in Teviot Row, at the southern end of George VI Bridge, and is very firmly based in the University quarter. So, too, is George Square, found immediately behind the Medical School, where a definite campus-like atmosphere prevails. In this most charming of Edinburgh squares (where, incidentally, Sir Walter Scott spent his childhood) a number of university departments are based, including the departments of English Literature and Celtic and the School of Scottish Studies. Other University buildings located here include the David Hume Tower, the William Robertson building, the University Library, and the George Square Theatre. These are modern buildings, which, when they were built in the late 1960s, caused some controversy, owing to the fact that the south side of George Square had to be pulled down to make way for them. Robert Garioch made his contribution to this debate with his poem, "George Square", written in 1973.

> *With two jets in its roof, the Library*
> *stands, a two-engined Handley Page, and roars*
> *with double blast right upwards at the sky.*

Action-reaction, equal-opposite,
hold down that cage, all windows and glass doors
and flimsy bars, making hard work of it,
an unsolved literary mystery?

The structure's even lighter than it looks,
perhaps; a trick of the Venetian blinds
may carry weight for eyes that see no books
from here, outside, as matter, but as thought
enclosed in tomes by men of soaring minds
who seem to us magicians, and who caught
their albatrosses, eagles, doves and rooks.

In the immediate vicinity, lying just behind the David Hume Tower, Buccleuch Place is a broad street almost exclusively occupied by academic departments. It was here, at No.18, in March 1802 that *The Edinburgh Review*, arguably the most influential literary journal of its time, was founded by Francis Jeffrey and others, including Henry Brougham and Sydney Smith. First published by Constable in Edinburgh and later by Longman in London, *The Edinburgh Review* appeared quarterly, setting a new standard in criticism. At the height of its renown, it had a circulation of 14,000, some of its issues proving so sought after that they were reprinted as many as ten times. This pre-eminence lasted, moreover, for over a century, the last issue of the journal appearing in 1929.

This area is full of literary associations. It was here in 1809 that the young Thomas Carlyle arrived—after a three day walk from his home in Ecclefechan—to study for a general arts degree. Thirty years earlier, Mrs. Agnes McLehose, better known as "Clarinda", had a house in nearby Alison Square, where she entertained her great love, Robert Burns. Just a few years later, Thomas Campbell arrived in Alison Square and it was here that he wrote his great poem "The Pleasures of Hope" with its immediately familiar opening:

At summer eve, when Heaven's ethereal bow
Spans with bright arch the glittering hills below,
Why to yon mountain turns the musing eye,

Whose sunbright summit mingles with the sky?
Why do those cliffs of shadowy tint appear
More sweet than all the landscape smiling near?
Tis distance lends enchantment to the view,
And robes the mountain in its azure hue.

Alison Square, where these lines were written, was demolished some time ago to create Marshall Street, a throughway between Nicolson Square and Potterow. Robert Chambers in his *Traditions of Edinburgh* describes Campbell's sojourn in this part of the city as follows:

In Alison Square Thomas Campbell lived while composing his Pleasures of Hope. *The place where any deathless composition took its shape from the author's brain is worthy of a place in the chart. A lady, the early friend of Campbell and his family, indicates their residence at that time as being the second door in the stair, entered from the east side, on the north side of the arch, the windows looking partly into Nicolson Square and partly to the Potterrow. The same authority states that much of the poem was written in the middle of the night, and from a sad cause. The poet's mother, it seems, was of a temper so extremely irritable that her family had no rest till she retired for the night. It was only at that season that the young poet could command repose of mind for his task.*

Yet another literary figure associated with this vicinity is Thomas de Quincey (1785-1859). Towards the end of his life, de Quincey had lodgings at 42 Lothian Street, where he completed the final version of *Confessions of an English Opium Eater*, first published in 1821. The house where he lived was demolished some years ago to make way for the Edinburgh University Student Centre.

Greyfriars

At the time of its foundation, the University of Edinburgh lay at the center of a cultural enclave, comprising a number of educational and religious institutions, including two monasteries: the Grey Friars (Franciscans) and The Black Friars (Dominicans). The Black Friars was the older of the two, dating back to the time of Robert the Bruce, who granted the monastery's charter in 1325. After the Battle of

Bannockburn, Bruce also gave the Black Friars the silks and tapestries he had taken from the pavilion of the English King. These, together with other treasures, were held in the monastery for centuries but, like the institution itself, did not survive the storm of the Reformation.

The Grey Friars became established in Edinburgh in the fifteenth century. Originally situated in the Grassmarket, this monastery flourished for just over a century until 1558, when the Earl of Argyll laid waste to it during the social upheaval that presaged the Reformation. Four years later, Queen Mary granted the monastery and its gardens to the Town Council for use as a graveyard and this remains its function today. It is situated very close to the juncture of Chambers Street and George VI Bridge. It was within this graveyard, in fact, that the first post-Reformation church in Edinburgh was built. Greyfriars was to become one of the most historic churches in the long and eventful history of the Scottish church—the scene of the signing of the National Covenant in 1638. The congregation was also to enjoy the services of many famous ministers, including the first principal of Edinburgh University, Robert Rollock, the Covenanters Robert Trail and Gilbert Rule, the historian William Robertson and, probably the most celebrated of all, Dr. Thomas Guthrie.

Guthrie (1803-1872) was ordained as one of the ministers of Greyfriars—which was at that time split into two parishes—in 1837. A physically large man, he was absolutely fearless and possessed of a conscience to match his courage. As his son Charles, himself to become a celebrated Scottish jurist, wrote of him in 1923: "He was eager, enthusiastic, quickly-responsive, ready to leap into the arena 'for the cause that needs assistance, for the wrongs that need resistance,' to use words he often quoted." Guthrie was also an extremely popular preacher. The announcement that he was to preach, in Edinburgh or anywhere else, always drew huge crowds. He used his eloquence to good effect and was always active in the social movements of his day. He took a leading part in the agitation for a national system of education that produced the Scotch Education Act of 1872, and was one of the first in Scotland to advocate compulsory education. But his name is principally associated with the cause of the so-called "ragged schools", providing education for the city's poor.

In 1843 Guthrie left Greyfriars (in circumstances that will be dealt with in a later chapter) and so has no connection with one of Edinburgh's most captivating fables, the story of Greyfriars Bobby. There are a number of different versions of this story but they all retain the essential details. Greyfriars Bobby was a little terrier whose master of many years, an Edinburgh policeman called John Gray, died in 1858. After the funeral, Bobby remained at the grave and could not be persuaded to leave. A local publican undertook to feed the little dog and, for the next fourteen years, Bobby spent part of each day keeping vigil at the graveside, where he died and where he was finally laid to rest. In 1873 Lady Baroness Burdett-Coutts, in recognition of this act of fidelity, erected a drinking fountain to commemorate Bobby, commissioning the sculptor William Brodie to make a bronze statue of the little dog. Both fountain and statue survive outside Greyfriars today and are still held in great affection by Edinburgh people.

George Heriot: "Jingling Geordie"

Next door to Greyfriars is one of Edinburgh's oldest-established schools, George Heriot's. The founder of this school, George Heriot, is a featured character in Scott's *The Fortunes of Nigel* (1822), where he is described as follows:

> *He might have seemed some secretary or clerk engaged in the service of the public, only that his low, flat, and unadorned cap, and his well-blacked, shining shoes, indicated that he belonged to the city. He was a well-made man, about the middle size, and seemed in firm health, though advanced in years. His looks expressed sagacity and good-humour: and the air of respectability, which his dress announced, was well supported by his clear eye, ruddy cheek, and grey hair. He used the Scottish idiom in his first address, but in such a manner that it could hardly be distinguished whether he was passing upon his friend a sort of jocose mockery, or whether it was his own native dialect, for his ordinary discourse had little provincialism.*

Although he occupies a justified place as "Jingling Geordie" in Edinburgh folklore (his nickname derived from his vast wealth), Heriot is far from being a fictional character. Born in 1563, he was an

Edinburgh jeweler who became goldsmith to King James VI and I and, through this connection, did business with most of the Scottish and English nobility. So successful was he that, on his death in 1623, he left a considerable fortune, which went to establish a trust to found a "hospital" for poor children. Investing the funds in land financed this philanthropy. By means of feu-duty—a remnant of the feudal system that survived in Scotland until the 1960s—the trustees derived income from lands they had sub-leased to property developers. A great part of modern Edinburgh is built on land that was, at one time or another, in the possession of the George Heriot Trust. The profits from these investments not only built and sustained George Heriot's Hospital (which was renamed George Heriot's School in1886) but also established some thirty additional "free schools" along similar lines. In 1879 the Heriot Trust took over the Watt Institute in Chambers Street to create the Heriot-Watt College, which was granted university status in 1964.

The school building is a rather dramatic structure in the style of a Tudor castellated hall. The quadrangular edifice encloses a court with Heriot's statue at its center and turreted towers at each corner. This design has been attributed to the English classical architect Inigo Jones and the building was completed in 1650.

Facing Heriot's is a location which, at the time of writing, is about to undergo a profound physical and cultural change. The Royal Infirmary of Edinburgh is the city's leading hospital and has occupied this site since 1870. Prior to that date, however, this was the location of yet another educational institution. George Watson, a Scottish merchant in Rotterdam, died in 1723 and left money for a school to be built in Edinburgh. This school—originally styled George Watson's Hospital, it later became known as Watson's Merchant Academy—stood across the road from Heriot's for more than a century. After the sale in 1870, George Watson's College removed to a new building further south and the Royal Infirmary occupied the site for the next one hundred and thirty years. It was, in fact, the third hospital of that name to be established in Edinburgh. The first infirmary, established in Robertson's Close, near the site of the old Blackfriars monastery, secured a Royal Charter in 1736. This hospital could hardly have been satisfactory, since the College of Surgeons (established in the Old Town since 1505) set up a rival hospital in their premises in nearby College Wynd. Fortunately, whatever differences existed between the infirmary and the surgeons were resolved and the two hospitals merged to create the Second Royal Infirmary in 1738. This is the hospital, standing for more than a century and a half in Infirmary Street, that, together with the associated medical school, established Edinburgh's international reputation as a center of medical education. It was here that Joseph Lister (1827-1912) revolutionized surgery by the introduction of antisepsis and it was here, too, that W.E. Henley composed his poem "Invictus", with its famous line "my head is bloodied but unbowed." Henley, friend and collaborator of Stevenson, is believed by many to have been the model for the character of Long John Silver in *Treasure Island*. Not a major literary figure in his own right, he owes his place in

literary history to his friendship with Stevenson and his ardent support, as editor of *The National Observer*, of the young Rudyard Kipling.

By 1870 this building had become too small for the demand that its excellence had created and a third Royal Infirmary was required. The land has, just recently, changed hands once more. A fourth Royal Infirmary has been built in the southern suburb of Little France, and the land and buildings of the old Infirmary have been taken over for the development of a new project, to be called Quartermile, Edinburgh. The aim of this project is to create a completely new residential and business precinct in the Old Town, including 600 new homes, speciality shops, cafés, bars, restaurants and a metro-style supermarket. All of this will take seven years to carry out and completion is anticipated no earlier than 2010. The road that runs between Heriot's and what we must now call Quartermile is called Lauriston Place and might be said to sum up this part of the city very tidily. At one end of this road is Edinburgh's famous Medical School, while at the other stands the Edinburgh College of Art. There is something of an irony, however, that so many educational institutions are to be found in a district of the city whose atmosphere is largely defined by dark deeds.

CHAPTER FOUR

"A Wholly Grand City": The New Town

"A more striking contrast than exists between these two parts of the same city could hardly be imagined. On one side a succession of splendid squares, elegant granite houses, broad and well-paved streets, columns, statues and clean sidewalks, thinly promenaded and by the well-dressed exclusively—the kind of wholly grand and half deserted city, which has been built too ambitiously for its population; and, on the other, an antique wilderness of streets and 'wynds' so narrow and lofty as to shut out much of the light of heaven; a thronging, busy and particularly dirty population; sidewalks almost impassable from children and other respected nuisances; and altogether, between the irregular and massive architecture and the unintelligible jargon agonizing the air about you, a most outlandish and strange city. Paris is not more unlike Constantinople than one side of Edinburgh is unlike the other. Nature has properly placed a great gulf between them."

Nathaniel Willis, *Pencillings by the Way*, 1845

The Jacobite rising in 1745 was an important episode in the development of Edinburgh, so it would be as well to begin this chapter with a brief outline of its history.

In 1688 the ruling dynasty of Great Britain changed when James II was deposed in favour of his sister, Mary Stuart and her husband, William of Orange. This event, known to history as "the Glorious Revolution", established the constitutional monarchy that remains in place today, but its importance was not nearly so evident at the time. After all, James' brother and predecessor as king, Charles II, had spent nine years in exile prior to his Restoration in 1660, so there was at least a possibility that the old regime could be restored once more. James had many supporters, known as "Jacobites" in both Scotland and England and, over the next fifty years, there would be no fewer than three attempts at restoring the Stuarts to the British throne. The most successful of these took place in 1745 and was led by the most charismatic leader ever to figure in Scottish history, James II's grandson, Prince Charles Edward Stuart, popularly known as "Bonnie Prince Charlie".

By this time, several monarchs had come and gone. William and Mary reigned jointly until 1694, when Mary died. William was sole monarch until his death in 1702, when Mary's sister, Anne, succeeded him. When the childless Anne died in 1714, she was succeeded by the Elector of Hanover, who became George I, later succeeded by his son, George II, thereby establishing the Hanoverian dynasty. This was the dynasty that the Jacobites proposed to evict from the British throne.

The Prince landed at Eriskay in the Outer Hebrides in July 1745 and quickly raised an army of some five thousand Highland clansmen. Moving south, the Jacobite army entered Edinburgh on September 15 and a few days later scored their first success when they defeated a Hanoverian army, led by Lieutenant-General Sir John Cope, at Prestonpans, a few miles east of the city. After this victory, the Prince remained in Edinburgh for another month, during which time his legend was born. For this brief period, the Scottish court, which had been discontinued when James I succeeded to the throne of England and moved to London in 1603, flourished once more in the balls and levees that were held at Holyrood. It was at this time, however, that the Prince made the tactical blunder that was to lead to his ultimate defeat.

Against the advice of a majority of the clan chiefs, he decided to march into England, believing that a substantial number of English Jacobites would flock to his colors. This simply did not happen, and before the end of the year the Prince's army was forced to retreat to Scotland. Two further battles followed: a Jacobite rout of the Hanoverians under Cope's successor, General Hawley, at Falkirk; and, only two months later, in April 1746, a crushing defeat by another Hanoverian army under the Duke of Cumberland at Culloden, which put an end to the Rising.

After Culloden, it became clear to even the most ardent Jacobites that neither Prince nor court was ever going to return to the city. This being the case, the Scottish aristocracy would have no reason to remain and, if Edinburgh was not to decline in status, it would need to be developed along completely different lines. In short, the city would have to re-invent itself.

At the time, of course, the city was much smaller than it is today, with a population of approximately 23,500 citizens, mostly crowded together in the area around the Castle and the Royal Mile. There were only two suburbs: Canongate in the east, most of which has since been absorbed into the Royal Mile; and Portsburgh to the south, both lying outside the city wall—built as a result of the Scottish army's disastrous defeat at Flodden in 1513—which enclosed Edinburgh on three sides. On the fourth side, the northern side, lay a large body of water called The Nor' Loch.

"To enlarge and beautify the town"

The leading promoter of change was Lord Provost George Drummond. Politically, Drummond was a Whig, who identified the Hanoverian succession with stability and progress. At the age of just eighteen, he had been appointed accountant-general to the Scottish Parliament and, as such, had been responsible for the financial computations involved in the Act of Union in 1707. In 1715 he took up arms against the Earl of Mar's unsuccessful rebellion and thirty years later became responsible for the defense of Edinburgh against the advancing Jacobite army. Drummond had been arguing for twenty years that the city needed extension and was quick to endorse the following set of *Proposals*, published by Sir Gilbert Elliot of Minto in 1752.

The magistrates and town council, the college of justice, and several persons of rank… propose
1. To build an exchange "upon the ruins on the north side of the high street";
2. To "erect upon the ruins in the parliament close" a building for law courts, the town council's "several registers", the advocates' library etc;
3. To obtain an act of parliament for extending the royalty; to enlarge and beautify the town, by opening new streets to north and the south,

*removing the markets and the shambles and turning the North Loch
into a canal with walks and terraces on each side.
4. That the expense of these public works should be defrayed by a
national contribution.*

These proposals were put into effect almost immediately. Work
began on the Exchange building in the High Street—now the City
Chambers—in 1753 and a design competition was initiated for a New
Town to be built on Barefoot's Parks, on the high ground to the north
of the city. This competition was eventually won in 1766 by James
Craig (1744-95), an architect who, until then, was best known as the
nephew of the poet James Thomson (1700-48), author of *The Seasons.*

Craig's original plan for the New Town was, in essence, very
simple. Two large squares—one to the west, another to the east—
would face each other along a wide avenue. This avenue would be
flanked by two long, one-sided streets running parallel with it, one
facing the Castle, the other facing the Firth of Forth, and these would
be crossed with smaller streets and the intersections marked with
statues to emphasize the pattern, which sought to imitate the Union
Jack.

Although this plan was never fully implemented, something of its
spirit is discernible in the New Town today, in which two squares, St.
Andrew Square in the east and Charlotte Square in the west, are
connected by the long avenue of George Street. Princes Street faces the
Castle, while Queen Street faces the Firth of Forth and these are
connected by Frederick, Castle and Hanover Streets. Two subsidiary
streets, Thistle Street and Rose Street, named after Scotland and
England respectively, reflect the aspiration of Craig's original intention.

Princes Street
Princes Street is probably the most famous of these streets. In his
Reminiscences (1887) Thomas Carlyle recalls Princes Street as Edinburgh's
"chosen promenade" and it still fulfils this function today, being the city's
most popular gathering place. On December 31 every year, it is the scene
of one of the largest street-parties in Europe, when tens of thousands
gather for the world-famous Hogmanay party. When it was originally
built, it was composed exclusively of town houses for the landed gentry,

but before long hotels, banks and warehouses began to establish themselves and, between 1830 and 1850, the first shops began to appear. The street is unusual, of course, for having buildings only on one side. H. V. Morton observed in his *In Search of Scotland* (1929):

> *Princes Street has been called the finest street in the kingdom. There are shops on one side only; the other side runs along the edge of a deep ravine, planted with gardens, above which rise the Castle Rock and the high roof-line of Old Edinburgh. On a calm autumn morning the ravine is filled with mist. The shops of Princes Street stand with their doorsteps against a grey wall, dense as the greyness that blows in from the Atlantic at Land's End. If you did not know that there are shops on the north side only, you might be excused the belief that, a landslide having occurred in the night, the south side had fallen into the grey abyss.*

Today the street is dominated by department stores, most of which are merely Edinburgh branches of national chains—Virgin, Debenham's, Marks & Spencers etc.—but there is one which remains quintessentially Edinburgh. This is Jenners, at the junction of Princes Street and St. David Street.

In 1838 two draper's assistants, Charles Jenner and Charles Kennington, were dismissed by their employers for attending a race meeting at Musselburgh. They decided to set up on their own and leased 47 Princes Street, the site on which the store still stands. After the death of Kennington in 1863, the business took the name of Charles Jenner and Company and by the end of the century it had become the largest retail shop in Scotland. Its impressive exterior makes a very substantial contribution to the grandiose architectural feel of Princes Street, but it is the interior of the store, with its sumptuously carved wooden staircases and galleries, that really makes Jenners unique. The overall effect is so theatrical that, when in Jenners, one feels that the shopping is being done in the public gaze.

This is a feeling that one often has in Princes Street generally, as described so well by Edwin Muir in his *Scottish Journey* (1935):

> *Princes Street in the evening is like a country platform where the train is late; there is the same intense and permitted scrutiny of one's fellow-*

passengers, the same growing expectation, and behind these the same sense, too, or rather a greater one, of wariness and prolonged disappointment. For the train never arrives at this platform, and so waiting becomes a thing with an existence of its own, which can no longer call up any definite image such as the arrival of a train, and is forced to find alleviation finally in distractions, in temporary liaisons with one's stranded companions. One of the advantages of this platform life is that it increases people's powers of observation, and of resistance to observation. In Princes Street you are seen, whoever you may be, and this knowledge, partly alarming and partly exhilarating like a plunge into cold water, forces the pedestrian to assemble his powers and be as intent as his neighbours. The concentrated force of observation sent out by the people he passes is sometimes so strong that he has the feeling of breaking, as he passes, through a series of invisible obstacles, of snapping a succession of threads laden with some retarding current. In London he can walk the most crowded streets for hours without feeling that he is either visible or existent: a disconcerting, almost frightening, experience for a Scotsman until he gets used to it. But the crowd in a London street is mainly composed of people who are going somewhere while the crowd in Princes Street is simply there; and even if you are going somewhere you cannot ignore it; it acquisitively stretches out and claims you. For it is there not only to observe but also to be observed, and if you omit one of these duties you strike at its amour-propre, and perhaps at its existence.

That was written almost seventy years ago but is as true today as it was then.

Register House

Queen Street, on the other hand, is in this sense altogether less public, being composed in the main of private residences and the offices of lawyers and accountants. Two of Edinburgh's most valued museums are located here, however: the Museum of Antiquities and the Scottish National Portrait Gallery. The Edinburgh offices and studios of the BBC were also located in Queen Street for some eighty years, prior to their removal, in 2001, to Holyrood.

The nomenclature of the New Town streets is interesting. Apparently, Princes Street was initially to be called St. Giles Street, but this was changed after George III objected, on the grounds that the name had associations with a rather squalid area of London. This may also account for the fact that so many of these streets have a definite Hanoverian ring to them. One street, however, has nothing to do with the royal family and may even have been coined as a joke. There is a tradition that St. David's Street, leading from Princes Street to St. Andrews Square, was named after David Hume who bought a house nearby and was, notoriously, an atheist.

The New Town began building from the east, starting with St. Andrew Square and moving westward to Charlotte Square. But here some difficulties were encountered and the Council called in Robert Adam to complete Craig's design. In Charlotte Square, Adam created one of the most beautiful squares in Europe, just one of a number of projects with which this famous architect became involved. Perhaps the most sumptuous of these is Register House, at the east end of Princes Street, funded by the government from forfeited Jacobite estates. This building, which Adam built in the Palladian style, has a visual charm that is quite overpowering, rendered even more so by the presence of Sir John Steell's larger-than-life equestrian statue of the Duke of Wellington, standing at its entrance. Inside, more than a hundred rooms are filled with national and legal documents, including all records of births, marriages and deaths in Scotland. In one of the largest rooms are the rolls of ancient parliaments, the records of the Privy Council, royal charters from the reign of William the Lion in the thirteenth century until Queen Anne in the eighteenth, and—most important of all—the Scottish copy of the 1707 Treaty of Union with England.

Theatre Royal

Across the road from Register House, the General Post Office stands on what was once Shakespeare Square, home of Edinburgh's first (and, for long, only) legal theater. The Act of Parliament granting powers to Edinburgh Corporation to build the New Town contains a clause enabling "His Majesty to grant Letters Patent for establishing a Theatre in the City of Edinburgh." At the time, it was against the law for any theater to seek to operate without such letters patent and, previous to 1769, Edinburgh's principal playhouse, the Canongate Theatre, had been completely illegal.

Far from being a popular venue, the official Theatre Royal was regarded by the general population as a somewhat disreputable place—and with good reason. It *was* a disreputable place. We should not make the error of thinking that the hostility that Presbyterian Scotland showed towards the theater generally was hypocritical or in any way unjustified. When Victorian ministers attacked the practice of theater going from their pulpits, it was not the theaters that we know today that they had in mind. Such clean, orderly, essentially respectable places of entertainment were completely beyond their knowledge and would remain so for another hundred years. In those days, theaters—and the Theatre Royal was no exception to this—formed a definitely louche part of city low life.

For instance, anyone entering the Theatre Royal would first of all have to run the gauntlet through a line of prostitutes thronging the foyer. These "flash molls", as they were called, were not there to see the play but to secure customers to take back to the New Town brothels. There would then be a serious risk of having one's pocket picked while the play was in progress, and a good chance of a mugging on the way home. The wealthier patrons, of course, would have their servants to protect them, but for the great mass of the population, an evening at the theater was not at all the attractive proposition that it would later become. Small wonder then, that in the early part of its existence, the Theatre Royal struggled to maintain profitability under a succession of managers, buoyed up by the occasional success and the continued support of its wealthy sponsors.

Then, in 1809, these sponsors were joined by one of the greatest names in Scottish history: Sir Walter Scott. Then plain Mr. Scott, he bought a share in the Theatre Royal and used his influence to secure the management for Henry Siddons, son of the great Sarah Siddons, the most popular actress of the age. Although he turned out to be a popular and competent manager, Henry Siddons was no more successful than his predecessors had been. Yet he did do two things that changed the fortunes of the theater completely. First, he engaged his brother-in-law William Murray as an actor with the company; secondly, six years later in 1815, he died and allowed Murray to take over as manager. As actor, playwright and manager, Murray ran the theater for more than 35 years between 1815 and 1851 and created many initiatives whose repercussions are still being felt today. It was Murray, for instance, who first identified the need for a Scottish national theater, an institution that has yet to be brought into being and is still the subject of much argument in theatrical circles. On a more practical level, he was one of the first theater managers to introduce a disciplined rehearsal period. At the time when he took over, rehearsals were little more than pre-performance discussions, in which actors would tell each other how they proposed to play their respective parts. Murray insisted that they behave in rehearsal exactly as they would in performance, thereby ensuring a much higher degree of preparation and professionalism.

In the course of the next four decades, the Theatre Royal was to become the most important single playhouse in the entire history of the Scottish stage. After Murray's retirement in 1851, Robert Wyndham, a manager who successfully maintained the reputation of the Theatre Royal and extended it beyond Scotland, succeeded him. In the days before the establishment of drama schools, the only way that a theatrical aspirant could receive any kind of training was through membership of a stock company—and Wyndham ran one of the finest stock companies in the British Isles. Wyndham would count among his students such future notables as the great Victorian comedian, John Laurence Toole, the playwright, Arthur Wing Pinero, and Marie Wilton, better known as Lady Bancroft, whose management of the Prince of Wales Theatre in London ushered in a new era in dramatic history. The most important apprentice of all, however, was the greatest of all Victorian actors, Henry Irving (1838-1905).

Irving spent three years with Wyndham, during which time he acquired an affection for Edinburgh that he never lost. In 1857, shortly after his arrival in the city, we find him writing to his cousin in the most glowing terms.

> It is indeed a city of poetry; I can hardly conceive a more beautiful unity of art and nature, town and country.
>
> Standing on the summit of the castle situated on a hill, you see a giant city, consisting of cottages surrounded by trees—buildings of most magnificent design and structure; old dilapidated streets erected centuries ago—new ones vying with Regent Street; village-looking churches—

small cathedrals; splendid statues, and one of Scott surpassing, I believe, any other erected; and the whole is surrounded by mountains and valleys seen for miles.

Another leading theatrical figure who loved Edinburgh was the actress Fanny Kemble (1809-93). The Kembles are possibly the most celebrated acting family in the entire history of the English-speaking stage and Fanny was one of its brightest stars. At the age of nineteen, she became, in her own words, "difficult and troublesome and unsatisfactory to myself and to others". Her parents, thinking that she might benefit from a change of scene, sent her to Edinburgh to spend some time with Mrs. Henry Siddons, to whom they were related through marriage. Fanny arrived in Edinburgh in the spring of 1828, intending to stay no longer than two or three months. In the event, she remained for a year.

Among the many friends she made at this time were two brothers named Combe, who lived in Northumberland Street, in the very heart of the New Town. Both became lifelong friends and both achieved distinction in their chosen professions. George, the elder, was a lawyer and writer on legal matters, who was to become a pioneer in the field of phrenology, while Andrew, the younger brother, was a doctor who became physician to the King of the Belgians and, later, to Queen Victoria. One of Fanny's most recent biographers, Dorothy Marshall, tells of the benefit the young actress received from this friendship.

The Combes' house—they were both bachelors when Fanny first knew them—was the centre of a group of brilliant men, including Duncan McLaren, the editor of The Scotsman, and the sculptor Lawrence Macdonald. It is a tribute both to Fanny's charm and to her intelligence that she was privileged to spend so many evenings with 'these grave men', as she called them. None of them would have willingly borne with the presence of some empty-headed teenager, however charming. Fanny, remembering with affectionate nostalgia the hours she had spent in their company, declared 'it was undoubtedly a great advantage to an intelligent girl of any age to hear such vigorous manly clear expositions of the broadest aspects of all the great political and governmental questions of the age'. For too long Fanny had read at random almost every type of book that had come her way and had fed her more than vivid imagination on the disturbing Byron. Now, at a vital stage in her intellectual development, she had come within the orbit of disciplined first-class minds and the benefit to her was incalculable.

On her return to London, Fanny made her debut as an actress and scored an immediate success as Juliet at Covent Garden. She never lost her love for Edinburgh, however, and returned in 1830 to play a season at the Theatre Royal. This included her performance as Juliet, later described by James C. Dibdin in *Annals of the Edinburgh Stage* as "a marvellously life-like impersonation" of the part. Although the reviewer from *The Scotsman* felt that her performance had shown signs of fatigue from her long journey from London, this was a judgment that was to be contradicted by an entry in Sir Walter Scott's journal concerning her performance in a different role.

June 17ᵗʰ, 1830—Went last night to the Theatre and saw Miss Fanny Kemble's Isabella, which was a most creditable performance. It has much of the genius of Mrs. Siddons, her aunt. She wants the beautiful countenance, her fine form and her matchless dignity of step and manner. On the other hand, Miss Kemble has very expressive, though not regular features and what is worth it all, great energy, mingled with and chastened by correct taste.

The Assembly Rooms: High Society

In creating the New Town, the intention was never to bring into being a separate city, and many of the customs of the Old Town were transported across the valley that was created between the two parts of Edinburgh. One of the most popular of these was the holding of dancing assemblies, supervised for many years by the Hon. Nicky Murray, one of the sisters of the Earl of Mansfield. These were held in Assembly Close, off the High Street, and, as described by Robert Chambers in his *Traditions of Edinburgh*, seem to have been rather tedious affairs:

There being but one set allowed to dance at a time, it was seldom that any person was twice on the floor in one night. The most of the time was spent in acting the part of lookers-on, which threw great duties in the way of conversation upon the gentlemen. These had to settle with a partner for the year, and were upon no account permitted to change, even for a single night. The appointment took place at the beginning of the season, usually at some private party or ball given by a person of distinction, where the fans of the ladies were all put into a gentleman's cocked hat; the gentlemen put in their hands and took a fan, and to whomsoever the fan belonged, that was to be his partner for the season.

The assemblies were held to raise money for charity and, perhaps for this reason, were always very select. In this regard, Miss Murray was something of a dragon. It was said of her that she was "manifestly cool" to any young lady who could not put a territorial addition to her name. Miss Napier of Merchiston would be warmly welcomed at the assembly, but the presence of plain Miss Napier would be considered presumptuous. On one occasion, she turned a leading Edinburgh merchant out of the assembly for no other reason that he was of lowly birth and had made his money in trade.

With the removal of what would no doubt be described by Miss Murray as "persons of quality" to the New Town, the situation of the Assembly Rooms was found to be inconvenient. The opportunity was therefore taken to open new Assembly Rooms in George Street, with a ballroom of enormous proportions: the ceiling rises to a height of forty feet and the floor area is 4,000 square feet. Since these premises opened in 1786 they have seen many brilliant nights, none more so than the Hunt Ball of 1887, at which the young Eleanor Sillar was a debutante. In her posthumous volume of memoirs, *Edinburgh's Child* (1961), she gave the following description of the experience.

Can I ever forget that first breath-taking glimpse of brilliance and splendour, which now opened, before my unsophisticated but enraptured eyes? Far above one's head, from the ceiling, lofty and aloof, the crystal chandeliers hang delicately as if on threads of gossamer. From them, innumerable lights shine down, illuminating the length and breadth of that stately hall, where the floor stretches from shining distance to shining distance; lighting up the raised seats under the high-windowed walls, where the velvets and satins of bediamonded dowagers crush and crowd together; sparkling on jewelled bracelets as delicate wrists wave in graceful greeting.

> *In front, restless, excited, smiling, chattering, stand the girls, golden and brown heads turning and nodding, debutante white mingling with the rainbow colours of the already "out", ribbons on the bouquets fluttering, bouquets and girls one glowing garden of colour.*
>
> *Among them stand I waiting, fidgeting with my programme. Partners swarm like bees round honey. The men I know find me quickly, and Charles, all aglow with pleasure and pride, the prince of brothers, introduces friend after friend. Bows, smiles.*
>
> *"May I have the pleasure?" over and over.*
>
> *"Yes!" and again "yes!" and again, and again, triumphantly, "Yes!"*

Sixty years earlier, on February 23, 1827, a rather famous literary event took place at a dinner held in the Assembly Rooms in aid of the Edinburgh Theatrical Fund. At one point during the evening, Sir Walter Scott, a director of the Edinburgh Theatre Royal, rose to drink a toast to the comedian, Charles Mackay. Although Scott had, by this time, written more than twenty successful novels, he had never admitted to the authorship of any of them. (His first novel, *Waverley*, had been published anonymously in 1814 and each subsequent work had simply been entitled "by the author of *Waverley*". This is the reason, incidentally, why the novels of Sir Walter Scott are often described as "the Waverley novels".) Mackay, the recipient of the toast, had recently been playing Bailie Nicol Jarvie in a stage production of *Rob Roy* and, in proposing the toast, Sir Walter used the following words: "I beg leave to propose the health of my friend, Bailie Nicol Jarvie. And I am sure that when the author of *Waverley* and *Rob Roy* drinks to Nicol Jarvie, it will be received with the just applause to which that gentleman has always been accustomed."

The Assembly Rooms—now known as the Assembly Rooms and Music Hall—are still in use, being the first location of the Festival Club and, these days, a popular venue for Fringe productions, particularly stand-up comedy.

St. Andrew's Church

On the other side of George Street, St. Andrew's Church was the scene of one of the most momentous episodes in Scottish history, involving an assembly of rather a different kind. The Great Disruption, which took place during the General Assembly of the Church of Scotland in May 1843, involved issues that now seem—superficially, at least—so obscure and removed from contemporary experience that a degree of explanation is necessary.

In 1707 some of the sting was taken out of Scottish opposition to the Union of Parliaments by a clause in the Treaty that guaranteed the survival of Presbyterianism in the Established Church. In those days, the Church of Scotland, which had responsibility for education and social welfare, was rather more important than parliament as far as the lives of ordinary people were concerned. Then, in 1712, the government of the United Kingdom introduced the Patronage Act, which gave landowners the right to appoint ministers to livings within their jurisdiction. This was completely unacceptable to the Church of Scotland, in which ministers were, and still are, appointed by their congregations. This form of appointment—it is known as "the call"—was an early form of democracy in which the heads of families examined a number of ministers and voted for the candidate of their choice. In the eyes of many, the Patronage Act, by depriving congregations of this right, affronted fundamental Christian principles.

Initially, there was little difficulty, since most landowners respected the views of their tenants and would only appoint those candidates who had been called by the congregation. But there was always the possibility of conflict. In 1833 the General Assembly passed a Veto Act, giving presbyteries the power to reject any minister who had not received a call from his congregation. In the autumn of 1834 this power was put to the test in the parish of Auchterarder in Perthshire, when the local landowner and patron, Lord Kinnoul, attempted to put in office a certain Robert Young against the wishes of the congregation. When the congregation conclusively rejected this candidate, the local presbytery refused to permit Lord Kinnoul's candidate to be ordained and the landowner, unaccustomed to having his decisions frustrated in this way, instituted proceedings in the civil courts. Matters reached crisis point when the Court of Session found in favor of the landlord. When two other similar cases followed Auchterarder, the situation became intolerable as far as the Church of Scotland was concerned. A special conference of the leading ministers, called a "Convocation", took place in Edinburgh in 1842 and action was planned for the following year.

> *We shall give them their stipends, their manses, their glebes and their churches. These are theirs, and let them 'make a kirk or a mill' of them. But we cannot give them up the crown rights of Christ, and we cannot give them up our people's privileges.*

These were the words of the Rev. Thomas Guthrie, one of the leading figures in the Disruption, in his last sermon as a minister of the Established Church, preached on Sunday May 14, 1843. Four days later, at the General Assembly in St. Andrew's Church in George Street, 472 ministers made good Guthrie's promise and walked out of the Church of Scotland in order to immediately re-constitute themselves as the Free Church of Scotland. The Disruption led to a whole series of ecclesiastical schisms, which would have a serious impact on Scottish culture. In Edinburgh, the legacy of this religious turmoil is the large number of church buildings that are to be found in the city. Although many of those no longer fulfill their original function, the church in which the Disruption actually took place—it is now called St. Andrew's and St. George's—is still in operation as a place of worship. This is a quite beautiful building whose circular interior creates simultaneously a sense of space and intimacy. The congregation, 500 strong, is drawn mainly from the New Town and the denomination is Church of Scotland. Apart from the historical significance of the building, there is no connection with the Free Church.

Stockbridge

Today, the Free Church is regarded as the most puritanical and conservative of all Scottish denominations. Such a view overlooks the fact that the people who created the Disruption formed part of a movement that was essentially progressive, involving organizations such as the Chartists and the trade unions. Most supporters of the Free Church—non-intrusionists, as they were called—were sympathetic to other radical initiatives that were being taken during the same period. One of the most successful of these took place in the New Town itself, and was made possible by the support of a group of men who were leading figures in the Free Church.

It happened in this way. In February 1861, after a dispute over a reduction in wages, a large number of building workers were "locked out" by their employers for a period of three months. During this time a group of stone masons began to discuss the possibility of creating a cooperative company, with the object of building houses that artisans could afford. One of their number, a certain James Colville, took their ideas to the radical Liberal MP, Hugh Gilzean Reid. Reid was immediately interested and secured the support of the journalist Hugh Miller, who edited the Free Church newspaper *The Witness*, and the Rev. Dr. James Begg, one of the first ministers of the Free Church. By May 1861 the Edinburgh Cooperative Building Company Ltd. had been formed and, by the following October, work began on its first project.

The style of architecture employed in the construction is rather interesting. At the time, the most common form of working-class housing was the tenement—great blocks of flats, connected by an internal staircase, rising to as much as seven or eight stories in some cases, are still to be found all over the city—and it would not have been at all surprising if the Edinburgh Cooperative Building Company had simply imitated this style. Instead, they opted for a cottage-like building, just two stories in height, laid out in terraces. When completed, the entire development provided rented homes for sixty-two families consisting of at least two rooms, access to a WC and a private garden. The upper dwellings were entered on the opposite side of the block from the ground-floor houses by means of an external staircase, and access to the front doors on both sides was provided by narrow paths running between the houses and their gardens.

The result was the creation of a working-class community in the heart of the New Town. The Colonies of Stockbridge, a district of some fourteen streets, lying between Craig's New Town and the course of Edinburgh's river, the Water of Leith, are now among the most desirable, and therefore most high-priced, properties in the whole of

Edinburgh. Between the 1960s and the 1980s, the value of these houses quadrupled, placing them beyond the means of the very people for whom they had been originally built. As a result, the character of the Stockbridge community has changed radically. No longer proletarian and democratic, Stockbridge has been absorbed by the wider community of the New Town and is now very much part of the turf of Edinburgh's middle-class elite.

This change of character is less surprising when one considers that Stockbridge is home to one of Edinburgh's most elitist institutions, Edinburgh Academy. Unlike so many other Edinburgh schools—Heriot's, Watson's and even Fettes (of Tony Blair fame)—the founders of Edinburgh Academy, Lord Cockburn and a linen merchant by the name of Leonard Horner, were not interested in creating a charitable institution. As Magnus Magnusson, an old Academy boy, has pointed out in his excellent history of the school, the aim from the start was to create an elitist educational institution that would stand comparison with the traditional English public schools. From an educational point of view, this aim may well have been accomplished, but no one today can possibly claim that an education at Edinburgh Academy carries the same social cachet as that of one at Eton.

This part of Edinburgh is also home to what is, in many respects, Edinburgh's most anonymous theater. Theatre Workshop in Hamilton Place was founded in 1965 as an arts and drama center for children, and became immediately popular with middle-class parents, many of whom would drive from miles around to bring their offspring to its play-making sessions. Concerned about this somewhat narrow social mix, the company tried to enlarge the range of participants by setting up an Outreach Programme, employing two community artists, Ken Wolverton and Neil Cameron. In 1976, Cameron explained their approach to Su Braden for her study of community art, *Artists and People* (1978).

> *We decided to reverse the process and take the Theatre Workshop to them. So we started programmes of street theatre. In the end we linked in with the play scheme network and we were able to get the input of the arts into that structure. We worked in a number of directions—training programmes for local people which taught them how to work with kids*

*and everything from football and safety to silk-screening and sculpture.
At that time, the Theatre Workshop concentrated on three main areas of
the city and gradually evolved from an arts centre into a community
group.*

Theatre Workshop has remained essentially a community
enterprise ever since. Although it houses a professional producing
company and stages a full program of performances throughout the
year, the company has never had the kind of city-wide profile that is
enjoyed by other Edinburgh theaters. Perhaps its location has
something to do with this; over the past fifty years, companies taking
part in the Festival Fringe have found that it is very difficult to attract
an audience to a New Town venue. There again, since Theatre
Workshop obviously attracts *some* kind of audience, it may have to do
with perceptions that have been created by the company's history.

The Mound and Princes Street Gardens
Originally planned as a residential area, the New Town's first residents
were professionals and men of business, whose offices and places of
work remained in the Old Town. Despite being depleted by the
inevitable incursion of business and commerce—particularly in Princes
Street, now a shopping precinct in which private homes have all but
vanished—this community has thrived in the New Town ever since.

In order to ensure that communication between the two parts of
Edinburgh could continue, work began in 1765 to build the North
Bridge across the valley that lay between them. But before this could be
completed, another means of communication was created in a
somewhat fortuitous manner. Six years earlier, the draining of the Nor'
Loch had begun. This work would take many years to complete and,
until then, the ground was a soggy marsh, although still the best means
of crossing from the New Town to the Old. A merchant in the
Lawnmarket called George Boyd decided to make life easier for his
customers by laying out a system of planks and stepping-stones across
the morass. This idea caught on, and other merchants began to add
refinements to the crossing. Additionally, site foremen, who had the
continual problem of disposing of the earth that was acquired from
digging foundations in the New Town, began to tell their men to "take

it to the mound", and eventually an enormous causeway came into being. This causeway, of course, is still there today, is still called the Mound and is still the quickest way to reach the Old Town from the New.

The Mound stands between the two parts of Princes Street Gardens, the open space created by the draining of the Nor' Loch. Today, this is one of the glories of Edinburgh, particularly in the summer when visitors and residents fill the Gardens with a joyous, holiday atmosphere, but this was not always the case. The eastern section of this open space has always belonged to the Council, but the Western Gardens were initially privately owned, held in common by the residents of Princes Street. These residents, known as the "Princes Street Proprietors", landscaped the Gardens and maintained them for many years. It was not until 1881, in fact, that the Town Council acquired Western Princes Street Gardens as a public resource. Before then, the rights of the Princes Street Proprietors were rigorously defended and the Gardens operated under a system that is still used today, on the other side of George Street, in Queen Street Gardens. This is quite simply a private park, access to which is gained by the possession of a pass key and is denied to all but local residents and their friends.

It was possible, however, to gain access to the Princes Street Gardens by taking out a subscription, and occasionally the Proprietors would confer access on a distinguished citizen. In 1827, for instance, the Clerk to the Proprietors received the following communication:

3 WALKER STREET,

May 21, 1827.

DEAR SIR,

I am honoured with your letter covering the pass key of the Princes Street gardens and acquainting me that the Committee have been pleased to admit me to the privilege of the gardens. I beg you will express to them my sincere thanks for an accommodation which circumstances and my increasing infirmities render extremely agreeable to me as my health requires exercise, which I can take much more easily and agreeably in its beautiful walks than along the public street.

I am, etc.

WALTER SCOTT.

The Scott Monument

It was perhaps the sentiment expressed in that letter that led the Scott Memorial Committee to site the Scott Monument in Princes Street Gardens. In 1836, just four years after Sir Walter's death, this committee invited architects to submit designs for a fitting memorial. The competition was eventually won, after some deliberation, by an architect called John Morvo. This, it transpired, was a *nom-de-plume* and members of the committee were no doubt surprised when they discovered the true identity of the winner. He was a journeyman carpenter who worked for an Edinburgh building firm and his name was George Meikle Kemp.

The story of George Meikle Kemp (1804-44) is one that is surprisingly common in nineteenth-century Scotland. A young man from a lowly background and severely lacking in education succeeds in his chosen profession by dint of hard work and application, animated by a sense of conviction of his own genius. Others of his ilk include the engineer Thomas Telford, the road builder John MacAdam, and the linguist John Leyden. Unlike these success stories, however, Kemp's career was to end in tragedy.

The foundation stone of the Scott monument was laid in August 1840. For the next four years Kemp worked tirelessly on the construction, which became something of an obsession with him. Eventually, though, all the problems were solved and by March 1844 completion was in sight. It was at this precise moment that the tragedy occurred. One evening, while on his way to his home in South Edinburgh, Kemp accidentally stumbled into the Union Canal and drowned. The monument with which he had been so preoccupied was completed just a few months after his death.

It has been a prominent feature of the Edinburgh landscape ever since, an open Gothic tower, 200 feet in height, with four arches supporting a central spire. These form a canopy, sheltering Sir John Steell's figure of Scott in Carrara marble. The great writer is represented in a sitting position, wrapped in a shepherd's plaid, with his favorite hound, Maida, at his feet. An interior staircase leads to a series of open galleries, encircling the spire. The first of these galleries affords access to a central apartment, fitted with carved oak cabinetwork and lighted by stained-glass windows. The chamber is used as a museum, and contains some interesting relics of Scott.

The arches accommodate niches, filled with statuettes representing characters featured in Scott's novels and narrative poems, including Prince Charles Stewart, The Lady of the Lake, Meg Merrilees and The Last Minstrel. Four flying buttresses spring into the open air to the height of 90 feet, terminating in pinnacles. All over the monument are additional niches containing statuettes of the principal characters in Scott's poems and in the Waverley novels. These include figures such as King James VI, Rob Roy, Dominie Sampson, Meg Dods, Dandie Dinmont Bailie Nicol Jarvie, Amy Robsart and Jeanie Deans. Most of these figures, instantly recognizable to devotees of Scott, were designed by the sculptor Amelia Paton, second wife of David Octavius Hill, whose career will be discussed in due course. The Monument is open to the public during the summer months, and a climb of 287 steps provides the visitor with one of the most sensational views of central Edinburgh.

Over the years, however, many of the monument's best features have become literally obscured by the existence of another Edinburgh institution that came into being at much the same time, and which can also claim an association with Sir Walter Scott. In 1842 trains began running from Waverley Station, named after the novels, and, for good or ill, the railway age had arrived. (This, incidentally, put paid to one of the *Proposals* of 1752, which promised to turn "the North Loch into a canal with walks and terraces on each side.") The smoke from the trains created a covering of soot that has turned the entire monument black, rendering most of the statuettes invisible. This choking smoke was to justify Edinburgh's nickname of "Auld Reekie", a phenomenon never better described than by the poet Robert Southey. Southey paid a short visit to the city in 1819, during which time he resided at McGregor's Hotel in Princes Street. His impressions were later collected by Maurice Lindsay for his *The Eye is Delighted: Some Romantic Travellers in Scotland* (1970).

> *The view from this hotel in the morning, when the fires are just kindled, is probably the finest smoke-scape that can anywhere be seen. Well may Edinburgh be called Auld Reekie! and the houses stand so one above another, that none of the smoke wastes itself upon the desert air before the inhabitants have derived all the advantage of its odour and smuts. You might smoke bacon by hanging it out of the window.*

The Scott Monument is far from being the only memorial of its kind to be found in Princes Street Gardens, which is something of a sacrarium as far civic Edinburgh is concerned. In addition to a profusion of war memorials, commemorating the Edinburgh and Scottish contribution to various conflicts, there are several statues, featuring figures such as David Livingstone, Dean Ramsay, and Sir James Young Simpson. The most recently created memorial is a grove of birch trees, designed by Iain Hamilton Finlay and planted in memory of Robert Louis Stevenson, while the statue of a much earlier Scottish writer is to be found next to the Gardens' most popular tourist feature.

The Floral Clock has stood at the corner of the Mound and Princes Street since 1903. The display is changed every year—in 2002, for instance, it commemorated Queen Elizabeth II's Jubilee—and is comprised of some 27,000 individual plants. A statue of Allan Ramsay, looking up towards his old home in Ramsay Garden, stands immediately above the clock. Ramsay, of course, is associated with the Old Town rather than the New, but on the other side of the Mound is a statue of a writer who was, in his day, one of the most familiar figures in the New Town.

John Wilson and *Blackwood's Magazine*
John Wilson (1785-1854) was born in Paisley and educated at Glasgow and Oxford. Although as a young man he won the prestigious Newdigate Prize, his subsequent poetry was not successful. Elected to the chair of Moral Philosophy at Edinburgh University, he owes his

place in literary history to his association with the publisher, William Blackwood. Blackwood (1776-1834), who had made his fortune in the antiquarian book trade, became involved in publishing in 1810 with the appearance of Sir David Brewster's *The Edinburgh Encyclopedia*. The following year he brought out Thomas McCrie's *Life of John Knox*, which became a minor classic. After the success of *The Edinburgh Review*, politically a Whig publication based in the Old Town, Blackwood decided to found a Tory alternative in the New Town. He enlisted the aid of Wilson, who wrote under the pen name of "Christopher North", and two other writers: Scott's son-in-law, John Gibson Lockhart, and the poet and novelist, James Hogg.

Originally appearing as *The Edinburgh Monthly Magazine* in April 1817, the first issues failed to impress. It was only with the appearance of the *Chaldee MS*—a satire of Edinburgh manners using scriptural language, jointly written by Hogg, Lockhart, and Wilson—that *Blackwood's Magazine* became established. Published from Blackwood's offices in George Street and affectionately known as "the Maga", it would become a permanent feature of literary life in Edinburgh over the next century and a half, before it finally ceased publication in 1980.

Its contributors during this long period included John Galt, Bulwer Lytton, Anthony Trollope, R. D. Blackmore, Henry James, Oscar Wilde, John Buchan (with *The Thirty-Nine Steps*), Walter de la Mare, J. B. Priestley, Ian Hay, Nevil Shute, and Neil Munro. *Blackwood's* also published all but one of George Eliot's novels. Her lover G. H. Lewes submitted *Scenes of Clerical Life* in 1856 and it was immediately accepted. *Adam Bede*, *The Mill on the Floss*, and *Silas Marner* quickly followed. In 1862 she moved to the *Cornhill Magazine* with *Romola* for an advance of £10,000, an extraordinary sum for the time, but returned to *Blackwood's* four years later with *Felix Holt*.

The initial success of the *Chaldee MS* was consolidated by the appearance of the series *Noctes Ambrosianae*, largely written by Wilson solely, although a visiting Irish writer by the name of William McGinn is said to have conceived the idea. There is probably no more eccentric work in all of literature nor another that more faithfully reflects the two abiding enthusiasms of Edinburgh society: drinking and conversation. Although the dialogue is imaginary and the characters fictional—or, at any rate, fictionalized versions of real, living people—the setting is absolutely authentic. Ambrose's Tavern on Gabriel's Road, situated immediately behind Register House, was later replaced by Edinburgh's Café Royal where, it may be safely said, the spirit of the *Noctes* lives on. While the *Noctes* is not a work that lends itself readily to quotation, the following brief extract may suggest something of its flavor. Tickler (Lockhart), the Ettrick Shepherd (Hogg) and North (Wilson) discuss the dangers of sobriety.

Tickler	*I never saw you the worse o liquor in my life, James.*
Shepherd	*Nor me you.*
North	*None but your sober men ever get drunk.*
Shepherd	*I've observed that many a thousand times; just as nane but your excessively healthy men ever die. Whene'er I hear in the kintra o' ony man's being killed aff his horse, I ken at aince that he's a sober coof, that's been getting himself drunk at Selkirk or Hawick, and sweeing aff at a sharp turn owre the bank, he has played wallop into the water, or is aiblins been found lying in the middle o' the road, wi' his neck dislocate, the doctors canna tell hou; or ayont the waa wi his harns sticking on the couping-stane.*
North	*Or, foot in stirrup, and face trailing the pebbly mire, swept homewards by a spanking half-bred, and disentangled at the door by shriek and candlelight.*
Shepherd	*Had he been in the habit of taking his glass like a Christian, he wad hae ridden like a Centaur!*
Tickler	*Your sober man, on every public occasion of festivity, is uniformly seen, soon after "the Duke of York and the Army", led off between two waiters, with his face as white as the table-clothe eyes upwards, and a ghastly smile about his gaping mouth, that seems to threaten unutterable things before he reach the lobby.*
North	*He turns round his head at the "three times three", with a loyal hiccup, and is borne off a speechless martyr to the cause of the Hanoverian Succession.*
Shepherd	*I wad raither get fou five hunder times in an ordinary way like, than aince to expose myself sae afore my fellow-citizens!*

Pubs and Poets

Alcohol and talk have always been boon companions in Edinburgh. In the eighteenth century no self-respecting Old Town merchant or professional would dream of passing any morning without his "meridian" (alcoholic refreshment taken around 11 a.m.) and, during the same period, there was a fashion for oyster cellar parties, as described by Robert Chambers:

In winter, when the evening had set in, a party of the most fashionable people in town, collected by appointment, would adjourn in carriages to one of those abysses of darkness and comfort, called in Edinburgh laigh shops, where they proceeded to regale themselves with raw oysters and porter, arranged in huge dishes upon a coarse table, in a dingy room, lighted by tallow candles. The rudeness of the feast, and the vulgarity of the circumstances under which it took place, seem to have given a zest to its enjoyment, with which more refined banquets could not have been accompanied. One of the chief features of an oyster-cellar entertainment was that full scope was given to the conversational powers of the company. Both ladies and gentlemen indulged, without restraint, in sallies the merriest and the wittiest; and a thousand remarks and jokes, which else-where would have been suppressed as improper, were here sanctified by the oddity of the scene, and appreciated by the most dignified and refined.

This tradition continues to thrive in Edinburgh, especially in the New Town, which abounds in hostelries and eating-places. But for lovers of literature, it is the pubs of the New Town that hold the most fascination. The Oxford Bar, for instance, situated in Young Street on the eastern edge of Charlotte Square, features in the crime fiction of Ian Rankin as the regular haunt of Rankin's hero, Inspector Rebus. Long before Rankin's first Rebus novel, however, the Oxford Bar had a reputation as the meeting place for people who were involved in publishing and the antiquarian book trade. It is a small, intimate pub, where even the most casual visitor cannot avoid participation in the conversation of the bar, which is usually concerned with books. It is, in short, a literary pub.

Such pubs abound in Edinburgh, and two of the most celebrated are found in the New Town. Milne's Bar on the corner of Hanover

Street, and the Abbotsford, at the east end of Rose Street, are famous as the regular haunts of the poets of the Scottish Literary Renaissance, which reached its apogee in the 1950s. The Renaissance was a campaign to revive an interest in the arts and serious literature in Scotland, and its success in doing so is evidenced by the much livelier arts scene that exists in Scotland today. This has given rise to a legend, promoted by an increasingly self-conscious Scottish media, that much of the strategy was conceived in one or other of these watering holes.

The truth, of course, is much simpler. Although the full story of the Scottish Literary Renaissance awaits the telling, it is generally agreed that a certain quickening of the literary pulse took place in the years immediately following the First World War. At the conclusion of any war, an initial feeling of relief that hostilities have ended is very quickly replaced by a fairly angry consideration of how they had come to be initiated in the first place. Among the survivors of 1918 was a young Scottish journalist called Christopher Murray Grieve (1892-1978), who was later to write that he "came back with an *idée fixe*—never again must men be made to suffer as in these years of war." This belief played its part in the development of a wider, even more deeply held conviction: that it was essential for the progress of humanity that the conventions of society be subjected to a rigorous and perpetual examination. If this seems a daunting task, Grieve's energy and intellect were equal to it. For the next sixty years he never so much as wavered in his unreserved acceptance of Thomas Hardy's definition of literature as "the written expression of revolt against accepted things." By 1921 Grieve was writing poetry and had adopted the pseudonym by which he is now most commonly known: Hugh MacDiarmid.

Hugh MacDiarmid

In dealing with MacDiarmid in the present context, it might be as well for us to take the greatness of his poetry for granted. Since his death in 1978, a number of substantial books (some of them as thick in volume as MacDiarmid's own) have been devoted to an exploration of his huge, complex, and fascinating genius. In any case, there is a sense in which the nature, as opposed to the fact, of MacDiarmid's genius is irrelevant to present concerns. On the other hand, MacDiarmid's poetry was to prove absolutely vital to the establishment and continued health of the Renaissance. Much has been made both by his admirers and his detractors of the almost superhuman efforts MacDiarmid exerted in promoting the movement. All of this—the articles, the books, the magazines he edited, the speeches he made, the yards and yards (one is almost tempted to say miles) of polemic that issued from his pen— would have been to little avail, had he not been able to practice as he preached. In particular, in the absence of "A Drunk Man Looks at the Thistle", one of the great poems of the twentieth century and arguably the greatest poem in the entire canon of Scottish literature, all this acreage of polemic would have been so much huff-and-puff.

Although MacDiarmid's early work was executed in Lowland Scots, it is quite fallacious to suggest, as a number of (mainly English) critics have done, that MacDiarmid revived a dead language. So far from doing that, MacDiarmid's work re-vivified and invigorated a living tradition. The matter of modern Scots usage has often been a subject of controversy, erupting at regular intervals over the years, usually in the correspondence columns of our leading newspapers, in which a couple of key phrases have emerged: "synthetic Scots" and "plastic Scots". MacDiarmid originally coined these expressions in an attempt at definition, but critics of Scots usage have tended to employ them in a pejorative sense. The suggestion here is there is something intrinsically wrong with a writer making use of an artificial language— as if the language of literature is ever anything other than artificial. The language of MacDiarmid's most famous poem about Edinburgh is just as artificial, although it is in straightforward English. It is entitled "Midnight".

> Glasgow is null,
> Its suburbs shadows
> And the Clyde a cloud.
>
> Dundee is dust
> And Aberdeen a shell.
>
> But Edinburgh is a mad god's dream,
> Fitful and dark,

Unseizable in Leith
And wildered by the Forth,
But irresistibly at last
Cleaving to sombre heights
Of passionate imagining
Till stonily,
From soaring battlements,
Earth eyes Eternity.

Although MacDiarmid was a borderer (he came from Langholm in Dumfriesshire), he had many connections with Edinburgh. He was educated in the city and received his training as a journalist on the staff of the now-defunct *Edinburgh Evening Dispatch*. For the last third of his life, moreover, his home was at Brownsbank, near the village of Biggar, a few miles to the south of the city center. A man of enormous charisma, who attracted many adherents to his cause, he was nevertheless selective in his friendships. Two of his closest friends, Norman MacCaig and Sydney Goodsir Smith, were leading Edinburgh poets and he was frequently to be seen in their company at both Milne's and the Abbotsford.

Alasdair Gray, the celebrated Glasgow novelist, has a scene in his novel *1982 Janine*, which describes a typical meeting between these three poets.

The bar was crowded except where three men stood in a small open space created by the attention of the other customers. One had a sombre pouchy face and upstanding hair which seemed too like thistledown to be natural, one looked like a tall sarcastic lizard, one like a small sly shy bear. 'Our three best since Burns', a bystander informed me.

These are fairly accurate descriptions of the physical appearances of the three poets, although—like all appearances—they tend to be misleading. MacDiarmid's expression may have been invariably somber, yet his personality was anything but. As his biographer Alan Bold wrote after his death, he was a restless man, always capable of intellectual provocation, but "in private, he was unfailingly friendly."

Edinburgh Poets

Sydney Goodsir Smith (1915-75), the "small sly shy bear", was a phenomenon—there is simply no other word to describe him. He was born in Wellington, New Zealand, and did not know anything of Scotland until he was twelve years old, when his father, Professor (later Sir) Sydney took up the Chair of Forensic Medicine. He came from a Scottish family, it is true, but it was an upper middle-class, and therefore highly anglicized, background. He received his education at Marlborough and Oriel College, Oxford, where he graduated in History. He settled in Edinburgh in the late 1930s, studying medicine briefly, but eventually embarking on the career of a freelance author and artist. His background does not suggest the ideal preparation for a poet whose work in the Scots language is so effective that he has been compared to Robert Burns, leading Dame Edith Sitwell to describe his work, in 1952, as "among the few poems by a poet now under forty to which the word 'great' can be applied."

One of his finest poems is called "Kynd Kittock's Land". The title comes from a character in a ballad by the medieval makar (or poet), William Dunbar, who described Kynd Kittock as a somewhat inebriate inn-keeper in Edinburgh's Grassmarket. She must have been nonetheless a woman of some virtue for, when she died, she was given a place in Heaven, a place that she did not like very much. Surrounded by so many respectable spirits, Kynd Kittock was bored out of her mind and St. Peter, in a special dispensation, allowed her to open a public house, half-way between Heaven and Purgatory, for the refreshment of weary travelers. According to Goodsir Smith, Kynd Kittock's spirit lives on in subterranean Edinburgh and his poem is a celebration of this. It ends as follows:

> I'm gettin gey and auld, and wearie
> Sleepie... my grey heid hings...
>
> And shall she get the richts o' it,
> A diadem for the brou?
> Shall Scotland croun her ain again,
> This ancient capital—?
> Or sell the thing for scrap?

Or some Yankee museum maybe?
I'll be here bidin the answer...
Here I be and here I drink,
This is mine.
Kynd Kittock's land,
For ever and aye while stane shall stand—
For ever and aye till the World's End.

Unlike Sydney, Norman MacCaig (1910-96)—the "tall sarcastic lizard"—was born in Edinburgh and spent his entire life in the city. While he was certainly tall, and could be devastatingly sarcastic when it suited him, Gray's description omits his rather stunning good looks, which led to him being idolized by poetry groupies even when he was in his seventies. MacCaig's relationship with MacDiarmid was essentially social—they had little in common artistically—and indeed could sometimes be combative. At MacDiarmid's funeral in 1978, MacCaig paid a very eloquent tribute to his friend, declaring that "he would walk into my mind as if it were a town and he a torchlight procession of one, lighting up the streets and some of the nasty little things that were burrowing into the corners."

In contrast to Sydney Goodsir Smith, MacCaig was never enthusiastic about MacDiarmid's use of Scots. Although he was as Scottish a Scot as one would wish to find, both in his personality and his knowledge of things Scottish, he never wrote in any language other than English. As a matter of fact, he always remained completely apart from the political and artistic commitments that were made by his friends. In spite of this, or perhaps even *because* of it, he did not receive the kind of critical recognition that many felt was his due until very nearly the end of his life. When his collected poems were published in 1990, Seamus Heaney was led to remark that MacCaig's work constituted "an ongoing education in the marvellous possibilities of lyric poetry". Although he was born and bred in Edinburgh, MacCaig gave remarkably few of his poems a specifically Edinburgh setting. An exception to the rule is "April Day in Edinburgh", written towards the end of his life.

The sun punches through the cloud gaps
with strong fists and the wind

buffets the buildings
with boisterous good will.

Bad memories are blown away
over the capering sea. Life
pulls up without straining
the jungle tangle between us
and the future.

Easy to forget
the last leaves thicken the ground
and the last roses are dying
in their sad, cramped hospitals.

For gaiety's funfair whirls
in the gray squares. Energy
sends volts from suburb to suburb.

And April, gay trespasser,
dances the dark streets of November,
Pied Piper leading a procession
of the coloured dreams of summer.

The conversation of these poets was often stimulating and witty, with much discussion of developments in the arts, but they were not the kind of people who had much enthusiasm for planning and organization. They were simply a group of like-minded friends who had found a congenial place to meet. Today, this period in literary history is remembered by the presence in Milne's of a collection of photographs of all these writers, plus a number of others, by Gordon Wright. This collection, with some notable omissions, recently featured in a high-profile exhibition of contemporary Scottish literature at the National Library, adding further to the potency of the legend of the Rose Street pubs.

Such fictions seem to be created quite readily in Edinburgh. The most persistent legend of all was initiated early in the nineteenth century, probably without any conscious design. In 1818 an Edinburgh painter by the name of Hugh William Williams, made a tour of Italy and Greece. As a result of this immersion in antiquity, he created a number of views of classical Athens, in which city the painter seemed to find certain correspondences with Edinburgh. This earned Williams the sobriquet of "Grecian" and, largely because of this, the term "Athens of the North" began to gain currency. As a description of the city, this term is, of course, quite spurious. Edinburgh, then as now, has little in common with the ancient capital of Greece that it does not share with any number of other cities. For better or worse, however, this expression was to have a potent influence in the further development of the city.

CHAPTER FIVE

Modern Athens: Calton Hill

"The view of Edinburgh from the road before you enter Leith is quite enchanting; it is, as Albert said, "fairy-like", and what you would only imagine as a thing to dream of, or to see in a picture. There was that beautiful large town, all of stone (no mingled colours of brick to mar it), with the bold Castle on one side, and the Calton Hill on the other, with those high sharp hills of Arthur's Seat and Salisbury Crags towering above all, and making the finest, boldest background imaginable. Albert said he felt sure the Acropolis could not be finer; and I hear they sometimes call Edinburgh "the modern Athens".

Queen Victoria, *Journal*, September 1842

The expression "Modern Athens" (a variant of "the Athens of the North") was to become something of a conceit for those Edinburgh citizens with the power and influence to promote it. In 1819 a committee was formed to organize the construction of a national monument to the heroism that had been shown in the Napoleonic Wars. By 1822 it was decided that this was to take the form of a replica of the Temple of Minerva Parthenon, to be erected on the summit of Calton Hill, to the east of Princes Street.

The Calton Hill occupies a curious place in Edinburgh folklore. During the seventeenth century it was reputedly a favorite meeting place for goblins, elves, demons, and all kinds of fairies. In 1688 a sea captain by the name of Burton met a young man in a Leith tavern who told him of an enormous underground cavern, lying within the Calton Hill, where such spirits would gather for feasting and dancing every Thursday night. When Burton expressed an interest in witnessing this gathering, the young man, who became known as the "Fairy Boy of Leith", agreed to take him there in exchange for a substantial sum of money. But on their arrival at the Calton Hill, Captain Burton reported that the Fairy Boy, having received his payment, simply vanished.

Architectural Aspirations

Today, the Calton Hill is considered to be a symbol of Scottish national aspirations, mainly because of two buildings that are located there: the Old Royal High School and St. Andrew's House.

The High School of Edinburgh has a very long history, tracing its roots as far back as the twelfth century. Until 1829 it was located in the Old Town, moving in that year to a new site on the western slope of Calton Hill. This building was designed by Thomas Hamilton (1784-1858) as a specimen of the purest Grecian Doric, with even its most minute detail copying the Temple of Theseus in Athens. While it can count among its most distinguished pupils Sir Walter Scott, Lord Cockburn, Alexander Graham Bell and the comedian Ronnie Corbet, it received its "royal" appellation because the future Edward VII received tuition from its then rector, Dr. Leonard Schmitz, during a two-month visit to Edinburgh in 1859. More than a hundred years later, in 1968, the school moved again—to Barnton, in the west of Edinburgh—and the building was refurbished in anticipation of the creation of a Scottish assembly.

When the government failed to deliver this assembly, the building became the focus of the campaign to create a Scottish Parliament. After the 1992 general election, which returned a Conservative government that had set its face against the establishment of such a body, a group of campaigners set up a vigil in a hut outside the Old Royal High School. This vigil remained in place, twenty-four hours a day, for the next five years, until the election of the new Labour government led to the creation of the Scottish Parliament in 1999. One of the first tasks of the new Scottish Executive was to decide on a home for the parliament. Everyone had assumed it would meet in the Old Royal High School, but the new First Minister, Donald Dewar, rejected this location on the grounds that it would give encouragement to nationalist opinion. Even so, there are many people in Scotland today who regret this decision and argue that an opportunity was missed. As a direct result of Dewar's decision, the building reverted to the ownership of Edinburgh City Council, who immediately converted it into office accommodation. It is certainly true that it would have made an extremely handsome parliament building, but perhaps there were other considerations to be taken into account.

Immediately opposite the High School is a monument to Robert Burns, also designed by Hamilton. Once again, the Greek theme is evident, in this case embodied by an exact reproduction of the peripteral temple of Lysicrates in Athens.

Although it was not opened until 1939, St. Andrew's House, the headquarters of the Scottish civil service, was conceived in 1928 as a concession to the emerging Scottish national movement. The failure to make such concessions in the case of Ireland had led to the loss to the United Kingdom of a large part of that island, not to speak of the civil disorder which has disfigured Northern Ireland ever since. Westminster had no intention of repeating the error in Scotland. At that time, government offices were scattered all over Edinburgh and it was proposed to bring them all together in one central location. Calton Jail, Edinburgh's principal place of incarceration since 1791, was closed down in 1924 as a result of the creation of Saughton Prison in the west of Edinburgh, and the new building was to be erected on this site. The proposal that the design was to be the responsibility of the Office of Works in London rather than any private architect was immediately seen as an affront to Scottish sensibilities and met with instant opposition.

A Scottish National Committee was formed, led by the Moderator of the Church of Scotland, including representatives from every part of Scottish society. This won the support of Queen Mary, who expressed a hope that "nothing unsightly would be built on Calton Hill that might spoil the outlook from her Palace of Holyrood." As a direct result of this intervention, the architect Thomas Tait was appointed in 1933 and the original idea of a simple office building became a project that would create a seat of government for the Secretary of State for Scotland. As David Bruce pointed out in *Edinburgh Past and Present* (1990), "Tait's St. Andrew's House bears some relation to the League of Nations building in Geneva and is probably the most significant piece of public architecture to have gone up in Edinburgh during the thirties."

Singers' Memorial

On the right-hand side of the steps facing St. Andrew's House, on a plaque affixed to the rock, is Edinburgh's most unusual monument. Known as the Singers' Memorial, it bears the simple inscription "In Memoriam" above the wreathed profiles of John Wilson, John Templeton, and David Kennedy — three singers who, in their day, enjoyed international reputations. Although they were not all Edinburgh men by birth, they all started their careers in the city in exactly the same way.

The Presbyterian form of worship, as is well known, rejects most kinds of ritual, and the use of musical instruments was long forbidden in Edinburgh churches. Instead, a precentor was employed to lead the congregation during the singing of psalms. Wilson, Templeton, and Kennedy had all performed this role in city churches.

John Wilson was born in the Canongate on Christmas Day, 1800. A printer by trade, he was on the staff of James Ballantyne, printer of Scott's Waverley novels. At the age of 25, after a spell as a precentor, Wilson abandoned printing to study music. In 1830, shortly after his stage debut at the Theatre Royal, Edinburgh (playing Henry Bertram in *Guy Mannering*) he was invited to join the Covent Garden company, and for the next eight years he performed exclusively on the London stage. His first American tour took place in 1837 and he continued to cross the Atlantic regularly to perform his repertoire of Scots songs. These appearances were extremely popular, particularly in Canada where his "Jacobite Entertainments" always attracted sell-out audiences. In 1849, while appearing in Quebec, Wilson was caught in a sudden downpour and, as a result of this, contracted cholera, leading to his untimely death.

John Templeton was Wilson's near contemporary. Born at Riccarton, near Kilmarnock, in 1802, Templeton, who came from an extremely talented musical family, arrived in Edinburgh at the age of twelve. Like Wilson, he began as a church precentor. At the age of sixteen, after his voice broke, he was advised to give up singing, but he continued with his study of music for the next four years. In 1822 he left Scotland and secured his first engagements as a professional singer, first at Worthing—where it is said that, in order to gain the experience, he worked for three weeks without salary—and later at Brighton, with the Southampton and Portsmouth Operatic Society. It was shortly after this engagement that Templeton was invited to join the company at Drury Lane. As so often happens, Templeton's big chance came unexpectedly. At Covent Garden, a production of *Don Giovanni* was in its final stages when the singer who had the part of Don Attavo suddenly withdrew and the management approached Templeton. Although he had only had five days to prepare, the Scottish singer scored a major success in the role.

Like Wilson before him, Templeton traveled extensively and Scottish songs were always featured in his concerts. His rendering of the songs of Robert Burns was particularly popular and, wherever he went in Britain, Ireland or the US, he unfailingly drew crowded houses. Despite these extensive concert tours, he did not completely desert the stage and appeared at the Theatre Royal twice in the winter of 1838. He sang the part of Elvino in *La Somnambula* and played the leading role of Francis Osbaldistone in *Rob Roy*.

Unlike Wilson, though, Templeton enjoyed a long and prosperous life. In 1852 he announced his retirement, but could always be prevailed upon to sing at charity concerts. He died in London 34 years later, at the age of 84, a much-respected figure in musical circles.

Wilson encouraged Templeton at the beginning of his career, and he, in turn, would later provide encouragement for the third member of the celebrated trio, David Kennedy. Kennedy was born on April 15, 1825 in Perth, where both his father and his uncle were precentors in local churches. In addition to this influence, he learned the traditional versions of farming community songs from his mother. Although he served an apprenticeship as a house-painter, he gave up his trade in 1857 when, shortly after his arrival in Edinburgh, he was appointed precentor at Nicolson Street United Presbyterian Church at a salary of £40 per annum. He held this position for the next five years, during which he studied music with a well-known teacher of the time, Edmond Edmonds.

According to the music critic John Forbes-Robertson, Kennedy was "by far the most perfect and dramatic exponent of Scots songs that Scotland has produced." His first appearance as a professional concert singer took place in 1859, when he was invited to appear at the Burns centenary celebration at the St. George's Hall, Liverpool. That same year, he gave twelve successful concerts at the Buccleuch Halls,

Edinburgh, followed by an extended tour of Scotland. In 1863, like Wilson and Templeton before him, he set out for London and scored a sensational success when he carried out a marathon season of one hundred concerts in the Egyptian Hall, Piccadilly. This season was also a considerable financial success, which probably accounts for Kennedy's loyalty to the concert stage. As far as can be established, he never appeared in either opera or theater although, as Wilson McLaren tells us in his *Edinburgh Memories* (1926), this was certainly not due to any absence of acting talent.

> *Kennedy's song-recitals in the Music Hall, Edinburgh, always drew crowded and enthusiastic audiences. Gifted with that pawky mother wit, on the platform as well as in private life, he rendered the auld Scots songs in a way that could never be forgotten. I can still recall his singing of 'The Barrin' o' the Door,' and his vivid interpretation of the poet's meaning, which he conveyed to his hearers by his gestures on the platform. Kennedy not only sang the songs but acted them as well, to the intense delight of the audience.*

With his wife Elizabeth, Kennedy raised a talented family of twelve children, the most celebrated of whom was their third daughter, Marjorie. In 1887, after studying singing in Paris and Milan, Marjorie married A.Y. Fraser, headmaster of Allan Glen's School in Glasgow. Her marriage, unfortunately, was to be rather short-lived. After just three years, her husband died in November 1890 and the young widow settled in Edinburgh, where she earned her living as a lecturer and teacher of music. It was during this time that she became interested in Gaelic folk song, and her work in creating English versions of songs such as *Mairi's Wedding* and *Ho Ro, My Nut-Brown Maiden* has added considerably to the Scottish choral repertoire.

She is, of course, better known today as Marjorie Kennedy-Fraser. During her lifetime, she would earn a special place in the hearts of the people of Edinburgh. When she died, full of honors, at her home at 6 Castle Street in November 1930, a huge congregation attended her memorial service in St. Giles.

Kennedy himself died at Stratford, Ontario in 1886, while on a farewell visit. His body was brought home for burial in Edinburgh and his last resting-place is marked by an imposing memorial-stone that takes up a large part of the wall of the Grange cemetery in the Southside. Unlike the Singers' Memorial, however, this is a family monument, carrying inscriptions in memory of Elizabeth Kennedy and all their children.

The National Monument: "Pride and Poverty"

In 1822 the Calton Hill must have seemed to be a most appropriate location for the siting of the National Monument. Only a few years earlier, after the death of Nelson at the battle of Trafalgar, a monument to the great naval hero had been erected there. This monument, still in existence today, takes the form of a tower some 100 feet in height. Taking the shape of an inverted telescope, it was designed by Robert Burn, and took eight years to build. Since its construction had been financed entirely by public subscription, the members of the National Monument Committee obviously believed that their more ambitious project could be accomplished in the same manner.

They were certainly not lacking in support, at least of the moral variety. Francis Jeffrey wrote enthusiastically of the national monument in the *Edinburgh Review,* declaring:

> *It is the peculiar boast of Edinburgh, the circumstance on which its marvellous beauty so essentially depends, is that its architecture is its landscape; that nature has done everything, has laid every foundation, and disposed of every line of its rocks and its hills, as if she had designed it for the display of architecture. It will also be the boast of our Parthenon that whilst it is the eye and centre of one of the noblest architectural landscapes of Europe, it will be everywhere supported by forms which will give to it additional importance and additional picturesque effect.*

The existence of this Parthenon, in other words, would create a cultural beacon for the city, guiding the good taste of the buildings that surrounded it.

By any standards, therefore, the National Monument was a very ambitious venture. It was also a very expensive one and, as a matter of fact, would have been for this reason completely out of the question just a few years earlier. Until 1815 access to the Calton Hill was restricted to one narrow street, rendering the transport of the required materials all but impossible. In that year, however, work began on a new eastern approach to Edinburgh—in itself an extremely difficult project, involving the bridging of a fifty-foot ravine—which would be completed in time for the state visit of the Prince Regent in 1822. Financed by Poor Relief and directed by the engineer Robert Stevenson, grandfather of Robert Louis, work on Regent Road (as it is now called) was completed by 1819, considerably extending the access to Calton Hill.

Work on the National Monument could therefore go ahead, and the man who was given responsibility for carrying it out was the architect, William Playfair. As mentioned earlier, Playfair was responsible for completing Adam's design of Old College and, since he received this commission when he was only 27 years of age, he must have been something of a prodigy. Four years later, Playfair set up his own practice and would go on to create many fine buildings, none more so than the two art galleries: the National Gallery of Scotland and the Royal Scottish Academy, which sit on Princes Street at the foot of the Mound.

The National Gallery of Scotland was opened in 1854 and today holds one of the most magnificent collections of paintings to be found anywhere in the United Kingdom. Indeed, this collection of great paintings by such artists as Rembrandt, El Greco, Monet, and Vermeer, not to mention the large collection of Turners that is shown every January, is so vast that the Gallery is simply not big enough to exhibit them all. At the time of writing, an extension is being created by burrowing into the Mound, but it is feared that even this imaginative attempt to create more exhibition space will prove insufficient.

Sharing an address with the National Gallery—and often mistaken for it—is the Royal Scottish Academy. This is, in fact, the older of the two buildings, first opened in 1826, and is the counterpart of the Royal Academy in London. Like that body, the RSA holds an annual exhibition, attracting artists from all over the UK, and frequently hosts touring exhibitions. These two important buildings, looking for all the world like a couple of Greek temples, sit at the very heart of Edinburgh. The Royal Scottish Academy, in particular, exudes a sense of power and permanence. Encased within a peristyle of Doric columns, it is constructed of a mixture of Culallo and Craigleith stone and there is a statue of Queen Victoria by Sir John Steell (1804-91) perched, rather eccentrically, on its north pediment. The National Gallery of Scotland, situated immediately behind the Royal Scottish Academy, has a more modest, or, at any rate, less ostentatious, appearance but the Greek theme is once more evident in the presence of Ionic columns.

Overlooking these galleries from the top of the Mound is a complex of buildings, created as a direct result of the Disruption of 1843. These include New College, established by the Free Church for the training of ministers, and the Assembly Hall of the Church of Scotland, temporary home of the Scottish Parliament. Playfair designed them both, as well as a number of other fine buildings, to be taken into account in due course.

The target figure for the building of the National Monument was set at £42,000. Most of this was to be raised by public subscription, although some attempt was made to secure government support. A large portion of this sum was obtained fairly quickly, leading Lord

Cockburn to declare that "we only want a public guinea for each of the private ones we have raised ourselves to give us a lift." In the event, however, this assistance was not forthcoming, the public subscription fell short of the target by some £18,000, and all that exists of the projected Parthenon is the structure of twelve columns standing on Calton Hill today. Writing of this structure in 1991, the architect Charles McKean made a rather valid point:

> *The contract began in 1826 to workmanship of Playfair's customary superlative quality, the massive stones for the columns from Craigleith Quarry requiring twelve horses and seventy men each for their transport. Three years later, the money was exhausted with only twelve columns to show for it. Notwithstanding, what was built was exactly that which the contract drawings specified should be built. In other words, it was a deliberate intention from the very first to build only the small section that we can see. It is therefore a deliberate folly: if money was insufficient to achieve the military Valhalla that had been hoped, at the least it could be used to crown Edinburgh's Athenian aspirations.*

In other words, if the National Monument Committee could not have their Parthenon, they were determined at least to have a semblance of it. No attempt was made to scale down the project, to use the available finances to create a less ambitious, more serviceable structure. In a rather bitter remark, Playfair was to describe the whole business as "striking proof of the pride and poverty of us Scots."

Modern Athenians

Playfair's involvement with Calton Hill was not restricted to the National Monument. In 1819 he was commissioned to build a number of high-quality houses on the eastern slope of Calton Hill and, as a result, Waterloo Place, Regent Terrace, Royal Terrace, and Carlton Terrace came into being. Within this community—one might almost call it "a new town in miniature"—lived a number of people who might, with justice, be described as "modern Athenians".

The painter, Francis Cadell (1883-1937), for instance, lived at 30 Regent Terrace towards the end of his life. Cadell was one of the four

"Scottish Colourists", whose work in the period immediately following the First World War, laid the foundations of modern Scottish painting. The other members of this group, S. J. Peploe, Leslie Hunter, and J. D. Fergusson, had, like Cadell, been deeply influenced by living in Paris and traveling throughout France, together with an enthusiasm for Manet and the Impressionists. Peploe was also an Edinburgh man— like Edinburgh's most celebrated painter, Henry Raeburn (of whom more presently)—while the others were from the west of Scotland. J. D. Fergusson was quintessentially a Glasgow painter, while Hunter, although his early work had been done in America, was also based in that city. All of them were committed, in principle at least, to living and working in Scotland.

The work of Cadell and his fellow-Colourists enjoyed a spectacular revival during the 1990s, when an exhibition of their work ran in Edinburgh for many months. In his youth, Cadell's work had been characterized by its jauntiness, but by the time he arrived in Regent Terrace in 1932 his style had become somewhat muted. One of his most interesting paintings from this period is *The Open Window*, which gives an atmospheric view of Arthur's Seat, as seen from his flat in Regent Terrace. The painter's sister was Jean Cadell, the actress whose sharp face and acidulous manner graced many a British film of the 1940s and 1950s.

Cadell would have had as a near neighbor one of Scotland's most influential academics, Sir Herbert Grierson—Regius Professor of Rhetoric and English Language at Edinburgh University for more than thirty years until 1953—who lived at 12 Regent Terrace with his wife and five daughters. One of those daughters, Janet, later wrote a memoir in which she recalled evenings of poetry and music in her childhood home. W. B. Yeats and G. K. Chesterton read the poems, while pianist and composer, Sir Donald Tovey, supplied the music.

I like to think our house still echoes with Tovey playing the piano, and my father and also W. B. Yeats reading poetry, and the conversation of all the exciting people that came to the house, and last but not least, G. K. Chesterton reciting Hilaire Belloc's Cautionary Tales for Children *when we were still young adolescents. I can remember my mother calling up to my sister Alice at the top of the house: 'Alice, are you coming*

to Mr. Chesterton's lecture?' and Alice's reply: 'Not bloody likely! I'm stay-
ing at home to read a detective novel!' and the long giggles that resounded
from Chesterton's room on the ground floor.

Tovey (1875-1940), once described as the "most learned musician
in Europe", lived nearby, at 39 Royal Terrace, until his retirement in
1939. In his day, Tovey's popularity in Edinburgh was very great. "You
can take it from me," says a character in Muriel Sparks' *The Prime of
Miss Jean Brodie* (1962), "you get a sight more religion out of Professor
Tovey's Sunday concerts than you do out of your kirk services." The
son of a schoolmaster, Tovey was born at Eton, where his father taught.
Something of a prodigy, he never went to school himself and was
educated privately. After winning a musical scholarship to Balliol
College, Oxford, his career as a concert musician began in 1900 with a
series of concerts in London, Berlin, and Vienna. His first appearance
in Edinburgh seems to have been in 1913, when he performed his own
piano concerto in the Queen's Hall, under the baton of Sir Henry
Wood. Appointed Reid Professor of Music at Edinburgh University in
1914, Tovey had a widespread influence as a writer, lecturer, and
teacher of composition. His own music includes *Sonata Eroica* (1913)
for solo violin, an opera, *The Bride of Dionysus* (1917), a symphony,
and a cello concerto written for his friend and frequent visitor, Pablo
Casals. He also set to music the poetry of Edward Lear, Lewis Carroll
and Hilaire Belloc.

Grierson had a profound interest in the metaphysical poets,
particularly John Donne. His edition of Donne's poetry, which first
appeared in 1912, is still considered to have set the standard for all
future editions. According to a contemporary critic, Cairns Craig, the
influence of Grierson's teaching can be discerned in the work of one of
his most brilliant students, the great Gaelic poet, Sorley Maclean
(1911-96). Maclean himself testified that although he had considered
studying either Celtic or history on entering university, he had opted
for English mainly because of the prospect of being taught by Grierson.

Always an extremely charismatic figure, Grierson was adored by
his students to the point of deification. No less appreciated was one of
his predecessors who, half a century earlier, had lived in the same street.
Professor David Masson (1822-1907), later Historiographer Royal for

Scotland, had occupied Grierson's Chair for thirty years until 1895 and lived at 10 Regent Terrace for part of that time. Masson, the close friend of John Stuart Mill and Thomas Carlyle, exercised an equally potent influence on his students. One of the most celebrated of those was the author of *Peter Pan*, J. M. Barrie (1860-1937), who would later pay tribute to this influence with the following anecdote.

> *There are men who are good to think of, and as a rule we only know them by their books. Something of our pride in life would go with their fall. To have one such Professor at a time is the most a university can hope of human nature, so Edinburgh need not expect another just yet... The test of a sensitive man is that he is careful of wounding the feelings of others. Once, I remember, a student was reading a passage aloud, assuming at the same time such an attitude that the Professor could not help remarking that he looked like a teapot. It was exactly what he did look like, and the class applauded. But next moment Masson had apologized for being personal.*

Another leading academic, who lived nearby, was Charles Sarolea (1870-1953), the first Professor of French at Edinburgh University. A Belgian by birth and a former political advisor to King Albert of Belgium, Sarolea was Belgian Consul from 1901 until his death. During both world wars he was very active as a campaigner for Belgian relief and addressed many mass meetings on this subject in Europe and America. He was famous in Edinburgh for being the owner of what was reputed to be the largest private library in Europe. This collection was so large that Sarolea needed two whole houses, 21 and 22 Royal Terrace, to accommodate it. Apart from his prowess as an assiduous, not to say fanatical, bibliophile, Sarolea was a prolific writer on contemporary politics and claimed a speaking knowledge of at least eighteen languages.

The Observatory
The Calton Hill may seem an appropriate place for the siting of an observatory, but the fact is that the location of such a building there has proved rather problematic. The first Calton Hill observatory was designed in 1776 by James Craig at the request of the optician Thomas

Short, as a showpiece for telescopes—but this structure, for some reason, proved to be unsuitable. It was replaced by the building that still stands there today, designed by William Playfair in cruciform shape with a central dome. In 1824 this became the Royal Observatory and was placed under the direction of the Astronomer Royal.

The holder of this post from 1870 to 1889 was Charles Piazzi Smyth (1819-1900), Professor of Astronomy at Edinburgh University from 1846. Born in Naples, Smyth was the second son of Admiral William Henry Smyth and had been named, somewhat prophetically, after the Italian astronomer Guiseppe Piazzi. Although he married a local girl, Jessie Duncan, and settled in Edinburgh, one cannot help but feel that his life in the city must have been rather frustrating. Apart from anything else, since his subject was not required for graduation in any degree, he usually had no students to teach. Furthermore, on becoming Astronomer Royal, he found to his dismay that there was practically no financial support from the government and that he had to pay for the repair and replacement of instruments out of his own pocket!

Piazzi Smyth's nineteen years in Edinburgh were spent mostly on travel and research. His most lasting achievement was his installation, in 1852, of the time-ball in the Nelson Monument. This time-ball, a sphere approximately the size of a cannonball, which slides up and down on a vertical mast, is raised every day to the top of the monument shortly before 1 p.m. and dropped on the hour, the movement determined by a special clock that is synchronized with Greenwich. Originally intended as an aid to shipping, this service was modified in 1861, since when it has been connected to the Castle, setting the time for the firing of the One O'clock Gun.

Platonic Love

Perhaps the most interesting street in the whole vicinity leads up the western slope and is itself called simply Calton Hill. This was the boyhood home of the antiquarian, Sir Daniel Wilson (1816-92), who was responsible for the rediscovery of St. Margaret's Chapel (See Chapter One). Sir Daniel's brother George was to become Regius Professor of Technology at Edinburgh University and was a leading expert on color-blindness. The Wilsons lived at 5 Calton Hill during the early years of the nineteenth century. Among their neighbors at this time was the street's most romantic resident, Mrs. Agnes McLehose. One of the great beauties of her age, Mrs. McLehose's place in literary history is due to her friendship with the poet, Robert Burns. The letters that passed between them, in which he addresses her as "Clarinda", while she calls him "Sylvander", are superb examples of the poet's underrated, although very polished, prose style. The lovers met at a tea party given by a certain Miss Nimmo and the correspondence began in December 1787, when Burns sent Mrs. McLehose (not yet "Clarinda") the following note.

> *Our worthy common friend, Miss Nimmo, in her usual pleasant way, rallied me a good deal on my new acquaintance; and, in the humour of her ideas, I wrote some lines which I enclose you, as I think they have a good deal of poetic merit; and Miss Nimmo tells me that you are not only a critic, but a poetess. Fiction, you know, is the native region of poetry; and I hope you will pardon my vanity in sending you the bagatelle as a tolerable off-hand jeu d'esprit.*

Mrs. McLehose replied, enclosing some verses of her own, and they did not actually meet until several letters had been exchanged. The true nature of their relationship has never been clear. In much the same way as George Bernard Shaw's so-called "love affair" with the actress Ellen Terry was conducted entirely by letter, their liaison was probably platonic—or, at the very least, unconsummated. Yet Mrs. McLehose did provide the inspiration for one of Burns' most poignant lyrics, "Ae Fond Kiss", of which the following are the first three stanzas.

> *Ae fond kiss, and then we sever,—*
> *Ae fareweel, and then—for ever*
> *Deep in heart-wrung tears I'll pledge thee*
> *Warring sighs and groans I'll wage thee!*
>
> *Who shall say that fortune grieves him,*
> *While the star of hope she leaves him?*
> *Me, nae chearfu' twinkle lights me,—*
> *Dark despair around benights me.*

I'll ne'er blame my partial fancy,
Naething could resist my Nancy;
But to see her, was to love her—
Love but her, and love for ever.

Mrs. McLehose spent the last forty years of her life at 14 Calton Hill, where she died in 1841, at the age of 82. After her death, the following note was found among her papers: "6ᵗʰ Dec. 1831. This day I never can forget. Parted with Burns in the year 1791, never more to meet in this world. Oh, may we meet in Heaven!"

Two years later, the photographer Robert Adamson (1821-48) came to live and establish a studio at 28 Calton Hill, known as Rock House. Almost immediately, David Octavius Hill (1802-70), with whom he formed a partnership that would create a new art form, joined him. Hill, the secretary of the Royal Scottish Academy, was a landscape painter and book illustrator who had recently been commissioned to paint a group portrait of the seceding ministers of the Disruption. In order to achieve this massive task—which can now be seen in the Free Church Assembly Hall on the Mound—he enlisted the aid of Adamson, whose pioneering use of calotype photographs allowed Hill to have permanent images of his 472 subjects before painting them.

Their partnership was not restricted to the Disruption painting, and they went on to create an archive of some 1,800 photographs. This archive—a unique record of mid-Victorian life—is currently located in the Scottish National Portrait Gallery in Queen Street. As for Rock House, it continued to provide both a home and studio for photographers for the next hundred years, until 1945.

Mixed Reputations

Although the atmosphere of the Calton Hill community may seem remarkably similar to that of the New Town, there have been periods in history when the excesses of the Old Town intruded here too. During the Regency period, for instance, a group of upper-class hooligans, known as the Sweating Club, were notorious for prowling the streets at night and attacking whomsoever took their fancy. In doing so, they were carrying out a tradition that had lasted for at least a century. In an earlier period, the Sweating Club was known by a more sinister name, and it is thought that the playwright John Gay (1685-1732), who was a regular visitor to Edinburgh, may have drawn inspiration from the Hellfire Club when writing his play *The Mohocks*. Certainly, the Mohocks' song is one that would have gone down well at gatherings of the Sweating Club, since it describes their activities exactly.

> *We will scour the town,*
> *Knock the constable down,*
> *Put the watch and the beadle to flight:*
> *We'll force all we meet*
> *To kneel down at our feet,*
> *And own this great prince of the night.*

> *Then a Mohock, a Mohock I'll be,*
> *No laws shall restrain*
> *Our libertine reign*
> *We'll riot, drink on, and be free. .*

Contemporary with the Sweating Club was a more civilized, and certainly better behaved, group of young men who met in the Boar Tavern and were known as the Boar Club. Although their rituals seem rather childish—members were known as "boars", their meeting place was called "the sty", and all conversation was described as "grunting"— their activities were mainly social. They seem to have been dedicated to nothing more strenuous than conviviality and the most interesting fact about this club is the identity of its founder.

J. G. Schetky (1737-1824) was a composer and cellist from Darmstadt in Germany, who settled in Edinburgh in 1772. He arrived to take up a temporary appointment, but found the musical life of the city so stimulating that he remained for the rest of his life. He married locally, sent his sons to the High School, and played an active part in Edinburgh cultural life. Although much of his work has been lost, his duets, trios, quartets and sonatas for cello and violin have all been published. He also wrote a cello tutor and sets of Scots tunes arranged for military bands.

In Edinburgh today, the Calton Hill has a somewhat mixed reputation. On the one hand, it enjoys a rather disreputable celebrity as a night-time "cruising ground" for homosexuals; on the other, it has retained its place as a preserve of mythic tradition. The ancient Celtic Festival of Beltane, in which cattle and crops are blessed, was revived on Calton Hill in 1988. Every year since then, the Beltane Fire has been lit on May 1, celebrated by a massive party, involving (mostly) young people from all over Edinburgh. Perhaps for this reason, it has come into increasing use as a venue for Fringe shows during the Festival.

In short, the Calton Hill has always provoked varied reactions. Charles Dickens plainly disliked the place, describing it in the magazine *Master Humphrey's Clock* (1841) as "a rubbish heap of the imaginative architecture". But for Robert Louis Stevenson, it presented the best possible view of Edinburgh. "It's a place to stroll," he wrote, "on one of those days of sunshine and east wind which are so common in our more than temperate summer."

CHAPTER SIX

Intangible Area: The West End

"A very old West End grocery shop is the sort of place where they let you taste the cheese before you buy, where the claret still comes in wooden cases, where truffles and tinned wild boar are commonplace. One has the feeling that they would deliver two ounces of salami to a good customer, then forget to send in the bill. If they sniff when you ask for a tin of beans, they do it very quietly."

W. Gordon Smith, *Edinburgh in Photographs,* 1979

"West End" is one of these expressions whose meaning varies according to its context. In Glasgow, the West End is simply the most prosperous part of the city; in Dallas, Texas, it is the center of the tourist trade; in John O'Groats it is one half of the village; and, of course, in London, the term is synonymous with glittering lights and nights out. In Edinburgh, though, the West End exists largely as an abstract expression, not so much a location as an ambiance, an atmosphere and a certain style of behavior. As such, this intangible quality is to be found in restaurants, bars, hotels, theaters, department stores, and—as the above quotation indicates—even grocers' shops throughout the city.

Yet there is also a *geographical* West End, found at the juncture of Princes Street and Lothian Road. From here, the road leads west, through Shandwick Place to Haymarket, where Edinburgh's second railway station is located. Haymarket is much smaller than Waverley, with just three platforms, and is mainly used by commuters from Glasgow and Fife. Opposite the station, at a crossroads, is one of the most unusual war memorials to be found in the British Isles. This takes the form of a clock and was erected after the First World War by the Heart of Midlothian Football Club to honor the many players and supporters who lost their lives in the conflict.

Football and Faith

Football has a long and colorful history in Edinburgh, a history, furthermore, which can be dated to one particular occasion in December 1873. In that month the Glasgow club, Queen's Park, played an exhibition match against Clydesdale in Holyrood Park. The aim of this match was to demonstrate the new rules that had recently been introduced by the Football Association in England, under which the first FA Cup competition had been played in the previous year.

Football, until then, bore little resemblance to the "beautiful game" that we know today. It was a very upper-class sport, played mainly at universities and English public schools, and even in this context, it was a very disorderly affair, in which brute strength counted for more than skill. Intended to provide an alternative to rugby, the early version of the sport had much in common with its physical counterpart. And although football had been around for centuries in one form or another, no one was quite sure of the rules. Even after a standard set of rules was drawn up—at Cambridge in 1848—the physical element continued to dominate, with every player getting behind the ball in order to force it over the opposition's goal line.

It was not the rules, however, that made the greatest impact, but rather the manner in which Queen's Park interpreted them. They moved the ball about the field, passing it between them skillfully, creating a spectacle that, as the Scottish football historian Bob Crampsie has put it, "was easy to understand and easy to talk about."

It was also easy to play—or must have seemed so. As a direct consequence of that Queen's Park match, football clubs were formed all over the city, and before too long a league competition had been established. Most of these clubs had a very short history, and in fact fewer than half-a-dozen survived to play in the era of professional football. Of these, only two now remain: Hibernian FC and the Heart of Midlothian FC, colloquially known as Hibs and Hearts respectively. Although these two clubs are, of course, bitter rivals, the nature of their rivalry should not be misunderstood.

Sectarianism in Scottish football is a product of the entry of professionalism into what had initially been an amateur game. Hibernian Football Club, for instance, was founded by a priest, Father Hannan of St. Patrick's in the Cowgate, as part of the activities of a Catholic boys' club. In order to qualify for membership, every player naturally had to be a Catholic. This restriction was all very well in the amateur days, but once the game became professional it meant that the club was open to the charge of discriminating against non-Catholic players. This led, in turn, to a demand from supporters of other clubs that a similar discrimination should be made against Catholics. In such conditions, it did not take long for tribal loyalties to assert themselves, with resulting conflict.

Hibs may have its spiritual roots in the Irish Catholic community and Hearts in that of Scots Presbyterianism, but religious differences play less of a part in their rivalry than is the case in other parts of Scotland. Sectarian bigotry may not be completely absent from this relationship, but it has always been less important than identification with territory. Hibs supporters tend to belong to the north and east of Edinburgh, while Hearts supporters (who outnumber their city rivals by a ratio of approximately two to one) are more usually found in the south and west.

On the other hand, those associated with Hibs have always prized their Irish identity, while Hearts have had a similar loyalty to the idea of the United Kingdom. This was why, on the outbreak of war in 1914, the entire playing staff of Hearts, together with some 400 shareholders and regular supporters, immediately volunteered for military service. Many of them did not survive and the memorial at Haymarket was built in their memory. Every year since, on Remembrance Day, a service is held at the memorial, which every employee of the club is obliged to attend.

Since both Hearts and Hibs originated in the Old Town, rivalry between the clubs was always inescapable. But in the main it is a fairly good-natured rivalry and, in fact, has not been without its productive aspects. In 1878, for instance, both clubs met in the final of the East of Scotland Football Association Cup. The match was drawn and they had to play another four games before the trophy was decided, in Hearts' favor, by a single goal. These were the games that established football as a spectator sport in Edinburgh. A crowd of some 4,000 supporters attended that fifth final, generating so much income that it became clear that football could not remain an amateur game for much longer. Furthermore, with some forty games a season attracting that level of business, football could no longer be restricted to public parks. In 1881 the Hearts' directors decided to establish a ground of their own and obtained a lease on some farm land in the west of Edinburgh, near the village of Gorgie.

It was a smart move, for the area was undergoing a degree of industrial development at the time. New factories were being built, together with housing for the people who would work in them. Most of these workers came from the Old Town and many were already Hearts supporters. This core support has been maintained over the years and, apart from the "Old Firm" of Rangers and Celtic, Hearts currently sells more season tickets than any other club in Scotland.

One view of Hearts' ground, Tynecastle Park, of more than average interest is that of a Hibs supporter. David Benning is a Glaswegian who, on coming to live in Edinburgh, immediately gave his footballing adherence to the club on the other side of the city. In his survey of Scottish football stadiums, *A Season in Hell* (1997), he describes his first visit to Tynecastle.

This area of the capital has always been a closed book to me, and unlike the environs of Easter Road it has not been put on the low-life literary map by the likes of Irvine Welsh (whose lugubrious Leithers and heroin-addicted Hibees must be more fun to read about than to share a close, landing or outside toilet with).

The crowd eventually totalled a remarkable 11,485, and although £13 seemed a bit steep for entry to the sepulchral Main Stand, the view from Row A of the wooden top level made the financial sacrifice seem less painful. The Wheatfield Stand opposite and the even newer School End Stand to our right were supported by exposed goalframe tubing, rather than yet more cantilevers, and both were serviced by mid-level concourses or walkways. Strangely, the steel supports were painted pink and somehow managed to appear not unattractive. Beneath our warped wooden floorboards, young boys were able to smoke in their bucket seats (in the concreted Paddock). Only the Gorgie Road end was unfinished, consisting of uncovered seating for away fans.

River and Canal

This whole area of Edinburgh stands on land that was occupied during the Middle Ages by the Royal Orchards. These Orchards—which were, in fact, market gardens, producing abundant quantities of fruit and vegetables—were once very extensive, covering a very large part of what is now western Edinburgh. Over the centuries, the area has become completely urbanized, absorbing villages such as Gorgie, Saughton, Stenhouse, and Roseburn so completely that their former existence is recalled mainly by street names. Yet something of a rural character continues to survive, in spite of the presence, as Charles McKean has it, of "a superabundance of supermarkets, bypasses and bungalows, tawdry industrial estates, filling stations, brick rejects from Welwyn Garden City, glass slabs and spotty construction." The area is also full of hills and green spaces, including Edinburgh Zoo, the national rugby stadium at Murrayfield, the Hearts' football stadium at Tynecastle Park, golf courses at Ravelston and Carrick Knowe, and the campus of Queen Margaret University. There is also much natural beauty to be found on the banks of two waterways that pass through the area. The course of Edinburgh's river, the Water of Leith, passes through the West End, while the Union Canal enters Edinburgh a little further to the south.

The Water of Leith rises at Craigengar in the Pentland Hills and runs through the center of Edinburgh until it reaches the sea at Leith. It is a rather pleasant but unremarkable little river, of which George Scott-Moncrieff wrote in 1947, "it comes into Edinburgh by chance, having had nothing to do with the foundation of the city." Nevertheless, it is a clear and sparkling stream, well stocked with brown trout and providing much sport for anglers, and its banks bustle with wildlife.

The Union Canal is not nearly so pretty. Built between 1817 and 1822, mainly as a means of transporting coal to Edinburgh, it runs between Edinburgh and Falkirk—a distance of some 32 miles—where it meets the Forth and Clyde Canal at the magnificent Falkirk Wheel, a spectacular conduit constructed as a Millennium project, which forms a link between the two canals. There has been little traffic since the 1950s, and this disuse has led to some deterioration in the canal's structure. Over the past few years, funding from the Millennium Commission, in partnership with others, has led to a program that aims to regenerate the canals of central Scotland.

At the time of writing, the Union Canal features in a new development that is currently in the planning stage. Edinburgh Quay is to be a large waterside development, incorporating shops, restaurants, office, and apartment blocks, which is to be centered on the Edinburgh end of the canal, at Lochrin Basin, in the district of Tollcross.

Tollcross: The King's Theatre

Tollcross, as the name suggests, is a crossroads at which several parts of Edinburgh come together. The Old Town lies immediately to the east, the New Town to the north and, of course, the Southside to the south. This is where, in Muriel Spark's *The Prime of Miss Jean Brodie*, Miss Brodie's pupils encounter the unemployed. This may also be the site, one ventures to suggest, which inspired Spark's most quoted poem, "Edinburgh Villanelle":

> *These eyes that saw the saturnine*
> *Glance in my back, refused the null*
> *Heart of Midlothian, never mine.*
> *Hostile High Street gave the sign.*

Holyrood made unmerciful
These eyes that saw the saturnine

Watchmen of murky Leith begin
To pump amiss the never-full
Heart of Midlothian, never mine.

Tollcross is also the home of Edinburgh's most popular theater, the King's, in Leven Street. Its story is a rather interesting one. An Edinburgh builder called Cruikshank built the theater in 1906, but shortly after completing the construction he discovered, to his great consternation, that the company that had placed the contract had gone bankrupt. If he wished to recover his outlay—not to mention making any kind of a profit—he would have to find a way of disposing of this very large theater. At the same time, he appreciated the value of the theater as an asset and was not about to sell it short.

As it happens, there was a theatrical impresario in Edinburgh who was more than willing to make a deal with Cruikshank. F. W. Wyndham, owner of the Royal Lyceum, was in the process of building a theatrical empire at the time. Over the next few years, Wyndham would create Howard & Wyndham Ltd., acquiring theaters in towns and cities all over the British Isles. His first acquisition, however, was the King's. Part of the deal that Cruikshank made with Wyndham involved the builder's son, Stewart, who was given a seat on the board of Howard & Wyndham Ltd.

Stewart Cruikshank was very young at this time and had had no experience whatsoever of theater management. He worked very hard at learning the business, though, and five years later was appointed director of the King's, the theater with which he was to be identified for the rest of his life. In time, he would not only become both chairman and managing director of Howard & Wyndham Ltd., but would hand over the succession to his son.

Cruikshank always maintained his base at the King's and, indeed, it was where his life eventually came to an end. One evening, on leaving the building, he died as a result of a traffic accident. In his youth, he had served his time as a joiner and had, in fact, worked for his father in the construction of the building. In the King's today, a memorial plaque that can be seen in the dress circle recalls a life devoted to the reputation of a theater that he had physically helped to build. Thanks to Cruikshank, the King's has earned, over the years, a considerable reputation for pantomime and big, lavish musicals. It is for this reason that of all the city's theaters it is the one that Edinburgh people know best.

Pantomime, in particular, has always been important at the King's. It is one of the lesser-known facts of theater history that Edinburgh has played a unique role in the development of this enduring popular form. Cruikshank's spectacular productions of the 1920s and 1930s were based on a code of practice that had been developing for more than a hundred years. Charles Farley, one of the most important pioneers of the modern pantomime, had trained William Murray, who made such a success of the old Theatre Royal. During his years at that establishment, Murray had modified the lessons he had received from Farley and perfected a style to suit his Scottish audience. Murray passed on his expertise to Robert Wyndham, who in turn trained his son, Fred. In the early decades of the twentieth century, Fred Wyndham's sumptuous pantomimes would be the last word in color and spectacle. This was the tradition that Fred Wyndham passed on to Stewart Cruikshank.

It would be wrong, though, to assume that the King's is restricted to popular theater. Even before the advent of the Edinburgh Festival, it served the city well as a venue for opera and ballet, and when the Festival was inaugurated in 1947 it provided a home for Glyndebourne Opera. Since then, as George Bruce has written, "the King's has echoed to more bravos than in the entire history of concert-going in Scotland."

Some of the most enthusiastic of such "bravos" were heard during the Edinburgh Festival of 1957, when La Piccola Scala, an opera company from Milan, performed Bellini's *La Somnambula,* with Maria Callas in the leading role of Amina. According to Christopher Grier of *The Scotsman,* the great *prima donna* "inflamed the audience to a fever of enthusiasm without parallel in the history of Festival operatic annals." Having done so, it is reported, Callas stormed out the theater and out of Edinburgh, never to return. Rumors abounded concerning this incident, which no one who was not directly involved could possibly understand. There was a degree of speculation concerning her relationship with the Festival management, the terms of her contract and even—absurdly enough—her need for publicity. It was only when a doctor's certificate was produced that it became clear that her withdrawal was a matter of her health; she had become exhausted to the point of breakdown.

On the other side of Tollcross from the King's, the north side, Lothian Road leads to Princes Street and the New Town. This street was originally built in 1785—in a single day, according to one story, as the result of a wager—in order to provide a link between the New Town and the suburb of Portsburgh. Today it is best known as the home of the leading Festival venues, which include the Usher Hall, Film House, the Traverse and Royal Lyceum theaters.

Festival Venues

The Usher Hall, which first opened its doors in 1914, was built as the result of a bequest of £100,000 made in 1896 by Andrew Usher, a prominent Edinburgh brewer. Usher's intention was to provide Edinburgh with a first-class concert hall and an open competition, won by an English architect, J. Stockdale Harrison, resulted in a building of great elegance and efficiency, with an auditorium that combines amplitude and intimacy to a quite extraordinary degree. It also retains a great deal of the atmosphere of its period, with mahogany fitments in the cloakrooms and panels of Sienna marble lining the staircases.

It was in the Usher Hall that the Edinburgh Festival experienced its most defining moment, for it was here in 1947 that Kathleen Ferrier sang Mahler's *Das Lied von der Erde* with the Vienna Philharmonic Orchestra under the baton of Bruno Walter. This great performance, which was later to be described by Walter as belonging "to the most beautiful music events of our time", set the seal on the Festival's success, ensuring its arrival as an annual institution in the life of the city. In the years that have passed since, orchestras and musicians from all over the world have played the Usher Hall at Festival time.

Apart from its role as an international concert venue, the Usher Hall also functions as a community resource, hosting many political rallies, school concerts and prize-givings. It is where the people of Edinburgh gather on important occasions, as when Sean Connery received the freedom of the city in 1991.

On each side of the Usher Hall are two theaters, each in its own way providing an example of the Edinburgh variety of "West End". The older of these is the Royal Lyceum, built in 1883 by two prominent Edinburgh actors, J. B. Howard and F. W. Wyndham, whom we have already encountered. Howard, a former member of Henry Irving's Lyceum Company in London, named the theater in honor of his former employer. (Originally called the New Lyceum, its appeal quickly eclipsed that of the Edinburgh Theatre Royal, also owned by Howard and Wyndham, with the result that the royal patent was transferred to the new theater.) Irving himself, whose illustrious career had its beginnings in Edinburgh, played a substantial part in the establishment of the Lyceum, contributing £1,000 to its construction. He also gave the enterprise the best possible start by opening the theater with a season of his most successful roles, featuring his full London company.

Over the past century or so, the Lyceum has played a notable part in Scottish, and indeed British, theatrical life. In the early days, although it maintained its own production company, it was chiefly a receiving house for the touring companies of actor-managers such as Irving. With the disappearance of such companies, it became identified with smart musical comedy, functioning as an out-of-town try-out house for such theaters as the London Gaiety. During the 1930s and 1940s, it provided a home for a popular repertory company—led first by Jevan Brandon-Thomas and later by Wilson Barret—and since 1947, it has been the leading theatrical venue of the Edinburgh International Festival. As such, it has featured dramatic premieres as different as T. S. Eliot's *The Cocktail Party* and the groundbreaking satirical revue, *Beyond the Fringe*. At other times of the year, it is home to a resident repertory company which, like all such companies, is highly influenced by (London) West End trends, with occasional departures into Scottish drama.

While the Lyceum is associated closely with the official Festival, the Traverse, on the other side of the Usher Hall, is more closely associated with the Fringe. Founded in 1963 by a group of enthusiasts led by Jim Haynes, the Traverse began life as a theater club, devoted to the production of experimental drama. For the next thirty years, it was firmly based in the Old Town, first in the Lawnmarket and later the Grassmarket, maintaining its club status until 1988, when it finally became a public theater. It was not until 1992 that it moved into its present home. Over the years, the Traverse has rather lost the reputation it once had for being at the leading edge of the *avant-garde*, and has taken on a rather more comfortable atmosphere. While it may lack radical potency as a theater, it nevertheless has a very nice bar and restaurant and is still a popular meeting place.

The site on which these three buildings stand has a long history in the entertainment business. In medieval times, the area was known as "the Barrace", a redundant Scots word which simply means tournament list, and it was where much chivalric jousting took place. Much later, during the Victorian period, it was the scene of an ill-fated scheme to create a grandiose entertainment complex, to be called the "Edinburgh Theatre and Winter Gardens". Only one part of this plan was ever put into effect. The Edinburgh Theatre, built at enormous expense in 1875, was a splendidly equipped and well-appointed playhouse. Unfortunately, after no more than two years of operation, it closed and the property was sold, for less than half of its original cost, to the United Presbyterian Church. In the best traditions of Victorian Presbyterianism, the Church authorities sold the furniture and fittings by public auction, pulled the theater down and built their own Synod Hall in its place. Many years later, the Poole family bought the building and added the Synod Hall to their chain of cinemas.

As recently as the 1960s, another hapless project came to grief on the same spot. This was the plan to build an Opera House, which began with the demolition of the Poole's Synod Hall. If this plan had come to fruition, both the Usher Hall and the neighboring Royal Lyceum would have been demolished and a magnificent Opera House would now be in place. Unfortunately—or fortunately, depending on how one looks at it—the funding was not forthcoming and, instead of an Opera House, Edinburgh was left with a hole in the ground. To the city's embarrassment, this gap site, which is now filled by an office building called Saltire Court, part of which is the Traverse Theatre, remained undeveloped for nearly thirty years.

The Exchange
On the other side of Lothian Road stands a landmark which, although it came on the market at much the same time, was developed over a much shorter period. The Caledonian railway station, once Edinburgh's gateway to the south, became redundant in the early 1960s, as a result of the notorious Beeching reorganization of the national rail system. In its place there is now a complex of modern buildings largely devoted to finance and commerce, known collectively as the Exchange. These include the Clydesdale Bank Plaza, the Standard Life building and the Edinburgh Conference Centre. The most prominent of all is the Sheraton Hotel, whose imposing presence at the head of Festival Square acts as a focal point for the whole complex.

On the south side of Festival Square, housed in a converted church, is Film House, headquarters of the Edinburgh Film Festival. This festival was founded at the same time as the Festival of Music and Drama, reflecting Edinburgh's long-standing love affair with the art of cinema. Although it was initially established, in the words of one of its founders Forsyth Hardy, as "an act of faith", this was rewarded from the first by a high level of achievement, summed up by the film critic Derek Malcolm, writing in the *Guardian* in 1973.

Not for the first time the Edinburgh Film Festival has comfortably exceeded expectations. It is now, in its twenty-seventh year, one of the most coherently planned and best-run of Europe's cinematic beanfeasts. The fact that it is put together by a group of young enthusiasts, led this year by Lynda Myles on an shoestring of a budget, makes this all the more remarkable.

One is now inclined to believe that if it spent half the money of most of its competitors it would be twice as good as them. It is already ahead of some on a mere £5,500, of which the Corporation contributes £2,000.

If the Edinburgh Festival may, in general, be accused of middle-aged spread, there could be no better way of dispelling that image than backing its film wing better. There are no hardening arteries at Film House.

The Edinburgh Film Guild, which initiated the Film Festival, was founded in 1930 in order to present "unusual films not normally seen in the ordinary cinema". This policy remains very much in place today at Film House, which is part art-house cinema, part festival headquarters, and part meeting place for everyone who is interested in the art of film.

On the other side of Festival Square, the Western Approach Road feeds traffic in and out of central Edinburgh. Crossing this road—by means of a bridge on the north side of the Exchange—is rather like making a journey from the twenty-first century to the nineteenth. One finds oneself in one of Edinburgh's most attractive places, Rutland Square, backing on to Shandwick Place, the heart of the true West End.

Henry Raeburn, Portrait Painter

This is an area of the city that might well be described as Edinburgh's Belgravia. These gracious streets and houses, almost exclusively Georgian in character, came into being in the early 1800s, when a number of landowners sought to exploit their properties as the city grew in prosperity. One of the most active of those was the great Edinburgh portrait painter, Henry Raeburn.

Raeburn was born in Edinburgh in 1756, the son of a textile manufacturer in Stockbridge. He was educated at George Heriot's Hospital (as it was then known) before being apprenticed to James Gilliland, an Edinburgh goldsmith. He began painting miniature portraits while still an apprentice, but his career did not make any progress until 1780, when he married Ann Leslie, a wealthy widow. After a brief sojourn of two years in Rome, he and his wife returned to settle in Edinburgh in 1786 and, over the next decade, Raeburn's reputation was established. During this time, he received many commissions for portraits of the Scottish aristocracy, leading lawyers, doctors, university professors, men of letters and ministers of religion. Possibly his most famous painting, in fact, is that of the Reverend Robert Walker skating on Duddingston Loch. There is something comical about this portrait of a black-clad Presbyterian divine skating joyously on one foot.

During the course of his career, Raeburn won many distinctions. Elected to the Royal Academy in 1815, he received his knighthood in 1822 and was appointed King's Limner and Painter for Scotland shortly before his death in 1823. His activities as a property developer, however, are less well known. A great deal of the area under discussion was built on land that was purchased with his wife's money, acknowledged by the fact that one of the streets is named for her. Even today, Ann Street is regarded by many as the prettiest street, not only in the West End, but in the whole of Edinburgh.

West End Scandals

This, of course, is one of the most beautiful parts of the city. But it is not without its dark side. Drumsheugh House, lying to the north of Shandwick Place in the very heart of the area, was the setting for one of the most sensational scandals of the nineteenth century. It was there, in the early 1800s, that two young teachers, Jane Pirie and Marianne Woods, established a boarding school for young ladies.

This academy was at first very successful, even fashionable, attracting the custom of the wealthiest families in Edinburgh. The trouble began when one of the pupils, a girl called Jane Cumming, told her grandmother, the Countess of Gordonstoun, that she had seen the two teachers in bed together, in the act of making love. Lady Cumming was scandalized, withdrew her granddaughter from the school, and persuaded other parents to do likewise. As a direct result of this action, the school had to close and Pirie and Woods immediately raised a lawsuit against the Cumming family. The question of whether or not the two teachers were actually in a lesbian relationship has never been determined—although some recent research on the case suggests that they probably were—but the fact is that they won the suit and were awarded damages. Their story later became the inspiration for a successful Broadway play of the 1930s, Lillian Hellman's *The Children's Hour*.

More than a hundred years after the Drumsheugh scandal, one of the most degenerate criminals that Edinburgh has ever known committed the first of his many crimes in a house that is just around the corner from where Pirie and Woods had their school. In March 1926 John Donald Merret lived with his mother at 31 Buckingham Terrace. Merret was, without any doubt, what used to be known as a "thoroughly bad lot". At the time, he was eighteen years old and nominally a student at Edinburgh University. Most of his time, however, was spent at a dancehall called the Dunedin, where he had become infatuated with a girl called Betty Christie, who worked there as a dance instructress. Merret squandered all his money on this girl and, when he ran out of funds, he simply cashed cheques on which he had forged his mother's signature. It was inevitable that Mrs. Merret would discover what Donald had been up to and, when she eventually confronted him about it, he responded by using an automatic pistol— which had also been bought with her money—to shoot his mother, at close range, through the head.

The terrible thing about this murder is that Merret actually got away with it. Although all the circumstances were against him, the defense counsel at his trial, Craigie Aitchison KC, was able to raise a doubt concerning his guilt by suggesting the possibility of suicide. Merret was jailed for twelve months for the forgery, but received the uniquely Scottish verdict of "not proven" for the murder.

Merret later changed his name to Ronald John Chesney and spent a large part of the remainder of his life in one kind of criminal activity or another. He was a thief, a forger, a black marketeer and, of course, a murderer. He killed at least two other people—his wife and his mother-in-law—and, finally, when he knew that he could no longer escape punishment for his crimes, he managed to cheat the gallows by killing himself. After his release from prison in 1927 after the twelve-month sentence, however, he had never again returned to Edinburgh.

The Village of Dean

Such episodes as the Drumsheugh Scandal and the murder of Mrs. Merret are, it should be said, scarcely typical of this part of the city, which is noted for its elegance and gentility. Queensferry Road, recalling the saintly Queen Margaret, runs through the heart of the area from Princes Street to the Firth of Forth, presenting its most enthralling view at the Dean Bridge. Here, the Water of Leith runs through the Dean Valley past St. Bernard's Well and the Village of

Dean. This bridge is 447 feet long and 106 feet high, consisting of four arches, each 96 feet in span. It was built in 1832 and financed by Lord Provost Thomas Learmonth in order to develop land that he owned on the northern bank of the Water of Leith. It is regarded by many as the finest of all Thomas Telford's works.

In *Edinburgh: Picturesque Notes*, Stevenson describes the view from the Dean Bridge as follows:

> *The river runs at the bottom of a deep valley, among rocks and between gardens; the crest of either bank is occupied by some of the most commodious streets and crescents in the modern city; and a handsome bridge unites the two summits. And yet down below you may still see, with its mills and foaming weir, the little rural village of Dean. Modern improvement has gone overhead on its high level viaduct; and the extended city has cleanly overleapt, and left unaltered, what was once the summer retreat of its comfortable citizens. Every town embraces hamlets in its growth; Edinburgh herself has embraced a good few; but it is strange to see one still surviving—and to see it some hundreds of feet below your path. Is it Torre del Greco that is built above buried Herculaneum? Herculaneum was dead at least; but the sun still shines upon the roofs of Dean; the smoke still rises thriftily from its chimneys; the dusty miller comes to his door, looks at the gurgling water, hearkens to the turning wheel and the birds about the shed, and perhaps whistles an air of his own to enrich the symphony—for all the world as if Edinburgh were still the old Edinburgh on the Castle Hill, and Dean were still the quietest of hamlets buried a mile or so in the green country.*

The Village of Dean was originally known as Water of Leith Village, and for almost three hundred years from the late seventeenth century it was an essentially agrarian community. Eleven mills supplied the whole city with flour; there was a tannery and a thriving colony of linen and damask weavers. Throughout the twentieth century, it suffered a long, slow decline—the last mill closed in 1956—but the hamlet is too valued an asset to permit dereliction. As early as 1884 flats were built at Well Court to replace old cottages and restore new life to the old village, which today is completely residential.

The picturesque St. Bernard's Well, found nearby on the south bank of the river, was built in 1789 on the site of a mineral spring that had been discovered on that spot thirty years earlier. The original design, by Alexander Nasmyth, featured a statue of the Greek goddess of health, Hygeia. When William Nelson and Thomas Bonnar restored the well in 1887, a new Hygeia by G.W. Stevenson replaced the original. A life-size statue of the goddess, complete with accompanying serpent and drinking cup, stands within a small Doric temple.

Art and Education

A love of the visual arts seems to be a recurring theme in this part of the city, in which Edinburgh's leading visual arts impresario has his home. Since 1966 Professor Richard Demarco has worked with tireless energy to ensure that Edinburgh art-lovers are exposed to the latest developments in contemporary European art. He is a true "modern Athenian", and although he has often appeared to become so disillusioned with Edinburgh that he has threatened to leave the city, he never seems to manage to do so. Although he no longer runs a gallery, he has made a photographic archive of over 500,000 items available for viewing by appointment.

Today, there are no fewer than seventeen public art galleries in the city, as well as some two dozen private galleries and art dealers. These include the Talbot Rice Gallery at Old College, the City Art Centre at the foot of the Mound, the Fruitmarket Gallery on the other side of the road at the same location, the Ingleby Gallery on Calton Hill and a whole clutch of smaller galleries in the New Town. In the West End, two excellent art galleries, the Dean Gallery and the Scottish National Gallery of Modern Art, offer excellent value to the viewing public.

The Dean Gallery provides temporary exhibition space for art of every period and style, and also contains a major library and archive center. The most striking feature of this gallery is the permanent presence of the work of Scotland's leading sculptor, Eduardo Paolozzi. The Scottish National Gallery of Modern Art, located literally next door to the Dean, houses a remarkable collection of twentieth-century painting, sculpture and graphic art, including work by leading artists from all over Europe, not excluding leading Scottish artists such as John Bellany, W. G. Gillies, S. J. Peploe and Anne Redpath.

Both of these institutions are housed in buildings that originally belonged to educational charities. The Dean was originally the City Orphanage, while the Scottish National Gallery of Modern Art took over John Watson's Hospital, a similar institution to those founded by George Heriot and George Watson. This would seem to indicate that the custom of leaving one's worldly wealth for the succor of the unfortunate was popular among the upper echelon of the Edinburgh bourgeoisie in times gone by.

The most spectacular example of this kind of bequest lies in the very heart of the West End. In 1842 James Donaldson, proprietor of the *Edinburgh Advertiser*, died and left a considerable sum of money for the construction of a school for children who were deaf and dumb. Donaldson's Hospital, designed by William Playfair and completed in 1851, was greatly admired by Queen Victoria, who declared that its palatial structure compared well with the best of the royal residences.

Another landlord who created a school in this area was Sir William Fettes, proprietor of the Comely Bank estate, which lay slightly to the north of the Dean Valley. It was here that Thomas Carlyle first set up house with Jane Welsh after their marriage in 1826. According to Carlyle's most recent biographer, Ian Campbell, the life the Carlyles led at Comely Bank prefigured the atmosphere of their later home in Chelsea.

> *Once a week, on Wednesday evenings, they held open house for their friends. These were brilliant but economical gatherings, the entertainment lying in the talk and the flow of ideas. Carlyle described his powers in these years as akin to 'fencing', a sharp repartee of ideas in which he could take as well as give points. Certainly Jane was a captivating hostess, and it emerges clearly from the circle of correspondents which they amassed in these Comely Bank years that they had established themselves not only as a social success, in their own terms, but that they retained these friends in later years. Francis Jeffrey, for instance, was quite willing to take time off from a very busy life in Edinburgh to travel a hundred difficult miles to visit the Carlyles in the 1830s. The attractions of their personalities, and their conversation, were very considerable.*

Like Henry Raeburn, Sir William Fettes must have been considerably successful in his activities. The architect David Bryce was able to build what has been described as "perhaps the finest exposition of the first revival of Scottish architecture" through Sir William's bequest. Fettes College, standing halfway down Comely Bank, began as a charitable institution, but very quickly transformed itself into "the Eton of the North". The school stands within its own campus of gardens and playing fields, the main building a resplendent marriage of the French Château and Scottish Baronial styles, bristling with turrets and topped by a lofty clock-tower. Fettes received rather more attention than usual in 1997, when one of its former pupils, Tony Blair, became Prime Minister of the United Kingdom. Aficionados of Ian Fleming, however, have always been aware that James Bond, after his expulsion from Eton, completed his education at this Edinburgh school.

Sean Connery

Fettes is not the only connection between Fleming's hero 007 and the West End. During the 1950s the West End Café in Shandwick Place was the heart of the Edinburgh jazz scene. Among the many bands to have played this venue perhaps the most successful was that led by the clarinetist, Sandy Brown, later acknowledged as one of the finest exponents of his instrument in Europe. Brown's band was very popular at this time, playing at dances and other events all over the city on a fairly regular basis. Unfortunately, since this was the period of the teddy-boy gangs, some of the dates they played could be disfigured by violence. Concerned for the safety of his musicians, Brown hired two bodyguards to protect them. One of these was an aspiring jazz singer called Jacky Macfarlane, a former commando and veteran of the Spanish Civil War in which he fought with the International Brigades on the Republican side. He was assisted by a young man whose home was practically on the banks of the Union Canal. His name then was Tommy Connery and, although he changed it for professional purposes to "Sean" on becoming an actor, he is still known in Edinburgh affectionately as "Big Tam". In cinema terms, he was the first—and for many remains the only—James Bond.

Connery's popularity is largely explained by the actor's reluctance to become cut off from his roots. This, in turn, may be explained by the fact that, as an actor, he is completely self-made. A near-contemporary, Ian Richardson, who grew up in approximately the same part of Edinburgh, had a more conventional training, studying at the Royal Scottish Academy and serving an apprenticeship in repertory before playing leading roles in the West End and on film. Yet Richardson is not nearly so recognizable in an Edinburgh context as Connery, who entered the profession via a "Mr. Universe" contest. Connery's career has been completely based on his rugged good looks, his magnificent physique and his readiness to work extremely hard. "I had to make it on my own or not at all," he remarked, during an interview in the mid-1960s, "and I would not have preferred it otherwise."

At the same time, Connery does appreciate how hard it can be for others. A few years later, he established a trust fund to provide scholarships and bursaries for talented young Scots from underprivileged backgrounds. In 1971 he instructed the producers of *Diamonds Are Forever*, his sixth film as James Bond, that his advance fee (a sum of $1.25 million) was to be made over to the Scottish International Educational Trust. Such acts of selfless generosity have enhanced Sean Connery's popularity with the Edinburgh public.

Fountainbridge, where Connery grew up, is a thoroughfare that runs between Tollcross and Gorgie, forming the southern boundary of the West End. The name, as it happens, is completely inapplicable—there never was any fountain at Fountainbridge. In the distant past, however, the course of a little stream called the Foul Burn was located here and the bridge that crossed it was known as the Foulburn Bridge. When the land was developed for urban use, the owners felt, not unreasonably, that Fountainbridge sounded better than "Foulburnbridge". At one time, its most prominent feature was the brewery where Connery's father worked, but this has since been demolished and replaced by a leisure complex called Fountain Park, comprising a number of bars, restaurants, nightclubs and cinemas.

Surviving Cinemas

This kind of development (there is another one, further west in the housing estate of Wester Hailes) seems to have replaced the old community cinemas that were common in this area in the period between the 1930s and the 1950s. Most of these have been demolished, but two of the buildings have survived. The New Tivoli, or "the Tiv" as it was affectionately known, was the kind of place that most people in the neighborhood would associate with "a night at the pictures". Situated at the northern end of Gorgie Road, it sparkled with welcoming light, the frontage was covered in neon and the interior had been designed in a prevailing motif of red and white. The staff all wore red and white uniforms and there was even a variety of Tiv coconut ices, in red and white stripes, on sale during the interval. The Tiv is now a bingo hall.

At the other end of Gorgie Road, the Poole's Roxy has become a furniture salesroom. The Poole family, who, as mentioned earlier, took over the Synod Hall from the United Presbyterian Church, have deep roots in the entertainment business in Edinburgh. The founding father, Charles W. Poole, a Gloucester man, first brought his Myriorama—a sort of magic lantern show, in which the pictures moved—to the city in the last years of the nineteenth century. His son, John R. Poole, built this magnificent cinema in 1927, planning the Roxy with an emphasis on glamour and modernity. In its heyday, the mood of the place was distinctly American and everything, from the sophisticated system of house lights to the brand of ice cream on sale, seemed devoted to the idea of a picture-house being essentially an extension of a Hollywood studio. When the bingo craze began to take over cinemas, Mr. Poole tried (unsuccessfully) to circumvent the fashion by combining bingo with film. The Roxy was one of the first cinemas in Edinburgh to convert to the wide screen and always seemed to be showing musicals, high quality westerns and American war films.

The loss of these local cinemas, not only in Edinburgh, is very much to be regretted. They promoted a degree of social cohesion that the bingo halls, video shops and even multiplex cinemas cannot match. During the middle decades of the last century, particularly on a Saturday night, whole families—sometimes, indeed, whole streets— would gather at their local picture-house. In Edinburgh today, only one such cinema survives. The Dominion was built in the late 1930s by Captain W. M. Cameron, who commissioned the famous cinema architect, T. Bowhill Gibson. The original Art Deco structure of pink-colored Craighall cast stone can still be seen today, although the interior has undergone many changes in the last thirty years. In 1972 two separate cinemas were constructed within the original building and

further changes followed in 1980 and 1997, with the introduction of four separate auditoria, a restaurant and a bar. Yet in two respects, the Dominion remains unchanged. It still maintains a family atmosphere and is still run by the Cameron family, who are devoted to the cause of presenting films in a building that has some elegance and style. Rejoicing in the title of "Scotland's leading independent cinema", the Dominion received a major industrial award in 1987 for the excellence of its comfort and décor.

Even if the Dominion is, in this sense, quite definitely "West End", it is not located in this area, but in another, which requires a separate chapter: the Southside.

CHAPTER SEVEN

"Lavender and Old Lace": *The Southside*

"Day by day, one new villa, one new object of offence, is added to another; all around Newington and Morningside, the dismallest structures keep springing up like mushrooms; the pleasant hills are loaded with them, each impudently squatted in its garden, each roofed and carrying chimneys like a house. And yet a glance of an eye discovers their true character. They are not houses; for they were not designed with a view to human habitation, and the internal arrangements are, as they tell me, fantastically unsuited to the needs of man. They are not buildings; for you can scarcely say a thing is built where every measurement is in clamant disproportion with its neighbour. They belong to no style of art, only to a form of business much to be regretted."
Robert Louis Stevenson, *Edinburgh: Picturesque Notes,* 1879

At the conclusion of the Napoleonic Wars in 1815, with Europe once more at peace, the United Kingdom began to enjoy the fruits of victory and Edinburgh, of course, had its share of the growing prosperity. This led, in turn, to another period of civic growth. As before, the movement took place in a southerly direction, centering on an area of common land known as the Borough Muir.

Immediately south of the Old Town, the Borough Muir lay on the banks of the South Loch, which supplied Edinburgh's drinking water until 1621. The water was piped from the loch to the city reservoir on Castle Hill—now home to the Old Town Weaving Co.—and distributed through a system of wells, the housings of which can still be seen on the Royal Mile. In 1657 the Town Council decided to drain the South Loch, a decision, it seems, easier to make than to carry out. As a matter of fact, it was more than a century later that the South Loch was completely drained and the park we know today as "The Meadows" was first laid out.

The Meadows

Although mainly used as a recreational area, with tennis courts, cricket pitches and other amenities, the high point in the history of the Meadows came in 1886, when it was the scene of an International Exhibition of Industry, Science and Arts, organized by the City's Dean of Guild, James Gowans, who earned a knighthood for his efforts. This exhibition featured displays of paintings by Constable, watches from America, rugs from Turkey and locomotives from Clydeside, and was a huge success, attracting almost three million visitors. Today, practically the only reminder of this occasion is an arch of whalebones, donated at the end of the exhibition by the Zetland and Fair Isle knitting stand. This arch stands at the very center of the park, at the end of a path that has become known as Jawbone Walk.

Adjacent to the Meadows is another park, Bruntsfield Links. Originally one of Edinburgh's main quarries, Bruntsfield Links is the last remaining fragment of the old Borough Muir. It must have been here that the Scottish army gathered, in a scene described by Scott in *Marmion* (1808), before setting out on the campaign that was to end so disastrously at the Battle of Flodden in 1513. But Bruntsfield Links also has a much happier historical association, as the city's earliest golf course. Many famous golf clubs were founded on these links, which even today is used for the game. Although it would hardly pose much of a challenge for any ambitious club golfer, the thirty-six holes of the "pitch and put" course is very popular with players who wish to improve their short game or, in fact, anyone who wishes to play there. There are no green fees and, as long as one has the necessary equipment, absolutely anyone can play the course. There is, at the same time, a club—the Bruntsfield Short Hole Club—that has produced several players who have gone on to greater things in the world of competitive golf. There are also a number of competitions, described by Charles J. Smith in *Historic South Edinburgh*.

The Tappit Hen or Tavern Trophy, an old pewter ale-measure, is the club's principal prize, and was donated by Mr. Michael Shaw in 1950. "Gang bring her ben, the Tappit Hen," is the invitation printed on the competition entry forms—which, translated into standard English, means: "After victory, fill her up at my place!"

One leading international golfer who almost certainly gained some early experience on this course was Tommy Armour. Born in Morningside in the late 1890s, Armour emigrated to the US in 1926 and was to become one of the most successful professionals in American golfing history. Apart from his competitive triumphs—he won the British Open Championship, the US Open Championship, the American PGA. Championship, as well as representing America in the Ryder Cup—he was in great demand as a teaching pro. Charging a tuition fee of $100 per hour from his millionaire clients, one of whom was future President Richard M. Nixon, he was based at the Boca Raton Club, New York, for twenty years until his death in 1968.

Hard by Bruntsfield Links is a hostelry of great antiquity, the Golf Tavern. According to a plaque on the wall, the origins of this public house go back as far as 1456 and there is some evidence that there may even have been a tavern here at an even earlier date.

Suburban Spread

The Borough Muir was gifted to the city by King David I in 1143. At that time, an ancient wood called the Forest of Drumselch largely covered the whole area. Almost four hundred years later, the authorities began to encourage Edinburgh citizens to begin clearing the area of trees by permitting anyone prepared to fell timber to use it as building material for their homes. People in the Old Town began to extend the frontages of their house, facing the stone with timber and building fore-stairs. Timber wrights living in a hamlet that became known as Wrychthoussis, later anglicized as Wright's Houses, undertook most of this work. While the hamlet has long since disappeared, the street on which the Golf Tavern stands is still known as Wright's Houses.

The clearing of the area was speeded up by the emergence of a number of villages, which emerged in and around the Forest of Drumselch. Many of these lay on the route out of Edinburgh to the southwest, running from the suburb of Portsburgh past Wright's Houses, Bruntsfield, Boroughmuirhead, Churchill, Morningside, Comiston and Fairmilehead. Traveling along this route, between Boroughmuirhead and Churchill, one passes Merchiston Tower, the central institution of Napier University.

Merchiston Tower is also the ancestral home of the Napier family, whose most famous member, the almost legendary mathematician, lived here between 1608 and 1617. Although he had a local reputation as a wizard—probably for no better reason than his preference for wearing a long, black cloak—John Napier (1550-1617) seems to have been a very private and extremely scholarly man. He is most famous, of course, for a book that he published in 1614. Entitled *Mirifici Logarithmorum Canonis Descriptio*, it is a mere one hundred and forty seven pages in length, but the system it elucidates—logarithms—served to open up the modern field of mathematical sciences. In the year after its publication, Napier brought forward another invention, a kind of abacus for shortening the labor of multiplication and division, known as "Napier's bones".

As well as Merchiston there were a number of estates that were ripe for development in much the same way as the similar estates of Henry Raeburn and William Fettes in the West End. Two of these estates formed the basis of the development that Stevenson described so scornfully in *Picturesque Notes*. This development began as early as 1806, when Sir George Stewart of Grantully acquired the Newington estate, on the east side of the area, on the death of its owner, Dr. Benjamin Bell, great grandfather of Dr. Joseph Bell, who would later become the prototype for Conan Doyle's Sherlock Holmes. As part of the purchase agreement, Sir George had to agree to do nothing to spoil local amenities and there was an additional proviso, prohibiting the establishment of certain industrial activities. As long as these promises were kept, Sir George was free to dispose of the land for building purposes.

Another landlord who took similar action was Sir George Warrender of the Bruntsfield estate, whose actions are described by Charles J. Smith:

> *Sir George Warrender, laird of Bruntsfield House in 1869, was a Member of Parliament and a man of considerable business tact and fore-*

sight. He saw immediately the feuing possibilities of his estate. His orig-
inal plan of feuing certain acres for the construction of terraced villas was
altered to permit a great building project which gave rise to the streets
which now surround Bruntsfield House. By about 1880, the high tene-
ments of Marchmont had arisen. Each new street name commemorated
some member of Sir George's family. Thirlestane and Lauderdale
honoured his mother, daughter of the Earl of Lauderdale whose family
seat was Thirlestane Castle. Sir George's wife Helen was the daughter of
the 5th Earl of Marchmont, hence the names of the whole surrounding
district. John Spottiswoode was another Warrender relation, while Arden
was the family name of the Earl of Haddington who married one of the
Warrender daughters. Thus from a family tree a whole district derived
its street names.

The district of Marchmont, since its establishment, has become
closely identified with the student community. Until a generation or so
ago, the most common form of student accommodation was
supervised by landladies such as Miss Jane Aitken, of whom Alasdair
Alpin MacGregor writes in *The Golden Lamp* (1964):

During my long sojourn with her, I never once needed to purchase a
pair of socks or of stockings, or a pullover, because her knitting needles
were constantly clicking away on my behalf, even as she sat reading in
her armchair. Long after I came south, and indeed until shortly before
her death, Christmas-time and Birthday-time always brought from her
a neat, little parcel containing a couple of pairs of socks she had knitted
for me. Much of her handiwork and industry in this category lies in a
drawer here, in Chelsea, most of it still perfectly serviceable.

One or two of the shirts Miss Aitken made for me, nearly forty years
ago, I have yet; and, although I have outgrown them, and they look a
little the worse for the wear, as the saying is, I just cannot bring myself
to throwing them out, or even having them cut up into rags for dusting
or cleaning purposes.

Such landladies have, unfortunately, all but vanished, replaced by
a phenomenon that is rather less appealing. In recent years it has
become common for wealthy parents to buy Marchmont flats as

accommodation for their offspring while attending university. Since this is being done largely as an investment and the flats are expected to sell at a profit once graduation has taken place, the practice has led to the inflation of property values, leading in turn to the disappearance of family homes. This is truly, to paraphrase Robert Louis Stevenson, "a form of business much to be regretted".

Stevenson's disapproval of the development of the Southside must be understood in the context of his affection for the area. It is a part of Edinburgh that he knew well, often passing through it in the early hours, after an evening's conviviality in the Old Town, on his way to his family's summer home at Swanston Cottage, and his hero spends quite a bit of time there in *St. Ives*. In that novel, however, the area is depicted, as it was when Stevenson first knew it, as countryside.

It was broad day, but still bitter cold and the sun not up when I came in view of my destination. A single gable and chimney of the cottage peeped over the shoulder of the hill: not far off, and a trifle higher on the mountain, a tall old washed farmhouse stood among the trees, beside a falling brook; beyond were rough hills of pasture. I bethought me that shepherd folk were early risers, and if I were once seen skulking in that neighbourhood it might prove the ruin of my prospects; took advantage of a line of hedge, and worked myself up in its shadow till I was come under the garden wall of my friends' house. The cottage was a little quaint place of many roughcast gables and grey roofs. It had something the air of a rambling infinitesimal cathedral, the body of it rising in the midst two storeys high, with a steep-pitched roof, and sending out upon all hands (as it were chapter-houses, chapels and transepts) one-storeyed and dwarfish projections. To appearance, it was grotesquely decorated with crockets and gargoyles, ravished from some mediaeval church. The place seemed hidden away, being not only concealed in the trees of the garden, but, on the side on which I approached it, buried as high as the eaves by the rising of the ground About the walls of the garden there went a line of well-grown elms and beeches, the first entirely bare, the last still pretty well covered with red leaves, and the centre was occupied with a thicket of laurel and holly, in which I could see arches cut and paths winding.

Stevenson must have felt that the activities of people such as Bell and Warrender would destroy this rural hinterland by absorbing it into suburbia.

Rural Idyll

If so, he was being overly pessimistic. In spite of everything that the property developers have done, the atmosphere of the Southside remains incorrigibly rural. Ringed on three sides by hills—from Blackford Hill in the east to Craiglockhart Hill in the west, with the Braid Hills in between—it is full of woods, streams and green places of every kind. At the foot of Blackford Hill, for instance, lies Blackford Pond, once a popular venue for winter sports, but today best known for its population of ducks, swans and wading birds. Adjacent to this is a wooded dell that leads to the most interesting of all Southside houses, the Hermitage of Braid.

This mansion house was built between 1770 and 1785, at a time when the property was in the hands of a solicitor called Charles Gordon. Gordon engaged the architect Robert Burn to design the house in a style that would be reminiscent of the work of Robert Adam. But it appears that he also required the introduction of mock battlements and corner turrets, recalling the fact that a fortified house

had once stood on the site. This has given the Hermitage a somewhat grotesque appearance that tends to mystify visitors.

Worse, the Gordon family had a rather unhappy history, full of early deaths, failed marriages and more than a touch of insanity, but the Hermitage remained in their possession until 1868, when it was taken over by a board of trustees. In the same year, the house acquired its most distinguished tenant, Sir John Skelton. Charles J. Smith provides an intriguing glimpse of Sir John and his tenancy.

Sir John was an advocate and Chairman of the Local Government Board for Scotland. He was also a distinguished essayist and historian. His Maitland of Lethington *and* Scotland of Mary Stuart, *important works in defence of Mary, Queen of Scots, are major contributions to the history of Scotland. In other vein, under the* nom de plume *"Shirley", he wrote a series of essays for* Blackwood's Magazine, *later published as books. During his tenancy of the Hermitage, the mansion-house became the mecca of many distinguished writers, notably James Anthony Froude, Robert Browning, Dante Gabriel Rossetti. Thomas Huxley, Thomas Carlyle and Principal Tulloch. Skelton's* Table Talk of Shirley *refers to these guests and others. Further insight into the gracious life of the Skelton family at the Hermitage comes from the letters and autobiographies of the literati who were his guests. His dinner parties were especially renowned. On one occasion Thomas Huxley proposed to wear the kilt, "to be as little dressed as possible". On another Froude recalled that Thomas Carlyle gave him his* Reminiscences *to read, and on yet another told him of the letters which his wife Jane was about to have published.*

Perhaps the most picturesque feature of the Hermitage is the stream that runs through it. This stream is called the Braid Burn and it flows all the way from the Pentland Hills in the west until it reaches the sea at Portobello. Bypassing the Braid Hills, where the chief municipal golf course is situated, it takes its name from a valley that lies immediately to the west of the Hermitage. This valley was purchased by Edinburgh Corporation from the local landowner in 1937 and laid out as a public park. Its most dominating feature is an open-air theater that can hold an audience of 2,500. The seating is cut into the valley slope, there is a sizable performance area and even a grove of trees that serves as a tiring-house. Unfortunately, due to the inclemency of the Scottish weather, this theater is not used very often, but there have been some notable productions, particularly in 1945, when the Wilson Barret company, then in residence at the Royal Lyceum, presented a season of Shakespeare. The sylvan setting no doubt added something to the Bard's verse.

Even some of the streets of the Southside are reminiscent of country lanes. One such street is Clinton Road, which lies to the south of Bruntsfield Links. Here at no. 5 is East Morningside House, once the home of the Victorian novelist, Susan Ferrier (1782-1854). Often described as "the Scottish Jane Austen", Ferrier was the daughter of an Edinburgh solicitor who was a friend and former colleague of Sir Walter Scott. Susan herself became a good friend of Sir Walter and was also acquainted with two other literary giants of her time: Christopher North (who married her aunt) and Thomas Carlyle.

After the death of her mother and the marriage of her three sisters, Susan became her father's housekeeper, writing fiction in whatever time she was spared from domestic duties. Her three novels, *Marriage* (1818), *The Inheritance* (1824) and *Destiny* (1831) are distinguished by her considerable skill in drawing character in a style of vivacious humor, but are somewhat marred by a degree of religious moralizing. In *The Inheritance*, for instance, there is an exchange between the heroine Gertrude and her lover Edward Lyndsay that gives some suggestion of Ferrier's strengths and weaknesses.

> *"I flatter myself I am a Christian," said she; "and yet I cannot help thinking there are people in the world who are very tiresome, very impertinent, and very disagreeable; yet, I don't think it would be a very Christian act were I to tell them so." "Certainly not," answered Mr. Lyndsay, with a smile; "you may think them all those things—but if you think of them, at the same time, in the spirit of kindness and Christian benevolence, you will pity their infirmities, and you will have no inclination to hurt their feelings, by telling them of faults which you cannot mend."*

Over the last twenty years, Susan Ferrier's work has become the subject of increasing public interest and, according to Charles J. Smith, the present owners of East Morningside House have laid out an exhibition of "Ferrierana" which groups of visitors can view by appointment.

Kippers and Pianos

Stevenson's rather disdainful reaction to the development that took place in South Edinburgh, however unjustified, is indicative not only of the extent of the expansion, but also of the degree of snobbery that accompanied it.

These properties were sold, in the main, to New Town residents who, for one reason or another, were dissatisfied with life in their district. The semi-rural nature of the location and the greater degree of privacy it afforded may have attracted some people. On the other hand, those to whom the post-war boom had brought greater prosperity, allowing them the luxury of a second home, certainly bought some of the houses. There is absolutely no doubt, however, that the sudden departure of many of their neighbors to what Stevenson sneeringly describes as the "villa quarters" was regarded by many New Town residents as a fall from grace.

This was an attitude that was to be sustained throughout the nineteenth century. Rebecca West, in her *Family Memories*, tells of her mother's reaction on learning that the family home was moving from the New Town to another part of the city: "Duncan Street?" she cried, almost choking in disbelief, "you mean Duncan Street, in *Newington?*" Rebecca West goes on to explain that her mother's feelings were not motivated by snobbery, but by history. Although precisely what this distinction means is rather difficult to understand, there is no doubt that a sense of social status has always figured noticeably in the culture of the Southside. As a matter of fact, it is where Edinburgh's universal image as a deeply respectable, strait-laced and thoroughly puritanical city has its origins. There is a somewhat hackneyed story (probably apocryphal) about a Glasgow woman who, on visiting her cousin in Edinburgh, receives the less-than-welcoming salutation, "You'll have had your tea?" This visitor cannot possibly be calling on anyone in either the Cowgate or the West End. Only in the Southside would such a greeting be possible.

That, at any rate, is the perception. The Southside is the home of what W. Gordon Smith calls "lavender and old lace Edinburgh, where mirrors are bracketed outside windows—all the better to see you with, from behind curtains—where *The Scotsman* used to be ironed flat and crisp every morning." This is a notion that is even shared by people from other parts of Edinburgh, who often characterize Southside residents with the phrase "kippers and pianos", the implication being that Southsiders like to pretend that they are more prosperous than they actually are.

The truth, of course, is rather more complicated. The genteel aura is evident enough and is made even more so by the presence of so many churches. There are probably more places of worship per head of population in the Southside than in any other part of Edinburgh. The Great Disruption of 1843 is probably responsible for this abundance of churches. When this schism took place, the number of congregations doubled, creating a need for new church buildings. When, however, the two sides were partially reunited in 1929, there was no corresponding *decrease* in congregations and the Free Church buildings were still needed. While by no means all Southside churches are Presbyterian or even, indeed, Christian (they include a Roman Catholic seminary, a Jewish synagogue and a rather spectacular mosque, its minaret standing out among a forest of spires), there are certainly a great many of them.

For instance, the crossroads where the road to Morningside meets the road that leads west to the village of Colinton is known locally as "Holy Corner", since four churches face each other at this spot. There is a Baptist church, an Episcopalian church, a Presbyterian church and a Congregational church—or, at least, there were until very recently. In 1992 the Congregational and Presbyterian congregations merged to form the United Reform church and the Presbyterian building was converted into a drop-in community center named in honor of south Edinburgh's greatest hero, Eric Liddell.

The son of missionaries, Eric Liddell was born in China—where he was later to die, in a Japanese internment camp—and received the first part of his education in the south of England. The family home had always been in Edinburgh, however, and Liddell spent a great deal of time in the city, taking a degree at the university and carrying out missionary work in the Old Town. His absolute dedication to Christianity was only equaled by his great sporting talent. He played rugby for Scotland and was selected to compete for Great Britain at the

Paris Olympic Games of 1924. On being told that the heats for his event, the 200 meters, were to be run on a Sunday, he refused to take part on religious grounds, thereby creating sensational headlines. Although he was later to win a gold medal at the same games—in the 400 meters—it is his staunch, uncompromising adherence to sabbatarian principle that has always been remembered. In 1981 the story became the basis for an Oscar-winning film, Hugh Hudson and Colin Welland's *Chariots of Fire*.

Thomas Chalmers: Architect of the Disruption

More than fifty years prior to Liddell's victory at the Paris Olympics, another man of principle lived very close to Holy Corner, in that part of the district that is known as Churchill. A villa that has since been named "Westgate" became the Edinburgh home of the Rev. Dr. Thomas Chalmers (1780-1847), first Moderator of the Free Church of Scotland and the man who, more than any other, was responsible for the success of the Great Disruption of 1843.

Chalmers was born in St. Andrews and had initially entered the ministry simply as a means of gaining time to study mathematics. Shortly after ordination, he underwent some kind of spiritual conversion and devoted the rest of his life to what he liked to call "Christian extension". It was, in fact, during a lecture on this very subject—by which he meant, presumably, simply the spread of the Christian gospel—that he first summed up, succinctly but with great dramatic force, the principles upon which the Disruption was founded. During a visit to London, he was invited to speak at a meeting in Hanover Square. His audience on that occasion included a number of leading churchmen, including no fewer than nine bishops of the Church of England. According to an eyewitness, his words were received with "a whirlwind of enthusiasm". This is what he said.

> *It should never be forgotten that in things ecclesiastical, the highest power of our church is amenable to no higher power on earth for its decisions. It can exclude, it can deprive, it can depose, at pleasure. External force might make an obnoxious individual the holder of a benefice, but there is no external force in these realms that could make him a minister of the Church of Scotland.*

There is nothing that the State can do to our independent and indestructible Church, but strip her of her temporalities. She would remain a Church notwithstanding, as strong as ever in the props of her own moral and inherent greatness. And though she shrivelled in all her dimensions, by the moral injury inflicted on many thousands of families, she would at least remain as strong as ever in the reverence of her country's population.

She was as much a Church in her days of suffering as her days of outward security and triumph—when a wandering outcast with nothing but the mountain breezes to play around her, and nought but the caves of the earth to shelter her—as now when admitted to the bowers of the Establishment. The magistrate may withdraw his protection, and she cease to be an Establishment any longer, but in all the high matters of sacred and spiritual jurisdiction she would be the same as before. With or without an Establishment, she, in these, is the unfettered mistress of her doings.

The King, by himself or his representative, might be the spectator of our proceedings, but what Lord Chatham said of the poor man's house is true in all its parts of the Church to which I have the honour to belong: "In England every man's house is his castle." Not that it is surrounded with walls and battlements; it may be a straw-built shed. Every wind of heaven may whistle round it, every element of heaven may enter it; but the King cannot enter—the King dare not enter!

As this passage indicates, Chalmers was an orator of great power and eloquence. Yet there was a great deal more to the man than that. While minister of St. John's parish in Glasgow, he developed a technique of ministry that became known as the "territorial mission". Working in a parish that comprised an amalgam of the wealthy and the destitute, Chalmers argued that in a Christian church community the better-off should be responsible for the material welfare of the poorer members, almost a practical application of the early Christian principle of "having all things in common". He relieved the Glasgow Poor Law authorities of the responsibility of making payments to the needy of his parish, and guaranteed that his wealthier parishioners would take care of the poorer. The parish was divided into "territories", with elders and others being given responsibility for each of these. The work involved finding work for the unemployed, housing for the homeless, and "schools for children where none existed". This Christian caring and sharing, Chalmers believed and wrote, was better and more dignified and humane than impersonal statutory dole payments which simply reinforced a pauper mentality. The experiment worked well in Glasgow, and Chalmers would later successfully repeat it in Edinburgh, setting up a similar system in the Grassmarket. Initial success, however, could not be sustained, for the simple reason that, as Thomas Carlyle would later point out, "to be universally successful, it would need a Chalmers in every parish."

Like all charismatic men, Chalmers had a legion of adherents who, after his death, marked his memory by naming churches in his honor. One of these was built very close to where the great Disruption leader lies buried, in Grange Cemetery. Originally known as the Chalmers Memorial Free Church of Scotland, a succession of mergers led to the name being changed several times and it is now known as the Parish Church of St. Catherine's in the Grange. The most celebrated communicant of this congregation—he was, in fact, an elder—was one of the most successful and influential writers of stories for boys, R. M. Ballantyne.

Ballantyne: Boyhood Hero

Robert Michael Ballantyne was born in Ann Street in 1825, into a family that included Sir Walter Scott's publisher. Ballantyne, who later became a publisher himself, began his working life at sixteen. At that age, he was accepted as an apprentice by the Hudson's Bay Company and spent some six years in Canada, taking part in trading expeditions and experiencing innumerable adventures in the wilderness.

On his return to Edinburgh in 1848, he published *Everyday Life in the Hudson Bay Company* and joined the publishing firm of Thomas Constable. It was at some point during this time that he decided to try his hand at an adventure story for boys and wrote his first great success, *The Young Fur Traders*. From then on, Ballantyne devoted himself completely to writing and over the next forty years produced two novels a year, plus a host of short stories for boys' magazines and annuals. The most successful of those was, of course, *The Coral Island*, which was first published in 1857. This has been translated into almost every European language and has never been out of print.

Ballantyne remained in Edinburgh until 1878, when he moved with his family to Harrow-on-the-Hill near London. Suffering from a condition that is now known to have been Meniere's disease (a disorder of the inner ear, affecting mainly middle-aged persons) he traveled to Italy for treatment in 1893. One evening in Rome, he suddenly became seriously ill and died. When the news of his death reached his legions of fans, there was an immediate campaign, initiated by the boys of Harrow school, to raise a memorial fund. Within a very short time, over £600 was raised, mostly from the pocket money of thousands of boys to whom "Ballantyne the Brave" was an outstanding hero. Ballantyne's most celebrated reader, Robert Louis Stevenson, who wrote many letters of support to newspapers, joined the boys in this enterprise. At Stevenson's suggestion, only a fraction of the money raised was used for a monument, with the balance going to Ballantyne's widow and family. Today, over Ballantyne's grave in Rome, the following inscription appears on a white marble tombstone.

IN LOVING MEMORY OF
ROBERT MICHAEL BALLANTYNE
THE BOYS' STORY WRITER
Born at Edinburgh, April 24th 1825. Died at Rome, February 8th 1894.
This stone is erected by four generations of grateful friends in Scotland and England

Ballantyne's Edinburgh home, at 6 Millerfield Place, lies between the Meadows and a district of south Edinburgh that once belonged to the church and was originally known as the Grange of St. Giles. It is still known as the Grange and it is here that two well-known Edinburgh institutions are to be found. The first of these is the Royal Edinburgh Hospital for Sick Children, known locally as the "Sick Kids", while the second—mentioned several times in previous chapters—is the Grange Cemetery, where many of Edinburgh's great and good are buried.

Unlike many cemeteries, the prevailing atmosphere of the Grange is by no means gloomy. On the contrary, it is a light, open and airy space, in which it is a pleasure to stroll. Alongside numerous civic dignitaries, politicians and church leaders, many of the people discussed in this and previous chapters—James Smith, Hugh Miller, Marjorie Kennedy Fraser, Sir James Gowans and Thomas Chalmers—found their final resting place here.

Poets and Doctors

The Southside has been home to some of Edinburgh's most able, successful, influential and distinctive personalities. Since the whole area abounds with hospitals of one kind or another, it is hardly surprising that many of these individuals were doctors. Furthermore, since the Southside is full of literary connections, it is hardly surprising that, at times, the disciplines of literature and medicine come together.

For instance, the Royal Edinburgh Hospital, first opened in 1813 as a "proper asylum for the insane", has a direct link with one of the most fondly remembered of Scottish poets, Robert Fergusson. As a twentieth-century Scottish poet, Maurice Lindsay, has remarked, "no other poet quite captured the Edinburgh atmosphere as surely as Fergusson." As a matter of fact, it was Fergusson who gave Edinburgh its most enduring nickname, reflected in the title of one his poems, "Auld Reekie".

Fergusson was born in Edinburgh in 1750, the son of an Aberdeenshire clerk. Educated at the High School of Edinburgh and Dundee Grammar School, he studied Divinity at St. Andrews University. After his father's death, his family found itself in financial difficulties and he was obliged to curtail his studies and return to Edinburgh, where he worked as a copyist in the office of the Commissary Clerk.

During his short life, Fergusson was a very popular figure in the Old Town, renowned for his wit and his sweet singing voice. His friends included the artist Alexander Runciman (who employed Fergusson as model for his work in St. Patrick's in the Cowgate), the landscape artist and painter of the famous Burns portrait, Alexander Nasmyth, the folk-song collector David Herd, and the actor William Woods. Inspired by the example of Allan Ramsay, Fergusson worked almost exclusively in the Scots vernacular tradition, and his output, though small, has had an influence on every Scots-writing poet since.

This influence is quite evident in one of his most successful poems, "Elegy on the Death of Scots Music", which begins:

On Scotia's plains, in days of yore,
When lads and lasses tartan wore,
Saft music rang on ilka shore
In hamely weid;
But harmony is now no more,
And music dead.

Fergusson had an important influence on the work of Robert Burns. Although the two poets never met, Burns acknowledged his debt to Fergusson in a number of ways, most famously by paying for a headstone for the man he called "my younger brother in the Muse" when he discovered that the Edinburgh poet lay in an unmarked grave. Fergusson had died twelve years earlier, at the extremely young age of twenty-four. On October 16, 1774, after a heavy fall, he appeared to be suffering from some kind of religious mania and was admitted to the City Bedlam. This was located at Bristo Port, on the north edge of the Meadows, almost directly opposite the Medical School. (Interestingly enough, this site is today occupied by a theater, the Bedlam, which is almost exclusively used for student productions.) In Fergusson's time, of course, little was known about mental illness and, apart from locking him up, there was nothing that could be done about his condition. This state of affairs so horrified the visiting doctor, a young man called Andrew Duncan, that he devoted the rest of his life to the welfare of the mentally ill.

Duncan (1744-1828) proved to be a physician of great distinction and boundless energy. His campaign to create a hospital for the mentally ill was to take almost forty years to reach fruition, but the foundation stone of the Royal Edinburgh Hospital was laid in 1809 and the first patients admitted in 1813. A department of the hospital, the Andrew Duncan Clinic, which was opened in 1965, almost two hundred years after Duncan first met Fergusson, commemorates the man himself.

Dr. Joseph Bell has already been mentioned as the prototype of Conan Doyle's Sherlock Holmes, but it would be an injustice if he were remembered simply for that reason. He was a very considerable figure in his own right, a capable surgeon, an efficient administrator, a popular and successful teacher and, perhaps most important of all, a pioneering writer on medical matters. In this respect, he had a deep interest in the training of nurses and his book, *Notes on Surgery for Nurses,* is dedicated to Florence Nightingale, for whom he had much admiration.

This being the case, it seems reasonable to assume that Dr. Bell would have been a supporter of another medical pioneer who was active in Edinburgh at this time. Dr. Sophia Jex-Blake (1840-1912), who successfully campaigned for women to be allowed to graduate in medicine, is remembered in Edinburgh, like her colleague Elsie Inglis, with a memorial in St. Giles. Motivated by a conviction that women have the right to be treated by doctors of their own sex, Dr. Jex-Blake established a hospital exclusively for women in her home at Bruntsfield Lodge, on the edge of Bruntsfield Links. Although this hospital closed down in the late 1980s, it flourished there for almost a hundred years.

Sisters of the Sciennes

Several centuries earlier, moreover, another group of medical women had practiced their craft in the Southside. During the sixteenth century Edinburgh experienced a number of plague epidemics, with which the authorities were powerless to deal. Among the measures taken was one that seems exceptionally brutal. Anyone who was infected—or, indeed, suspected of being so—was banished from the city and dumped unceremoniously on the Borough Muir. The only place where such people could expect any kind of treatment was the Convent of St. Catherine of Sienna, located in the neighborhood that is still known as the Sciennes, a corruption of Sienna, pronounced "Sheens".

This order had been established as a direct result of the defeat of the Scottish army at Flodden. Founded in 1517 by Lady Jane Setoun and some other ladies—all of them either the widows or daughters of knights who had fallen—the convent was in existence for a comparatively short period of little more than sixty years before being abolished at the Reformation. The Sisters of the Sciennes, as they came to be known, at first intended to simply lead a life of seclusion and contemplation. Yet with the passage of time, they began to take an interest in the welfare of the sick and maintained a hospital, not only in their convent but a mile or so further south, in the district of Morningside, at the Chapel of St. Roque. While no trace remains of the original convent, the graves of plague victims are marked on the site of Chapel of St. Roque, which is now part of the grounds of Morningside's Astley Ainslie Hospital.

At a time when the Church of Rome was increasingly being accused of venality and corruption, the Sisters of the Sciennes were held in the highest regard. Sir David Lyndesay of the Mount, the author of *Ane Tryall of the Thrie Estaitis* and regarded as Scotland's national poet until the advent of Burns, praises them in his satirical poem, "The Papyngo", despite being a merciless critic of the medieval Church. In this poem, the papyngo or popinjay is a pet bird of King James V and is looking for Dame Charity. At one point the bird visits a group of corrupt monks and says:

> *Where be she? Nocht among you, I do declare;*
> *I trust she be upon the Boroughmuir*
> *besouth Edinburgh, and that richt mony means*
> *professed amang the sisters of the Scheens.*
> *There has she found his mother, Poverty,*
> *and Devotion her ain sister carnall;*
> *There hath she found Faith, Hope and Charity,*
> *Thegither with the virtues cardinall;*
> *There she has found a Convent yet unthrall*
> *to Dame Sensuall, nor with Riches abusit,*
> *Sae quietly those ladies inclusit.*

Close to where the convent once stood is a tenement building that was once part of Sciennes Hill House, sometimes known as Sciennes Hall, the home of Professor Adam Ferguson. It was here, one evening in the winter of 1786-87, that the only recorded meeting took place between the two giants of Scottish literature, Robert Burns and Sir Walter Scott. Scott was only fifteen years old at the time, as he recalled later in a letter to his son-in-law John Gibson Lockhart.

Of course, we youngsters sat silent and listened. The only thing I remember which was remarkable in Burns' manner was the effect produced upon him by a print of Bunbury's, representing a soldier lying dead in the snow, his dog sitting in misery on one side; and on the other his widow, with a child in her arms. These lines were written underneath:

Cold on Canadian hills, on Minden's plain,
Perhaps that parent wept, her soldier slain
Bent o'er her babe, her eyes dissolved in dew,
The big drops mingling with the drops he drew,
Gave the sad presage of his future years,
The child in misery baptized in tears.

Burns seemed much affected by the print, or rather the ideas, which it suggested to his mind. He actually shed tears. He asked whose the lines were and it chanced that nobody but myself remembered that they occur in a half-forgotten poem of Langhorne's called by the unpromising title of The Justice of the Peace. *I whispered my information to a friend present, who mentioned it to Burns who rewarded me with a look and a word, which though of mere civility I then received and still recollect with very great pleasure.*

Literary Links

The Southside is full of literary associations of every kind and from every period in history. Not so very far from Sciennes Hill House, in the very heart of Marchmont, in fact, is Arden Street, where Ian Rankin's Inspector Rebus has his home. Directly behind Arden Street is a school that provided the inspiration for one of the greatest fictional creations of the twentieth century.

James Gillespie's High School for Girls was yet another of these Edinburgh educational institutions which began with charity and ended in elitism. James Gillespie, the founder, was a snuff merchant who, on his death in 1797, left part of his fortune to found a school for poor boys and girls. Today, Gillespie's is simply James Gillespie's High School, co-educational and publicly owned, one of Edinburgh's twenty or so comprehensives. From the 1920s to the 1970s, however, it was a

fee-paying school for young ladies, whose pupils were presumed to be the *crème de la crème.*

For twelve years, between 1923 and 1935, one of these pupils was a girl called Muriel Camberg, later to become one of the most successful novelists of her generation. At Gillespie's, she was taught by a lady called Christina Kay, of whom Dame Muriel Spark was to write in 1992:

> *I fell into Miss Kay's hands at the age of eleven. It might well be said that she fell into my hands. Little did she know, little did I know, that she bore within her the seeds of the future Miss Jean Brodie, the main character in my novel, in a play on the West End of London and on Broadway, in a film and a television series.*
>
> *In a sense Miss Kay was nothing like Miss Brodie. In another sense she was far above and beyond her Brodie counterpart. If she could have met 'Miss Brodie' Miss Kay would have put the fictional character firmly in her place. And yet no pupil of Miss Kay's has failed to recognize her, with joy and great nostalgia, in the shape of Miss Jean Brodie in her prime.*

The literary associations are not always fictional. At the other end of the Southside is a building that will forever be associated with the poets, Wilfred Owen and Siegfried Sassoon. Today this building forms part of the campus of Napier University, but in August 1917, when the two poets first met, it was Craiglockhart Military Hospital. Both were being treated for shell shock, although there seems to have been some doubt about this in Sassoon's case. In July 1917, he took a public stand against the war, refusing to serve further in a cause he considered unjust. As a serving officer, he should have faced a court-martial, but the authorities had every reason to avoid this. Since Sassoon's courage could not be doubted (he had already been awarded the Military Cross) it was simply not possible to charge him with cowardice, so perhaps the decision to send him to Craiglockhart, on the grounds that he seemed to be suffering some kind of nervous breakdown, may have been a face-saving exercise. Sassoon came from a fairly upper-class background and spent a great deal of his time in Edinburgh playing golf and frequenting gentleman's clubs such as the New Club in Princes Street and the Scottish Arts Club in Rutland Square.

Owen not only came from a quite different background, he had a rather different personality from his friend. A schoolmaster by profession, he was much less outgoing than Sassoon, more serious and introverted. During his time at Craiglockhart, he undertook some teaching at Tynecastle School, in the working-class district of Gorgie. In spite of their differences, however, the two became firm friends and their friendship was to produce work that would have a serious impact on the very nature of English poetry.

Prior to being pressed into service as a military hospital, Craiglockhart had been a hydropathic hospital, patronized by wealthy seekers of good health, where permanent guests were accommodated for an annual fee of £100. While most of the services that these people had enjoyed disappeared with the war, one surviving relic of the pre-war days was the house magazine, *The Hydra*. Almost immediately, Owen and Sassoon gained control of this publication, in which some of the greatest war poetry ever written first appeared. Owen's famous, much-anthologized "Anthem for Doomed Youth" made its first appearance in *The Hydra*, as did some of the finest of Sassoon's work, poems such as "The General", "Base Details" and "Attack".

Curiously enough, only a few years later, when the war had ended and Owen and Sassoon had long departed, Craiglockhart received regular visits from another, very different, poet. In 1920 the building was taken over by the Society of the Sacred Heart and became a convent that would, in time, become a training college for Catholic teachers. Of all the priests who visited this convent, one was a particular favorite with the nuns: Canon John Gray of St. Peter's in Morningside.

Father Gray had been born in Woolwich, and as the eldest of a large working-class family he had been obliged to leave school at fourteen in order to help provide for his younger brothers and sisters. He continued his studies at night classes, nevertheless, and eventually secured a well-paid position in the Foreign Office library. It was at this time that he began to publish his poetry and first made the acquaintance of Oscar Wilde.

Gray was always a very good-looking man and, it is said, became the model for Wilde's novel *The Picture of Dorian Gray*. Wilde certainly introduced him to the London literary scene and it was through Wilde that Gray first met Marc Andre Raffalovitch, a rather wealthy young man, whose father had been an international banker and whose mother was a society hostess, well-known for her fund-raising activities among the rich and famous of the day. The friendship between Gray and Raffalovitch, which began in 1888, was to last for another forty-six years.

Ten years later, in the autumn of 1898, Gray suddenly threw up his job and the Foreign Office and left for Rome to study for the Catholic priesthood. After ordination in Rome, he was sent to the Archdiocese of St. Andrews and Edinburgh in 1901. When he was appointed curate at St. Patrick's, the impression he made on the people of the Cowgate was immediately favorable.

During these early Edinburgh years, Raffalovitch paid his friend regularly visits, and in 1905 decided to establish his residence in the city. He bought a large villa at 9 Whitehouse Terrace and moved in with his housekeeper, the formidable Miss Florence Gribbell. This house was to become the location of a literary salon such as Edinburgh has seldom seen. Raffalovitch's Sunday lunches and Tuesday dinner parties became famous for their excellent hospitality, stimulating conversation and distinguished guests. These included luminaries such as Henry James, Max Beerbohm, Eric Gill, Gordon Bottomley, Herbert Grierson and Compton Mackenzie.

By this time, Raffalovitch, who had been born Jewish, had also embraced the Church of Rome. As a man of considerable wealth, he could afford to express his commitment to his new religion by financing the building of a new place of worship for Catholics. St. Peter's Roman Catholic Church, Falcon Avenue, Morningside, was duly designed by Sir Robert Lorimer and built in 1907. It is, in the opinion of many, the most beautiful church building of any denomination to be found anywhere in Edinburgh. Its first parish priest was Canon John Gray.

The story of Canon John Gray and his close friend Andre Raffalovitch is one of the most heart-warming in the annals of south Edinburgh. These men were devout Catholics, who lived in the heart of a Presbyterian community at a time—as described in a previous chapter—of considerable sectarian tension. Their relationship, moreover, was, in spirit if not in fact, essentially homosexual and, to make matters worse, there was a direct link between Canon Gray and the most sensational scandal of the Edwardian age. In 1900, the year before Gray's ordination as a priest, the friend of his youth, Oscar Wilde, had died in Paris, having served two years hard labor in Reading Gaol for homosexual practices. It would not have been surprising, therefore, if Raffalovitch and Gray had endured a degree of hostility from their neighbors. Yet, if anything, the contrary was true. Both men were held in the greatest respect by nearly everyone in Edinburgh, and their friendship was recognized as the beautiful thing it undoubtedly was. The fact that this is so is a testament to the liberality and generosity of spirit to be found among the people of this agreeable though much-maligned area of Edinburgh.

CHAPTER EIGHT

Roads to the Sea: Leith and the Coast

"We went this morning to behold and take a view of Leith, where is the haven belonging to this city; which is a pretty little haven, neither furnished with near so many ships as it is capable of, nor indeed is it a large haven capable of many ships. There are two neat wooden piers here erected, which run up into the river, but not one ship saw I betwixt them. There are two churches in this town, which belongs unto and is subordinate to the city of Edinburgh. This town of Leith is built all of stone, but it seems to be but a poor place, though seated upon a dainty haven: the country betwixt this and Edinburgh, and all hereabout this city is corn, is situated betwixt the hills and the sea."

The Diary of Sir William Brereton, 1636

Although Edinburgh is not, strictly speaking, a seaport, it does have a certain relationship with the sea through its assimilation of a number of neighboring coastal communities. Even so, this assimilation is comparatively recent, and the people of Newhaven, Leith, Portobello and Musselburgh continue to maintain their own sense of identity. While this distinctiveness, to some extent at least, places these communities beyond the scope of this book, it would be useful to take a brief look at each of them.

Leith

Leith is probably the most individual of these communities. Indeed, until 1920, this old seaport, which had achieved burgh status in 1833, enjoyed an existence that was quite separate from that of Edinburgh. Even today, most Leith people—Leithers, as they are known—are at pains to point out to visitors the essential difference between their town and its nearest neighbor.

For some peculiar reason, Leith has a reputation for being less conservative than Edinburgh. While there seems little justification for this suggestion—which, somewhat erroneously, takes Edinburgh's conservatism for granted—it is certainly the case that Leith businessmen can often be more enterprising than their Edinburgh counterparts. For instance, it was a Leith publisher, Thomas Sturrock, who first came up with the idea for the marketing of greeting cards during the Christmas season.

The first of these cards appeared in 1841, two years before an English businessman, Henry Cole, formulated a similar idea, although, in line with the Scottish custom of the time, it was the New Year rather than Christmas that this card celebrated. Sturrock's design was reproduced on copper plate by an Edinburgh engraver, Alexander Aikman, and the finished article was printed and published by a Leith bookseller, Charles Drummond. The following description of the design, supplied by an unidentified correspondent, appeared in the *Edinburgh Evening News* in the early 1930s.

The card showed the curly head of a boy, open-mouthed (minus a tooth in the upper row) with fat, chubby cheeks, merry twinkling eyes and an expression of such hearty laughter that the happy combination, by the natural infectious process, produced the desired result on the onlooker, who was greeted with the wish of 'many happy years'.

During the course of this correspondence, Thomas Sturrock's grandson, Douglas L. Sturrock, informed readers of the *News* that a copy of this card had hung in Leith Town Hall for many years until it was returned to the Sturrock family at the time of the amalgamation with Edinburgh in 1920.

This amalgamation, although no doubt resisted, was always inevitable. Leith has a long history as Edinburgh's gateway to the wider world and was, for centuries, the principal source of Edinburgh's commerce. In 1799 a writer on economic matters, Robert Heron, gave a glowing account of the port in his book, *Scotland Delineated*.

The commerce of this place is very considerable. The vessels employed in the London trade, called Berwick Smacks, have good accommodation for passengers. The largest ships at this port are those employed in the Greenland whale-fishery, and in the trade to the West Indies. The port of Leith is happily situated for the navigation of the eastern seas. To Germany, Holland, and the Baltic, are exported, lead, glassware, linen and woollen stuffs, and a variety of other goods. From thence are imported, immense quantities of timber, oak-bark, hides, linen rags, pearl ashes, flax, hemp, tar, and many other articles. From France, Spain and Portugal; wines, brandy, oranges and lemons. From the West Indies and America; rice, indigo, rum, sugar and logwood. Ships of considerable size are built at this port, and several extensive rope-works are here carried on. The flourishing manufacture of bottle-glass, window-glass, and crystal, under the direction of gentlemen possessed of great ingenuity and opulence, well merits notice. Three glass-houses have long been employed in this business, and three others have lately been erected. A carpet-manufacture, a soap-work, and some iron-forges are also worthy of being mentioned.

It was only the arrival of other forms of transport that led to the decline of shipping and, inevitably, to the degeneration of the old port. By the second half of the twentieth century, the Leith community had all but perished. As businesses closed down and the people who relied on them for employment were cleared out to occupy soulless housing estates on the fringes of Edinburgh, Leith suffered the most severe depression in its long history.

Yet Leithers are nothing if not resilient, and over the past twenty years or so something of a revival has taken place. The old warehouses have been redeveloped as high-priced apartment buildings, and new businesses have been established in such fields as advertising, public relations and telecommunications. In 1995 the Scottish Office moved from St. Andrew's House to a new home in Leith at Victoria Quay. Two years later, tourism was given a boost, when the Royal Yacht *Britannia* was permanently docked in Commercial Quay. As a result of this renaissance, Leith has become a fashionable residential district, full of expensive restaurants and designer bars and bistros. Even so, it retains something of its old raucous self and can, at times, be an extremely violent place, notorious for vice and drug dealing; all the guidebooks warn visitors to be careful after dark.

Newhaven and Musselburgh

Newhaven, which lies about a mile to the west, has a completely different character from Leith. While the town, in days of yore, was a center of commerce and industry, Newhaven was a thriving fishing community, famous for its oysters and its colorful fisher lassies. As recently as the 1950s, these women were a common sight on the streets of Edinburgh, carrying carried creels on their backs from which they sold their wares, mostly fresh herring, but oysters and other shellfish, too. They dressed in a sort of uniform, which was so attractive and distinctive that, for a short time in the 1880s, it became the rage of fashion in London. Couturiers copied the style of the dress, substituting silk for the homespun materials that the Newhaven fisher lassies used. An unsigned article in *Chamber's Edinburgh Journal*, quoted by Leith historian James Colston in 1892, provides us with the following description.

A cap of linen or cotton, surmounted by a stout napkin tied below the chin, composes the investiture of the hood; the showy structures with which other females are adorned being inadmissible from the broad belt, which supports the creel, that is, fish-basket, crossing the forehead. A sort of woollen pea-jacket (usually of dark blue colour), with vast amplitude of skirt, conceals the upper part of the person, relieved at the throat by a liberal display of handkerchief. The under part of the figure is invested with a voluminous quantity of petticoat, of substantial material and gaudy colour, generally yellow, with stripes, so made as to admit a very free inspection of the ankle, and worn in such numbers that the bare mention of them would be enough to make a fine lady faint.

Not all of these women came from Newhaven. The town of Musselburgh, no less than Leith, is proud of its own distinctive identity, which it celebrates in two annual local ceremonies that reflect the dual nature of the town. There are two communities in Musselburgh, divided by the course of the River Esk, which effectively splits the town in half. On the west bank of the Esk lies a country market town, while on the east is a fishing community, Fisherrow. The annual Musselburgh ceremony involves two representative figures—selected from the ranks of the youth of the community—known as the "Honest Lad" and "Honest Lass". Fisherrow, for its part, celebrates its own identity through the annual choosing of a "Fisher Boy" and "Fisher Lass" who take part in a march called the Fisherman's Walk. Both ceremonies, affirming the independence of their respective communities, have their roots in an even older ceremony, the Musselburgh Common Riding. But this ceremony, resembling similar annual festivals in Border towns such as Hawick, Galashiels, Selkirk and Langholm, has not taken place for many years and will probably never be revived.

In days gone by, fisher lassies from Fisherrow traveled by horse-lorry to Newhaven fish market, where they picked up the fish they would sell in Edinburgh. As recently as 1979, Mrs. Betty Millar, the last of the Musselburgh fisher lassies, was still making this journey and could be seen at the corner of Riselaw Crescent, in the very depths of the Southside, selling fresh fish from her creel. Today, there would be no fish to sell, since no fishing is carried out at either Newhaven or

Musselburgh. The harbors of both are now given over completely to pleasure craft.

Musselburgh is the birthplace of one of Scotland's most prolific female writers, Mrs. Oliphant (1828-97), the only female member of the group of writers, including Christopher North, John Gibson Lockhart and James Hogg, who were associated with *Blackwood's Magazine*, to which she made over 200 contributions. Francis Russell Hart, in his *The Scottish Novel: A Critical Survey* (1978) describes Mrs. Oliphant as Scotland's "most talented and tireless novelist". In an article that appeared in *A Companion to Scottish Culture* (1981), Maurice Lindsay tells us that:

> *Her fiction can be broadly divided into two categories: the novels based on Scotland and Scottish manners, and those with an English setting, of which the most famous were those forming* The Chronicles of Carling-ford *(1861-66).* Miss Marjoribanks, *the first of them and a minor masterpiece, filling a gap in English fiction by women novelists between Jane Austen and George Eliot (on whose* Middlemarch Mrs. Oliphant *seems to have exerted some influence), is her only novel available in a modern edition, edited by Q. D. Leavis. Its central male character, Dr Marjoribanks, is a Scottish medico happily settled in England, while his daughter has 'large Scotch bones' and 'moral solidity', standing in the way of her appreciation of English humour. The novel is in part thus a study of the impact of Scottishness on English rural life.*

Most of Mrs. Oliphant's work has a rural setting and she wrote little of Edinburgh or any other city. Her first novel, *Margaret Maitland*, written when she was a mere twenty years old and published in 1849 with great success, may be set against the dramatic events of the Great Disruption, but she is more concerned with the religious— as opposed to the social—aspects of that struggle. Her posthumous *Autobiography* (1899) confesses to some embarrassment regarding the praise it received.

> *When I read it over some years after, I felt nothing but foolishness and shame at its foolish little polemics and opinions. I suppose there must have been some breath of youth and sincerity in it which touched people,*

and there had been no Scotch stories for a long time. Lord Jeffrey, then
an old man and very near his end, sent me a letter of sweet praise, which
filled my mother with rapture and myself with abashed gratitude.

Portobello

In the previous chapter, mention was made of the Braid Burn, which reaches the sea at Portobello. By the time it does so, the name of the stream has changed and it is now the Figgate Burn, after an area of grazing ("figgate" is a corruption of an old Saxon word for grazing) where the town of Portobello had its origins.

Lying between Musselburgh and Leith, this small town has played an important recreational role in the lives of the Edinburgh population. Portobello's long sandy beach, its funfair and, perhaps most of all, its large open-air swimming pool long made the town a popular attraction in the summer months. Unfortunately, the pool closed some years ago and the funfair has diminished to the extent that Portobello is now a shadow of its former self. It owes its Spanish-sounding name to its first inhabitant, a retired mariner called George Hamilton, who built a cottage there to which he gave the name *Puerto Bello*, after a port of that name on the Isthmus of Panama. Tradition relates that Hamilton had fought under Admiral Vernon during his capture of that port in 1739.

Portobello prospered through two, quite different, industries. The first was brick-making, which enjoyed a considerable boom during the building of the New Town. An Edinburgh builder named Jamieson discovered large deposits of brick clay at Portobello and excavations began in 1764. Fifteen years later, some three million bricks were being produced annually, many of which were exported to Europe and North America. Jamieson also built cottages for his workers as well as a number of summer houses, still to be seen in Portobello today, which are a spin-off from the other activity which led to the town's growth: sea-bathing.

This pastime first became popular in Portobello around the end of the eighteenth century, when the building of chemical works near Leith destroyed the amenity of Leith sands. After the establishment of a stagecoach service between Edinburgh and Portobello in 1806, a steady stream of visitors flowed into the town for this purpose. Since most of these visitors were fairly wealthy, and since the Portobello lodging-houses offered only indifferent accommodation, it was not long before there was a demand for summer houses and weekend cottages. The town became very fashionable as a result, with many of the celebrities of the period acquiring houses there. In the main, these were army and naval officers, university professors and ministers of religion, all mostly forgotten now. Perhaps the most celebrated of all—at least, the most remembered, for there is a plaque in his memory outside his old home—was the writer and geologist, Hugh Miller (1802-56).

Born in the northern Scottish town of Cromarty, Miller was both an autodidact and a polymath. After serving an apprenticeship as a stonemason, he developed his interest in rocks to such an extent that, at his death, he was regarded as Scotland's leading geologist. Yet in his time he turned his hand to many disciplines, including banking and literature. At the time of the Disruption, he was editor of the Free Church newspaper, *The Witness*, and as such took an active role in church affairs. He seems, in fact, to have been something of a workaholic and this is often used as an explanation for the derangement that preceded his death. In the autumn of 1855 he began to suffer hallucinations, which convinced him that the house was about to be burgled, and he took to sleeping with a loaded revolver at his bedside, with other weapons, a dagger and a sword, close to hand. Early in the morning of December 24, 1856, after scribbling a note of farewell to his wife and children, he picked up the revolver and shot himself through the heart. A compulsive worker to the end, he had just finished an important work, *The Testimony of the Rocks* (1857) and had been preparing some lectures on the geology of the area, due to be given in Portobello. William Baird, in his *Annals of Portobello* (1898), records that Hugh Miller was a popular figure in Portobello and gives the following description of the Miller family home in Shrub Mount.

It would not be considered by any means an elegant or even a commodi-ous house nowadays. It ceilings were low and its rooms were by no means large: but though it stood close on the High Street it had then an air of comfort and retirement which made it an excellent family residence. It was one of the old original Portobello mansions of the previous century, and its well-stocked garden, which at one time extended to the sea, though in Miller's time only half the original size, gave ample recreation ground for his family. Here he erected a museum, into which he gathered the geological specimens that his researches in the neighbourhood were constantly bringing to light.

Leith Walk

All of these places, with the exception of Musselburgh, which now comes under the political jurisdiction of East Lothian, are now regarded, for most purposes, as being part of the city of Edinburgh. Indeed, a great deal of north Edinburgh is composed of routes leading from the city in the direction of these communities.

It will be recalled from an earlier chapter that one of the New Town proposals of 1752 included a plan to turn "the North Loch into a canal with walks and terraces on each side". This particular proposal, of course, was never carried out, being finally superseded by the arrival of the railways, but it did create the germ of an even more ambitious proposal that was at one time given serious consideration. This was to extend the Union Canal down Lothian Road, through Princes Street Gardens and on through the city until it reached the sea at Leith. This proposal—the object of which was to connect the west coast of Scotland with the east—would likewise prove unfeasible, but if it had been carried out, the canal would now be running down the great street known as Leith Walk.

Leith Walk was created as a direct result of an act of war. After Oliver Cromwell's crushing defeat of the Scottish army in 1650, Cromwell began a move that would lead to the capture of Edinburgh. In an attempt to defend the city, the Covenanting General Leslie arranged his troops in a line between Calton Hill and Leith and, as part of the fortifications, ordered that a trench be dug along the length of this line. Although this was completely ineffective, Cromwell simply circumventing these fortifications and entering Edinburgh by another route, the earth that had been dug to form the trench became a mound, which later became a footpath for travelers between Edinburgh and Leith. By the time of the New Town proposals, this had matured, according to a contemporary description, into "a very handsome gravel walk, twenty feet broad, which is kept in good repair at the public charge, and no horses suffered to come upon it." It was only after the opening of the North Bridge that the ban on horses was lifted and the Walk became used by carriages. The arrival of traffic inevitably led to further development of business and, indeed, housing on Leith Walk.

As the name of the street suggests, part of Leith Walk is in Edinburgh and part in Leith. Halfway down, at the point where both entities meet, is a place once known as the Gallow Lee, where public executions took place. This site, occupied today by a public house called the Boundary Bar, later became a sand quarry where the masons who were building the New Town obtained their supplies. It also has a rather curious literary association. Thomas Carlyle's long philosophical and autobiographical essay *Sartor Resartus* tells of the author's spiritual trials, in which he rejects the Devil, defined as "The Everlasting No". In Chapter VII of the book, Carlyle's protagonist, Teufelsdrockh, while walking along a street in Paris, receives a spiritual revelation. According to his friend, Professor David Masson, Carlyle himself had a similar experience at this part of Leith Walk: "Thus had the EVERLASTING NO pealed authoritatively through all the recesses of my Being, of my ME; and then it was that my whole ME stood up, in native God-created majesty, and with emphasis recorded its Protest."

"Antique" Smith: Literary Forger

This is by no means the only literary connection to be found on Leith Walk. Practically round the corner from the Boundary Bar is Brunswick Terrace, former home of Edinburgh's most literary criminal, Alexander Howland Smith. "Antique" Smith (as he became known) was a clever forger, dealing exclusively in the correspondence of famous authors. Although the proceeds of his criminal activities were not very great—he would receive between one and two pounds per letter—he was very industrious and must have completed, during the course of his late nineteenth-century career, many thousands of counterfeit inventions. It may have been his Edinburgh location that allowed him to fool so many collectors.

In 1892, for instance, a certain John Kennedy of New York donated a packet of two hundred documents to the Lenox Library in that city. This donation included letters from such celebrated writers as Robert Burns, Sir Walter Scott and William Thackeray and had been bought from a "bookseller" in Edinburgh. All of these letters, after close examination by experts, were found to be spurious and were eventually traced back to Antique Smith.

Smith did not seem to have worked from originals and actually *composed* his forgeries, so he must have been a highly literate man. He obtained his materials from the many second-hand bookstores that, then as now, thrive in Edinburgh. The proprietor of one of these shops became suspicious when he noticed that Smith was buying up ancient tomes that no other customer seemed to want. Further suspicions were aroused when Smith declined the proprietor's offer to have these books delivered (this, of course, would mean divulging his address), leading the bookseller to take the matter to the police. When Smith was caught and brought to justice, the reason for his purchases became clear. He had not bought these books for their contents but for their flyleaves, which he used to lend authenticity to his forgeries. In 1893 he was tried, found guilty and sentenced to twelve months imprisonment, which he served in Calton Jail.

Willie Merrilees: Edinburgh Vice

At the head of the street, directly opposite the Playhouse, is Picardy Place, where Sir Arthur Conan Doyle was born. Although the house in which the birth took place was demolished many years ago, the event is marked with the presence of a statue of Conan Doyle's most successful fictional creation, Sherlock Holmes.

Conan Doyle (1859-1930), in fact, spent only a short period of his life in Edinburgh. After receiving a public school education at Stonyhurst, he returned to the city to study medicine and it was at this time that he came in contact with Dr. Joseph Bell, whose method of deductive reasoning inspired the creation of Sherlock Holmes. Once he had taken his MD, however, he left to go into general practice in Hampshire and never really returned. He was firmly based in southern England and although his success as a writer enabled him to enjoy a comfortable living for the remainder of his life, it was his experience as a doctor, serving with the British army during the Boer War, that led directly to his receipt of a knighthood. Born into a Catholic family, he experienced a crisis of faith when his son was killed in the First World War. He became a convert to spiritualism and his last years were spent promoting his unorthodox religious views.

This part of the city is also associated with another detective—a real one—who made his most successful coup here. Willie Merrilees was a native of Leith and is remembered today as Edinburgh's most celebrated policeman. In time, he would rise to the rank of Chief Constable of Lothian and Borders police, a future that no one could have predicted for him when he entered the police force in 1924. As a matter of fact, there must have been some question at the time regarding his suitability for the job. He was shorter than the regulation height, had received only a rudimentary education and, as a result of an accident in the rope factory in which he had worked as a teenager, had lost four of his fingers. These handicaps do not seem to have impeded him, and by 1933 he was a sergeant in the Vice Squad.

There has always been a high incidence of prostitution in Edinburgh, a state of affairs that the City Council has recently sought to bring under control by the licensing of sauna parlors (brothels under another name) all over the city. These saunas, incidentally, have attracted a large number of visiting "sex tourists" (originating chiefly, curiously enough, from Newcastle-upon-Tyne), and must make a substantial contribution to the city's economy.

In the 1920s, on the other hand, this traffic was perceived as being too evil to be tolerated, particularly when it was found that young children were involved. After no fewer than twenty-seven prostitutes were arrested for soliciting at the coffee stall at the Mound, it was decided that a major initiative had to be taken to eradicate prostitution from the streets of Edinburgh. The traditional center of the traffic lay at the head of Leith Walk. It was here that, in Victorian times, two famous madames had carried out their business. Jean Brash ran a brothel in St. James's Square, now a shopping center, while Clara Johnston had a similar establishment in Clyde Street, which today forms part of the bus station. Both of these brothels operated at the upper end of the market, catering for a clientele of wealthy and influential men.

By 1933 the nature of the business had changed to become less concerned with the privileged few. In Picardy Place, the Dunedin Palais de Danse, favored haunt of the murderer Donald Merret, may not, strictly speaking, have been a brothel, but the way that the place was managed would have offered much scope to any enterprising prostitute. The ballroom employed "professional partners", who could be booked out for fifteen shillings per evening. Once this booking was made, there was no way of knowing what additional arrangements were agreed between partners and customers.

Across the road from the Dunedin was a place where such niceties were unknown. The Kosmo Club operated in much the same way as the Victorian madames had done. Brash and Johnston had kept control of their staff by keeping them in debt, supplying the girls with appropriate clothes and jewelry for which they would be obliged to pay. Ashley Barnard, who ran the Kosmo Club, did exactly the same thing. Brash and Johnston would send their girls—"flash molls", as they were known at the time—out into the streets and bars to pick up custom. Ashley Barnard followed the same principle, but had no need to send the girls out. He simply advertised their availability in the newspapers. It was this, perhaps, that was to prove his undoing.

The decision to raid the Kosmo Club was probably taken by someone other than Willie Merrilees, but it was the Leith detective who carried it out. In his methods, Merrilees had at least one thing in common with Sherlock Holmes—both men enjoyed reputations as "masters of disguise". There are all sorts of stories, some of them rather fanciful, about the disguises that Merrilees adopted, but he does seem to have had a degree of skill in this respect. (In 1938, five years after the raid on the Kosmo Club, a German spy named Werner Walti was apprehended, with all sorts of incriminating material in his possession, in Waverley Station by a railway porter, who turned out to be Willie Merrilees.)

In preparation for the raid, Merrilees spent some time at the door of the Kosmo Club, disguised as an elderly streetwalker, gossiping with the girls. The raid itself went like clockwork, Ashley Barnard went to prison and the Kosmo Club was closed down. As for the customers, over a hundred people were found that night, some of whom occupied prominent, and therefore influential, positions in the community. It has sometimes been suggested—perhaps with justice, perhaps not— that the meteoric rise in the police career of Willie Merrilees is entirely due to his readiness to keep silent about some of the more embarrassing discoveries of the raid. Whatever the truth, there is no doubt that the distinguished career of William Merrilees OBE was given a vital boost by the events of that night. Bearing this in mind, it seems oddly unfair that it should be the fictional creation of Conan Doyle, rather than the legendary exploits of Willie Merrilees, that is commemorated in this spot.

At the other end of the Walk—the Leith end—a rather different, although no less potent, fictional creation awaits commemoration. Hidden from the road by another public house, the Central, is all that remains of the old Leith Central Railway Station. During the 1980s, this became a so-called "shooting gallery" for users of heroin, giving rise to the expression "trainspotting", which Irvine Welsh adopted as the title of his first novel. While opinions vary, particularly in Scotland, regarding the lasting quality of that book, there can be no doubt about the sensational impact it made on an entire generation and it deserves to be remembered on that basis alone.

Irvine Welsh was born in Leith in 1958, but brought up in Muirhouse, the sprawling council estate in the north of the city that forms the background to much of his fiction. Educated at Portobello High School, he took a Diploma in Business Management at Heriot Watt University and, before achieving literary success, worked for some years as a training officer with Edinburgh's Housing Department. His origins notwithstanding, there is little of Edinburgh in his writing. His outlook tends to the cosmopolitan rather than the specifically local, and his main theme is the trapped and disaffected nature of the life of young urban males. Although a sense of place is certainly not absent in his writing, Welsh's stories might easily be taking place in any British or, indeed, American city. The only aspect of his work that relates directly to Edinburgh is his use of street dialect, but even the authenticity of this is questionable. Welsh's dialogue is always careful to avoid Scots idiom, which, although deemed unfashionable, remains a prominent feature in all Edinburgh speech.

Trainspotting (1995) is one of those books whose success is likely to become a burden to its author. The huge impact it made on its publication, particularly on the young, to whom a copy of the book became almost a fashion accessory, has led to a certain loss of perspective regarding Welsh's fiction. Enormous praise for *Trainspotting* has led to an unreasonable level of expectation that his subsequent books seem unable to satisfy. There has been a tendency to forget that *Trainspotting* is the first novel of a maturing talent. The nature of this talent is clearly demonstrated in the following scene, which comes from Welsh's second book *The Acid House* (1996). The central character is a Hibs casual (in Edinburgh, football hooligans are called "casuals") who finds himself in hospital after a drugs overdose.

The youth they called Coco Bryce had learned to speak. At first it was thought that he was repeating words parrot fashion, but he then began to identify himself, other people and objects. He seemed particularly responsive to his mother and his girlfriend, who came to visit regularly. His father never visited.

His girlfriend Kirsty had cut her hair short at the sides. She had long wanted to do this, but Coco had discouraged her. Now he was in no position to. Kirsty chewed on her gum as she looked down at him in the bed. —Awright, Coco? she asked.

- Coco, he pointed at himself. —Cawlin.

- Aye, Coco Bryce, she said, spitting out the words between chews.

His heid's finally fried. It's that acid, they Supermarios. Ah telt um, bit that's Coco, livin fir the weekends', raves, fitba. The week's jist something tae get through fir him, and he'd been daein too much fuckin acid tae get through it. Well, ah'm no gaunny hing aboot waitin fir a vegetable tae git it thegither.

Family Business

Lionel Daiches, brother of the essayist and scholar David, and one of the most eloquent advocates that Edinburgh has ever known, used to enjoy telling the following story, which illustrates the particular atmosphere of Leith Walk. It concerns a young man called Max Rosenbloom who, sometime toward the end of the nineteenth century, found himself in a spot of trouble in his native Russia. His relatives managed to smuggle him out of the country, putting him on a ship for New York with instructions to get in touch with a family called Cohen, who ran a business in that city. They omitted to tell him that the ship would not be sailing directly to America but would make a brief stop in Scotland—so when he arrived in Leith, he naturally thought he had reached New York...

Having very little English, he was unable to make any kind of inquiry regarding the Cohen family, but he made his way out of the port and began walking up Leith Walk. He had not gone very far, when he spotted a shop with the name "Cohen" on the door. He entered this shop and immediately found that, while these were not the Cohens he had been looking for, they were a Russian Jewish family and were happy to help. They provided him with lodging and supplied him with some knickknacks to sell in the street. This was the beginning of what became a successful business career, leading to a string of music shops and a prominent place for Max Rosenbloom in the Edinburgh Jewish community.

Almost a hundred years earlier, an even more successful business career had been launched on the same street. As was the case with Max Rosenbloom, it began with a period of serious difficulty. The Chambers family from the border town of Peebles had been financially ruined by the collapse of their haberdashery business and moved into Edinburgh, where they were living in reduced circumstances. To make matters worse, the father of the family became seriously ill, and so it fell to the eldest son, William, to become the main provider.

William found a job as an errand-boy for an antiquarian bookseller and, in this way, began to acquire a working knowledge of the book trade. After a period of very hard work, during which he accumulated a substantial quantity of second-hand stock, he found himself able to open his own bookshop. Meanwhile, his younger brother Robert, the scholar of the family, had been offered a place at Edinburgh University, which he had been obliged to decline because of the family finances.

William's shop on Leith Walk was not, perhaps, an immediate success, but it did provide the family with a living. With William's help, Robert opened a similar establishment next door—and this, too, proved viable enough. But William was the kind of man who would never be content to rest on his laurels and was possessed of a degree of vision and energy that would, in later life, make him one of Edinburgh's most successful Lord Provosts. In this role, he brought much improvement to the Royal Mile, ruthlessly abolishing many of the old slum closes and replacing them with habitable streets, introducing decent sanitation and creating open spaces wherever possible. He also played an important part in the restoration of St. Giles.

As a publisher, he was no less energetic. The publishing partnership of W. & R. Chambers, born in the back room of his Leith Walk shop, was to become one the great Edinburgh publishing houses and, for the best part of two hundred years, remained a family business. The company's earliest success was one of the most popular of all periodicals of the Victorian age, *Chambers' Edinburgh Journal.* This monthly publication had a popular sale that reached, at its highest point, a circulation of 50,000 copies. From the beginning, Chambers tended to specialize in educational publishing and, even today, are probably best known for their famous dictionary.

The brothers played different, if complementary roles. William was always primarily a businessman, responsible for production and general management, while Robert's contribution was that of author and editor. As well as contributing many articles to the *Journal,* all manner of books flowed from his pen: histories, biographies and reference works of every description. Although he is remembered today as an antiquarian and folklorist—and that wholly in a Scottish context—he was, in fact, the author of a book that created a high degree of controversy on publication and which might, in other circumstances, have had a major influence on modern civilization.

Vestiges of the Natural History of Creation (published between 1843 and 1846) is a scientific work which seeks to explain the development of life on earth without reference to any kind of deity. It was written between 1841 and 1844, during the time in which Robert Chambers was living in St. Andrews (he would later move, permanently, to London) and was described by one reviewer as "as great a source of wonder as *Waverley* itself". Chambers always knew that this book would cause argument and controversy, and had completed the work in conditions of the utmost secrecy. In spite of this, the identity of the author had somehow become known and Chambers had found himself at the center of an acrimonious dispute, which persisted for the best part of a decade. Indeed, it was only in 1859, when Charles Darwin published *The Origin of Species by Natural Selection*, a work whose ideas had largely been prefigured by *Vestiges*, that Chambers found that the hostility began to decrease.

As it is, Robert Chambers is chiefly remembered for his *Traditions of Edinburgh*, first published in 1825 in a series of "parts", collected in a final, revised edition by Chambers himself in 1868. Bearing in mind the humble beginnings of his career, it is interesting to read what he has to say about Leith Walk.

> *If my reader be an inhabitant of Edinburgh of any standing, he must have many delightful associations of Leith Walk in connection with his childhood. Of all the streets in Edinburgh or Leith, the Walk in former times was certainly the street for boys and girls. From top to bottom, it was a scene of wonders and enjoyments peculiarly devoted to children. Besides the panoramas and caravan-shows, which were comparatively transient spectacles, there were several shows upon Leith Walk, which might be considered as regular fixtures and part of the country-cousin sights of Edinburgh. Who can forget the waxworks of 'Mrs. Sands, widow of the late G. Sands,' at the door of which, besides various parrots and sundry birds of Paradise, sat the wax figure of a little man in the dress of a French courtier of the ancien regime, reading one eternal copy of the Edinburgh Advertiser? The very outsides of these wonder-shops were an immense treat; all along the Walk it was one delicious scene of squirrels hung out at doors, and monkeys dressed like soldiers and sailors, with holes behind where their tails came through. Even the half-penniless boy might here get his appetite for wonders to some extent gratified.*

Such attractions are no longer to be found in Leith Walk. Although it continues to be primarily a street of traders—and, as such, must still provide a promising starting place for any embryonic business career—one is more likely to find car dealerships than waxworks on the street today.

Stage and Screen

Yet it is still possible to have one's "appetite for wonders" gratified at the Playhouse Theatre, which stands at the head of the Walk. This is Edinburgh's leading commercial venue, a receiving house for the most successful and spectacular shows from London. In recent years, touring productions of Andrew Lloyd Webber's *Cats* and *Phantom of the Opera*, Boublil and Schonberg's *Les Misérables* and the Irish dance extravaganza *Riverdance* have all played successful seasons at the Playhouse, a former cinema with a capacity of fifteen hundred seats, making it one of the largest to be found in the entire United Kingdom.

The Playhouse is not, moreover, the only theater to be found on Leith Walk. A matter of yards away is the Gateway, nowadays used as a teaching resource by the Drama Department of Queen Margaret University, to whom the theater belongs. Like the Playhouse, the Gateway was originally a cinema; in 1946, as a result of a bequest it came into the possession of the Church of Scotland. To those who regard Presbyterianism as a joyless, naysaying sect, it must have come as something of a surprise when the Church decided to establish a repertory company in the building.

Surprising or not, it certainly worked. Between 1953 and 1965, the Gateway was a vibrant addition to the Scottish theatrical community and a popular feature of Edinburgh life. Its final demise was due entirely to the fact that the financial support it received from Edinburgh Corporation and the Scottish Arts Council was required elsewhere. It certainly had nothing to do with any decline in its popularity. It is to be hoped that now its stage is operational once more, albeit for student productions, this will lead to a revival of its fortunes.

Easter Road

Running parallel with Leith Walk is Easter Road, the home of Hibernian Football Club. Although, like Hearts on the other side of the city, the Hibs originated in the Old Town, the club has, for many decades now, been regarded as Leith's own. Like Tynecastle and Hearts, Easter Road and Hibs have featured in the poetry of J. T. R. Ritchie (1908-98). Ritchie, a life-long Hearts supporter, was unique among Scottish poets, in that the main (although by no means exclusive) subject of his poetry was football—and Edinburgh football at that. The following verses come from "Easter Road", his poem about Hibs.

> *Frae Arthur's Seat to Restalrig*
> *The blue's their roof eternally*
> *Where is the team as jimp and trig*
> *As Hybees in their Arcady?*

> *When racketies like crickets chirr*
> *The reeds in Lochend swee as bonny*
> *To whisper words that must be myrrh*
> *For Hybees in their Arcady*

> *Lang afore Parkheid saw the Cup*
> *Or Rangers showed sae vauntily*
> *Never forget it was held up*
> *By Hybees in their Arcady.*

Apart from the fact that it is thronged with football supporters every other Saturday afternoon, there is little to recommend this rather dreary street. But it may be that Easter Road will, in the years to come, become a magnet for literary tourists, because of its part in the most sensational publishing event of recent times.

In the early 1990s a young woman was regularly to be seen pushing a pram up Easter Road, on the long walk between her home in South Lorne Place, Leith and Nicolson's coffee shop in the South Bridge. This journey has since entered the realms of legend, for it was in Nicolson's—and presumably while walking up Easter Road—that Joanne Rowling reflected upon the book that was to become *Harry Potter and the Philosopher's Stone*. A graduate of Exeter University, Joanne Rowling came to Edinburgh with her daughter in 1993 after the breakdown of her marriage to a Portuguese called Jorge Arantes. Although she had experience of teaching—her subject is French—she found that she could not teach in Scottish schools without obtaining a postgraduate certificate of education in order to register with the General Teaching Council in Scotland. Until she could obtain this certificate, which she did by entering Moray House College as a full-time student in 1995, she was obliged to depend on state benefits. This is the basis of the legend about the single mother writing a bestseller in coffee bars, although Rowling was, in fact, able to resume her teaching career, albeit briefly. Her biographer, Sean Smith, describes her time at an Edinburgh school during her period of assessment.

The strengths Joanne brought to teaching were evidently the same ones she brought to writing: careful planning, an understanding of children and what they like, and sackloads of imagination.

Summer term was still to come but, if Joanne could maintain this level of progress, then her teaching career looked every bit as promising as her writing ambitions. This time her placement of six weeks was more convenient, at Leith Academy, no more than 600 yards from her home. Opened in 1991, the Academy, which has a thousand pupils, is an amazing modern architectural specimen just off Easter Road. It is like a giant greenhouse full of labyrinthine passages bounded by exotic palms and ferns - a quantum leap from the wooden desks, inkwells and chalky blackboards of traditional schools. Most importantly for Joanne, it had a crèche for the children of staff and mature students.

As a student teacher Joanne came into her own at Leith Academy. She liked the pupils and she liked the teachers. Her supervising teacher Elaine Whitelaw was impressed: 'She had some of my classes and was very good. She was very organized and professional but also had a very good relationship with the kids. She was a very good person in the classroom.' The French classrooms were light and airy and Joanne's looked out on to a small green area, which was much better than many urban schools enjoyed.

To the east of Leith Walk and Easter Road, the London Road runs south along the coast. On its way to Portobello and Musselburgh, it passes Edinburgh's premier sports center at Meadowbank. Originally a railway station, known as the Queen's Station after Queen Victoria arrived there in 1850, this venue was developed for the

Commonwealth Games in 1970. Although it is best known for hosting athletics meetings, this is, in fact, a multi-sports complex, with fitness rooms, squash courts, a velodrome and indoor as well as outdoor facilities. In 1993, however, it was utilized for a rather different purpose.

In that year, one of the leading attractions of the Festival was the Mark Morris Dance Company from the US. Apart from the fact that Mark Morris has always been, in Festival jargon, "one of the hottest tickets in town", he is one of a small band of performers—of whom Kathleen Ferrier was the first—by which the quality of the Festival is defined. Little wonder, then, that something of a panic took place in the Festival office when, shortly before the company's season was due to open at the Playhouse, the theater caught fire.

Mercifully, this was not a serious fire and was extinguished quite promptly, but enough damage was done to put the building out of commission until refurbishment could take place. It took some quick thinking from the Festival's director, Brian McMaster, not to mention a great deal of hard work by his technical staff, to save the day. With less than four days to do the job, a performance space was fitted up, and both the Mark Morris season and that of the Canadian Opera (which had also been due to appear at the Playhouse) were able to go ahead at Meadowbank.

Lost Talents

Beyond Meadowbank, the London Road passes through the district of Piershill, birthplace of the actor Ian Charleson, one of the finest actors of his generation. Born in 1949, Charleson was educated at Parsons Green Primary School (where one of his teachers was the poet Norman MacCaig) and the Royal High School, later attending Edinburgh University, where he took a degree in Architecture. He found his dramatic vocation while acting with the Edinburgh University Drama Society and, on leaving university, gained a place at the London Academy of Music and Dramatic Art.

Although he is best known for his film work, particularly his performance as Eric Liddell in the award-winning *Chariots of Fire*, Charleson was essentially a stage actor. In 1989 his quite exceptional portrayal of the prince in *Hamlet* drew the following comment from

John Peter in the *Sunday Times*: "The way Charleson can transform a production is a reminder that actors are alive and well, that directors can only draw a performance from those that have one in them, and in the last analysis, the voice of drama speaks to us through actors."

Ian Charleson's death from Aids in 1990 robbed the theater of one of its brightest talents and Edinburgh of one of its most accomplished sons. As with the death of all young men—Charleson was only forty-one—one is left to speculate concerning how much more they might have achieved, had they lived. In the year following Charleson's death, such thoughts would occur again, as the life of another Edinburgh artist came to an end. The filmmaker Bill Douglas, like Ian Charleson, died before the full potential of his talent was fulfilled.

Newcraighall, once a mining village, lies south of Piershill, on the way to Musselburgh. It was here that Douglas was born in 1937. His route to self-realization was long and painful and is chronicled in his autobiographical trilogy of films: *My Childhood*, *My Ain Folk* and *My Way Home*. These three films, although they constitute almost the totality of Douglas' work, have been collectively hailed as a masterpiece of the filmmaker's art. Shot in black and white and using an economy of dialogue, Douglas' camera dwells on every image with a relentless intensity. There is no sight whatsoever of any of the more comfortable parts of Edinburgh, and pinched faces, empty coal bunkers and cloudy skies are used to communicate a sense of perpetual bleakness. The entire work, in fact, is a brave attempt to return to the roots of the medium. As Douglas himself has written:

> *Surely it is imagery that is the language of cinema, a brand new language that almost a hundred years after its discovery is still to be properly learnt! The silent cinema started to learn it but, ironically in my view, the 'talkies' put back the process. And television isn't helping today. Sometimes I fear it may be a lost language.*

This approach is reflected in his films, in which he invests each shot with an obsessively bleak view of humanity. Like his near-contemporary Ken Loach, Douglas shunned the use of professional actors, preferring to use "real" people in his films. Stephen Archibald, who played the young Bill Douglas in the trilogy, has not acted since and still lives in Newcraighall. For all his technical mastery, Douglas' films make no attempt to entertain and his work challenges the audience while refusing to acknowledge any need to relate to it. The point of view, such as it is, is expressed in a style that, as Leslie Halliwell has remarked, is "spare, austere, non-committal".

Bill Douglas' last years were spent in London at the National Film and Television School, where he was apparently a gifted teacher, and after the trilogy he made only one other film, a somewhat idiosyncratic account of the Tolpuddle Martyrs entitled *Comrades*. This, too, is a work of some consequence, but suffers from the fact that Douglas never really seemed to understand the nature of cinema's appeal. There is thus a certain irony in the fact that Newcraighall is today known mainly for a cinema multiplex devoted to the commercial film industry that Douglas seemed always to scorn.

Inverleith

On the other side of Leith Walk—the western side—the Water of Leith, running through the West End and passing behind the New Town, enters an area which, despite appearances, has actually come down in the world. Comfortable, middle-class housing today covers the lands of Inverleith and related territories, yet when this area was originally developed, it was to create villas for the wealthier inhabitants of the New Town to use as summer homes. These are Edinburgh's true "villa quarters", a concept that Robert Louis Stevenson sniffed at with such disdain in *Picturesque Notes*. It is something of an irony, therefore, that Stevenson was actually born in this part of town.

Although the area has undergone many changes since then, there is at least one reminder of previous grandeur. This is Inverleith House, once the home of the extremely wealthy Rochead family, the senior member of whom is described as follows by Lord Cockburn in his *Memorials* (1856).

> *Except Mrs. Siddons in some of her displays or magnificent royalty nobody could sit down like the lady of Inverleith. She would sail like a ship from Tarshish, gorgeous in velvet or rustling in silk, and done up in all the accompaniments of fan, ear rings and finger rings, falling sleeves, scent bottle, embroidered bag, hoop and train—all superb, yet all in*

purest taste; and managing all this seemingly heavy rigging, with as much ease as a full blown swan does its plumage, she would take possession of the centre of a large sofa, and at the same moment, without the slightest visible exertion, would cover the whole of it with her bravery, the graceful folds seeming to lay themselves over it like summer waves. The descent from her carriage too, where she sat like a nautilus in its shell, was a display which no one in these days could accomplish or even fancy.

Mrs. Rochead's old home is now the centerpiece of the Royal Botanic Gardens, which has been established here since 1820. This is a quite remarkable open space of some 72 acres, containing a very wide variety of plants and trees, collected from all over the globe. The new Chinese Garden, featuring the largest collection of Chinese wild plants outside China, is particularly striking. Other attractions include the outdoor rock garden, the truly astonishing Glasshouse Experience, and the perfectly enormous Victorian Palm House.

Stevenson's old home in Howard Place lies directly opposite the entrance to these gardens. It is still a private residence, a fairly nondescript town house with a garden at the front door. In 1887 Stevenson wrote a poem about it.

*MY house, I say. But hark to the sunny doves
That make my roof the arena of their loves,
That gyre about the gable all day long
And fill the chimneys with their murmurous song:
Our house, they say; and mine, the cat declares
And spreads his golden fleece upon the chairs;
And mine the dog, and rises stiff with wrath
If any alien foot profane the path.
So too the buck that trimmed my terraces,
Our whilom gardener, called the garden his;
Who now, deposed, surveys my plain abode
And his late kingdom, only from the road.*

Frank Worthing: Edinburgh Actor

Not so far away, in Laverockbank Gardens, Francis George Pentland, a man with whom Stevenson would have found much in common (although the likelihood of their ever meeting seems extremely remote) was born in 1866, just sixteen years after Stevenson. After attending the Royal High School, Pentland entered Edinburgh University in order to study medicine. But after some experience with the University Dramatic Society, he gave up all medical ambitions and decided on an acting career. His brother David was already on the stage, working under the name of Nicol Pentland, and probably helped him get his first theater job, that of a prompter and small-part player with a playhouse in South Shields. The younger Pentland worked hard and learned quickly, eventually finding a more substantial job with a theater company at Worthing. It was at this time, in order to avoid confusion with his brother, that he adopted the name by which audiences would come to know him: Frank Worthing.

Frank Worthing's career was comparatively short, yet almost continuously busy. As a light leading man, he played opposite most of the most glamorous leading ladies of his time: Mrs. Patrick Campbell, Lily Langtry and, on Broadway, Maxine Elliot and Grace George. He never acted professionally in Scotland, however, and in fact the greater part of his work took place in the United States. From 1894 until his death in 1910, his life followed a regular pattern. The winter months would be spent in New York and, at the end of the season, he would take ship and return to his family home in Edinburgh for the summer.

Frank Worthing's great misfortune was to be at the height of his powers during a decidedly uneventful period in the history of drama. His career missed both the exciting barnstorming days of the actor-managers, and, of course, he died before the arrival of cinema and the mass media. In order to gain some idea of the nature of his talent, therefore, one must rely on the testament of those who were of his time and saw him act. His most celebrated role was that of Charles Surface in Sheridan's *The School for Scandal*, of which the American theater critic, William Winter, had this to say:

> *In his impersonation of Charles Surface, Mr. Worthing gave the finest performance of his career. He made the part sympathetic and winning, as well as merry and dashing, by reason of the fine, honest spirit, prodigal but not depraved, which he allowed to gleam through the extravagance of the character. His ideal of Charles was correct—a graceful, gay*

young fellow, reckless, generous and wild but without a taint of vice in his composition—and his performance was remarkable for the even sustainment of an assumed personality and for fluency of expression. His fine, mobile face greatly aided him in that performance. He took much care with every detail of it—more than with any other part that he ever played. It was a custom of his to wear fresh violets when acting Charles Surface—a custom which had brought him into conflict with his arbitrary manager, Augustin Daly, whose rules forbade the wearing or use of real flowers on his stage. Mr. Worthing's object, which was as nearly attained as it could be in a play of which the very life is an atmosphere of studied artificiality, was to present a veritable human being, and by the right artistic expedients—delicate exaggeration, studied but seemingly spontaneous movement, judicious pause, inflection, facial play—to create the effect of Nature. In doing that he was more successful in the part than any actor who has preceded him in it upon the stage in many years.

The part of Inverleith in which Frank Worthing grew up is called Trinity and has strong maritime associations. Once a popular area for sea captains, there may be some connection with Trinity House in Leith, which is now a maritime museum. Until very recently, it was the home of one of the most influential playwrights that Scotland has ever known.

Radical Playwright
John McGrath, who died in 2001, was based in Edinburgh for the last thirty years of his life. Born in Birkenhead near Liverpool in 1935, he was an Oxford graduate and a successful playwright and screenwriter before making his home in the city. In April 1973, in the George Square Theatre, he launched a company that was to change Scottish drama forever. A statistic in the *Guardian* newspaper had recently revealed that eighty-four percent of the wealth of the United Kingdom was held by no more than seven percent of the population. McGrath, a committed Marxist, seized on this figure and formed the 7:84 Theatre Company, first in England—where it had a limited success as just another agitprop company—and then in Scotland, where it set the whole theater world on its ears. Both as writer and director, McGrath used the techniques of popular culture to confront the most pressing

contemporary issues. For some reason, this seemed to work much better in Scotland than it did in England, and McGrath's legacy of some forty plays has changed completely the way that Scottish writers think about theater.

7:84 (Scotland)'s first production, *The Cheviot, the Stag and the Black, Black Oil* explores the history of exploitation in the Scottish Highlands, from the Clearances of the eighteenth century, in which people were evicted from their homes to make way for sheep, to the discovery of oil in the North Sea in the 1960s. The present author was in the audience at the premier of this play and recalled the experience in an essay that he wrote almost thirty years later.

> *I was more than a little disappointed when MacGrath came on stage to tell the audience that, since rehearsals were not quite complete, a full performance of the piece was not possible. What would be given, we were told, was not much more than a reading, a run-through with actors still having scripts in their hands, and the musical numbers added. I'm glad to say that this most unpromising introduction did nothing to prepare us for what was to follow.*
>
> *In all my years of play going, I can truthfully say that I have never, before or since, witnessed scenes of such excited jubilation as took place in the George Square Theatre that night.* The Cheviot *may not have been quite ready for the audience, but the audience was certainly ready for* The Cheviot. *It took us all by storm, creating an effect that would be replicated, over and over again, throughout the length and breadth of Scotland that summer. It wasn't so much a matter of the talent on display—although talent was there in abundance, with such as Bill Paterson, John Bett, Alex Norton and Dolina MacLennan in the cast—but of an idea being expressed at exactly the right time.*

It is absolutely typical of Edinburgh that such a revolutionary should choose to make his home in one of the most conservative and bourgeois areas of the city.

Pilton: Poverty and Culture

To the northwest of Inverleith is an area of Edinburgh that has all the social diversity of an eighteenth-century high street close. On exclusive golf courses, the members tee off within sight of some of the most miserable housing estates in the UK. In the districts of Muirhouse, West Pilton and Drylaw, the weekly family budget often does not exceed the green fee for a single round at Silverknowes and Barnton. It was in this part of Edinburgh, during the 1980s, that the explosive rise of the drug culture took place. An already deprived population suffered additional deprivation as the result of the policies of a heartless government that used the scourge of unemployment as a tool of social policy. As a direct result, many young people were persuaded to seek oblivion through the use of hard drugs, particularly heroin, with the consequence that many young lives were destroyed beyond repair.

This is true "trainspotting" country, a part of Edinburgh that has been portrayed in novel and film as a community of victims. Writers such as John Hodge and Irvine Welsh, while expressing a degree of sympathy for the area, tend to celebrate its ugliness and vulgarity. This rather tends to over-simplify the cultural outlook of this part of Edinburgh, as was proved by an event that took place in Pilton in 1958.

The great concert violinist, Yehudi Menuhin, was appearing at the Festival that year. Two years earlier, Menuhin had formed a trio with two colleagues, Louis Kentner and Gaspar Cassado, and they were to perform works by Mendelssohn and Beethoven in the Usher Hall. It was Menuhin's third appearance at the Festival and, on this occasion, he and his colleagues decided to try an experiment. They booked the Embassy cinema in Pilton for a concert that would enable them, as Menuhin declared at the time, "to get acquainted with people who really belong to Edinburgh and have no opportunity to get to the concerts."

The entrance fee for the concert was a shilling and they hoped to raise enough money to pay for the hire of the cinema. If this could be accomplished, the experiment would be counted a success. Nobody, not even the musicians themselves, expected to achieve more. Wilfred Taylor of *The Scotsman* drove Louis Kentner to the Embassy and later, in his regular column, reported the scene that greeted them.

When we reached the outskirts of Pilton, the streets were lined with cars, and crowds of children were being escorted along the pavements. In the distance we could see a number of policemen and a big crowd of people.

"There must be something on here," said Mr. Kentner, looking out of the window. "You're on," we said. He seemed genuinely surprised.

In the event, the concert played to a packed house and, at the conclusion, the musicians received warm and responsive applause. "You'll aye be welcome here!" one Piltonian matron called out to Menuhin as he left the Embassy—and so it proved. Over the next decade or so, the Embassy would be the venue for concerts by artists such as Kerstin Meyer, David Oistrakh and Isaac Stern, and the 1958 experiment would be successfully repeated in other Edinburgh cinemas.

Cramond: Treasure Island
As one travels through this area, one finds that the urban landscape grows progressively more affluent. Coming closer to the coast, the council estates gradually give way to the more prosperous districts of Davidson's Mains, Barnton and Cammo, until one finally reaches the village of Cramond, with its yacht club, its pretty whitewashed houses and its Roman excavations.

Cramond is yet another part of Edinburgh that boasts a strong association with Robert Louis Stevenson, who, like many another Edinburgh middle-class boy of his generation, spent part of his

childhood summers there. As a matter of fact, it is quite impossible for anyone who cares for Stevenson to be in Cramond without being reminded of him. Cramond Island, close enough to be reached on foot when the tide is out, is thought by many to have provided him with the geography of *Treasure Island*. The Hawes Inn, still in business, certainly provided the model for the "Admiral Benbow". Cramond is where *Kidnapped* begins and its sequel, *Catriona* ends. The first novel contains a description of the area, which is worth quoting at length.

> *Just then we came to the top of the hill, and looked down on the Ferry and the Hope. The Firth of Forth (as is very well known) narrows at this point to the width of a good-sized river, which makes a convenient ferry going north, and turns the upper-reach into a land-locked haven for all manner of ships. Right in the midst of the narrows lies an islet with some ruins; on the south shore they have built a pier for the service of the ferry; and at the end of the pier, on the other side of the road, and backed against a pretty garden of holly-trees and hawthorns, I could see the building which they called the Hawes Inn.*
>
> *The town of Queensferry lies farther west, and the neighbourhood of the inn looked pretty lonely at that time of day, for the boat had just gone north with passengers. A skiff, however, lay beside the pier, with some seamen sleeping on the thwarts; this, as Ransome told me, was the brig's boat waiting for the captain; and about half a mile off, and all alone in the anchorage, he showed me the Covenant herself. There was a seagoing bustle on board; yards were swinging into place; and as the wind blew from that quarter, I could hear the song of the sailors as they pulled upon the ropes.*

Today, the view that Stevenson describes has changed very little, but is perhaps best seen from the point of view of a more recent addition, within whose shadow it lies. The great Forth Railway Bridge, with the more recent Forth Road Bridge lying upstream, ensures that passing travelers are given a comprehensive view of the entire Firth.

CHAPTER NINE

Royal City: Holyrood

> *"We set out upon our walk and went through many streets to Holyrood House, and thence to the hill called Arthur's Seat, a high hill, very rocky at the top, and below covered with smooth turf, on which sheep were feeding. We climbed up till we came to St. Anthony's Well and Chapel, as it is called, but it is more like a hermitage than a chapel—a small ruin, which from its situation is exceedingly interesting though in itself not remarkable. We sat down on a stone not far from the chapel, overlooking a pastoral hollow as wild and solitary as any in the heart of the Highland mountains: there, instead of the roaring of torrents, we listened to the noises of the city, which were blended in one loud indistinct buzz,—a regular sound in the air, which in certain moods of feeling, and at certain times might have a more tranquiliz-ing effect upon the mind than those which we are accustomed to hear in such places."*

Dorothy Wordsworth, Recollections, 1803

Edinburgh, like Rome, is a city that is built on a number of hills. Apart from Castle Rock and Calton Hill, these include Blackford Hill, Craiglockhart Hill, Corstorphine Hill, the Braid Hills and (at the furthest southern extremity) the Pentland Hills. The most conspicuous hill of all is Arthur's Seat, which, at a height of 823 feet, is also the highest.

This hill is an extinct volcano, which, prior to corrosion caused by the Ice Age, was twice its present height. The name, incidentally, seems more likely to relate to an ancient and obscure Prince of Strathclyde than, as many suppose, to the half-legendary hero of Arthurian romance. (Another explanation argues that the name is simply a corruption of the original Gaelic *Ard-na-Said*—"height of arrows".) Crouching protectively over the city like some enormous lion, Arthur's

Seat is set in an area of natural wilderness of approximately 650 acres, known to Edinburgh people as "the Park".

Although the area is officially styled Holyrood Park, many continue to refer to it as the Queen's Park. This is a purely colloquial title, completely dependent on the reigning monarch. Prior to the accession of the present Queen, it was known as the King's Park—but perhaps a more appropriate title would be the "Prince's Park", since it was Queen Victoria's consort who was responsible for the park as we know it today. In 1844 Prince Albert instigated a number of schemes that were designed to improve the park in various ways, such as cutting back unsightly vegetation and installing a drainage system.

The green space that was created so close to the heart of the city holds possibly the unique distinction of being simultaneously a Site of Scientific Interest and a Scheduled Ancient Monument. It has a cultural topography that is entirely its own, and is rich in folklore and tradition, signified by the meaningful names that have been given to each of its features.

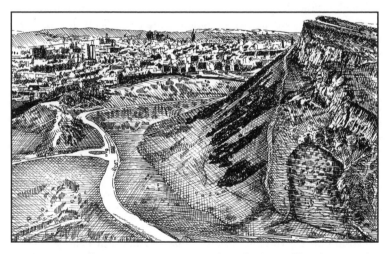

In 1778, for instance, a group of Seaforth Highlanders sought refuge in the Park after taking part in a mutiny in Edinburgh Castle. There had been a rumor that they were to be sent to serve in the East Indies, and in protest some six hundred soldiers left the Castle and set up a camp on Arthur's Seat. Among their number was a piper, who would play to them every evening. The path that he used while piping is still known as Piper's Walk. In the 1820s Sir Walter Scott instituted a scheme that would, he felt, simultaneously help the unemployed and dissuade them from radical action. He arranged for a group of unemployed weavers from the west of Scotland to construct a path around the base of Salisbury Crags. This path has long been popular with walkers and is now known as the Radical Road.

The Celtic festival of Beltane, recently revived on Calton Hill, was once celebrated at the summit of Arthur's Seat, and a fragment of this ancient ritual is still observed. Every year, on May 1, people gather at daybreak to bathe their faces in the dew, an ancient pagan rite. Today, this is accompanied by a Christian service.

The Park has not always been a recreational area. The industries of brewing and stone quarrying were once established here and, for centuries, much of the land was under cultivation. Although arable farming came to an end four hundred years ago, sheep farming featured within living memory, when flocks of sheep were a common sight throughout the Park. The last shepherd to work these sheep lived in a group of cottages that have become celebrated in Scottish song, *The Wells o' Wearie*. These cottages were associated with a number of wells once used for washing clothes but which have since gone dry.

The Park includes three substantial bodies of water: Dunsappie Loch, St. Margaret's Loch and Duddingston Loch, several distinctive rocky outcrops: Salisbury Crags, the Foxes Holes and Samson's Ribs, and a number of sites which have historical, literary and, indeed, romantic associations.

Writers' Haunt

There is a suggestion that Sir Arthur Conan Doyle, as a young medical student, often walked through the Park, which gave him the inspiration for the setting of his novel, *The Lost World*. This may seem a little fanciful, but it is certainly true that the area has provided inspiration for writers as diverse as James Hogg, Robert Fergusson and William MacGonagall. The Park was also a favorite haunt of Sir Henry Irving in the days when he was learning his trade with Robert Wyndham at the Theatre Royal. In 1888, during a visit to Edinburgh, Irving told J. Wilson Maclaren that he would regularly climb Arthur's Seat to study "his humble part". What he failed to mention was that, while the parts might have been humble, there were a great many of them. In Laurence Irving's biography of his grandfather, *Henry Irving: The Actor and his World* (1951), more than two hundred separate parts are listed for this period:

September was a breathless month. On the 7th Irving played a farmer in a farce 'Twas I, and the Governor in The Governor's Wife. *On the 8th he played Monks in* Oliver Twist *and, on the following night, the programme reverted to the popular mixture of national drama, patriotic melodrama and farce. On the 16th Irving had to play Lord Lyndsay in* Mary Queen of Scots, *and Birkie in another national drama,* Cramond Brig. *The following night saw him playing McKay in* The Battle of the Inch, *and as Hector Frampton in a farce,* Brother Sandy MacDonald; *on the playbills all such farces were hopefully announced as 'laughable', as though implying that it was the actor's fault if they were not. On the 18th he appeared again as McKay and as Kenmore in another Highland melodrama,* The Falls of Clyde. *On the 21st he was able for a time to drop his hastily acquired Scottish brogue, when, in the course of a triple bill, he played a Frenchman in* The Lady of Lyons, *and an Italian in* The Hunter of the Alps—*a cosmopolitan sandwich of drama layered with a farce,* The Ladies' Club, *in which he played a Mr. Bookly. Two new farces and a drama,* Thérèse, the Orphan of Geneva, *were billed for the 22nd, in each of which he had a speaking part. The month's work ended on the 26th when he appeared in an 'interesting' drama,* The Last Man, *as Alfred Fitzfrolic in* The Dancing Barber, *and as Monsieur de Rosembert, Seigneur of the village, in the 'favourite' drama,* The Somnambulist or The White Phantom of the Village. *Thus in thirty days, he had to learn and rehearse seventeen new parts, each of which required a carefully considered make-up and costume*

"I should like to stay there long enough," wrote the poet Gerard Manley Hopkins in 1871, "to allow the landscape of Arthur's Seat and

Salisbury Crag to grow on me." Another artist who found inspiration in the Park was the composer, Felix Mendelssohn. During his visit to Scotland in 1829—the visit which inspired both his *Hebrides Overture* and his 3rd (Scottish) Symphony—he spent some time in Edinburgh and described his feelings in a letter to his family.

> *It is Sunday when we arrive in Edinburgh; then we cross the meadows, going towards two desperately steep rocks, which are called Arthur's Seat, and climb up. Below on the green are walking the most variegated people, women, children, and cows; the city stretches far and wide; in the midst is the castle, like a bird's nest on a cliff; beyond the castle come meadows, then hills, then a broad river; beyond the river again hills; then a mountain rather more stern, on which towers Stirling Castle; then blue distance begins; further on you perceive a faint shadow, which they call Ben Lomond.*
>
> *All this is but one half of Arthur's Seat; the other is simple enough, it is the great blue sea, immeasurably wide, studded with white sails, black funnels, little insects of skiffs, boats, rocky islands, and such like. Why need I describe it? When God Himself takes to panorama-painting, it turns out strangely beautiful.*

The Park has often provided a setting for fiction. In Scott's novel *The Heart of Midlothian*, Jeanie Deans keeps her tryst with George Robertson at Muschat's Cairn, situated close to the Park's northern exit.

> *It was situated in the depth of the valley behind Salisbury Crags, which has for a background the north-western shoulder of the mountain called Arthur's Seat, on whose descent still remain the ruins of what was once a chapel, or hermitage, dedicated to Saint Anthony the Eremite. A better site for such a building could hardly have been selected; for the chapel, situated among the rude and pathless cliffs, lies in a desert, even in the immediate vicinity of a rich, populous, and tumultuous capital: and the hum of the city might mingle with the orisons of the recluses, conveying as little of worldly interest as if it had been the roar of the distant ocean. Beneath the steep ascent on which these ruins are still visible, was, and perhaps is still pointed out, the place where the wretch Nicol Muschat*

had closed a long scene of cruelty towards his unfortunate wife, by murdering her, with circumstances of uncommon barbarity. The execration in which the man's crime was held extended itself to the place where it was perpetrated, which was marked by a small cairn, or heap of stones, composed of those which each chance passenger had thrown there in testimony of abhorrence, and on the principle, it would seem, of the ancient British malediction, "May you have a cairn for your burial-place!"

This was where a famous murder took place in 1720, when Nicol Muschat, a trainee surgeon, slit the throat of his wife Margaret. The rather grisly event has led to stories of witchcraft and the supernatural becoming associated with the spot where the murder occurred. On July 16, 1836, for instance, the following article appeared in *The Scotsman*:

STRANGE DISCOVERY. About three weeks ago, while a number of boys were amusing themselves in searching for rabbit burrows on the north-east range of Arthur's Seat, they noticed, in a very rugged and secluded spot, a small opening in one of the rocks, the peculiar appearance of which attracted their attention. The mouth of this little cave was closed by three thin pieces of slatestone, rudely cut at the upper ends into a conical form, and so placed as to protect the interior from the effects of the weather. The boys, having removed these tiny slabs, discovered an aperture about twelve inches square, in which were lodged seventeen Lilliputian coffins, forming two tiers of eight each, and one on a third just begun!

Each of the coffins contained a miniature figure of the human form cut out in wood, the faces in particular being pretty well executed. They were dressed from head to foot in cotton clothes, and decently "laid out" with a mimic representation of all the funereal trappings which usually form the last habiliments of the dead. The coffins are about three or four inches in length, regularly shaped, and cut out from a single piece of wood, with the exception of the lids, which are nailed down with wire sprigs or common brass pins. The lids and sides of each are profusely studded with ornaments formed of small pieces of tin, and inserted in the wood with great care and regularity. Another remarkable circumstance

> is that many years must have elapsed since the first internment took place in this mysterious sepulchre. It is also evident that the depositions must have been made singly, and at considerable intervals—facts indicated by the rotten and decoyed state of the first tier of coffins and their wooden mummies, the wrapping cloth being in some instances entirely mouldered away, while others show various degrees of decomposition, and the coffin last placed, with its shrouded tenant, are as clean and fresh as if only a few days had elapsed since their entombment.
>
> As before stated, there were in all seventeen of these mystic coffins; but a number were destroyed by the boys pelting them at each other as unmeaning and contemptible trifles. None of the learned, with whom we have conferred on the subject, can account in any way for this singular fantasy of the human mind. The idea seems rather above insanity, and yet much beneath rationality, nor is any such freak recorded in "The Natural History of Enthusiasm." Our own opinion would be —had we not some years ago abjured witchcraft and demonology—that there are still some of the weird sisters hovering about Muschat's Cairn or the Windy Gowl, who retain their ancient power to work the spells of death by entombing the likenesses of those they wish to destroy.

These wooden figures are today held by the National Museum of Scotland and, although they are obviously items of great interest, their exact purpose has never been explained. The matter, incidentally, is featured in one of Ian Rankin's Rebus novels, *The Falls*.

The ruined chapel that Dorothy Wordsworth mentions in this chapter's epigraph overlooks Muschat's Cairn. St. Anthony's Chapel was built sometime in the fifteenth century as an oratory for a well that supposedly possessed healing powers. This well, which dried up long ago, apparently had some connection with the Knights Hospitallers of St. Anthony in Leith, a medieval order of knights devoted to tending the sick. (Although it was abolished at the time of the Reformation, this order was revived in 1831 and later founded the St. John's Ambulance Association.) The area was also apparently once used as a burial ground. Recent archaeology has uncovered a number of burial sites, possibly created in the sixteenth and seventeenth centuries, when victims of the plague found refuge in huts that had been specially built nearby.

Duddingston

On the eastern edge of the Park is Duddingston (possibly the most picturesque of all the villages that have been absorbed by the city of Edinburgh) whose place in Scottish cultural history has been given, perhaps, too little recognition. Henry Raeburn's painting of the Rev. Robert Walker skating on Duddingston Loch is one of Scotland's most compelling images, while another minister—who was also, incidentally, a leading landscape painter—was to achieve a rather different form of immortality. The Rev. John Thomson, parish minister of Duddingston at the time of the Disruption, was very popular with his flock. Thomson's great benevolence and sense of common humanity gave rise to one of the most common of all Scottish expressions. When Scots wish to identify with humanity in its entirety, the phrase that we're all "Jock Tamson's bairns" is often used.

Scarcely less common in its usage is the song, *Will Ye No Come Back Again*, which is frequently sung at leave-takings. This was one of the many popular songs written by Caroline Oliphant of Gask, better known by her married title, Lady Nairne. In all, Lady Nairne wrote some eighty-seven songs, many of which are still sung regularly, and include *The Rowan Tree, The Land o' the Leal, A Hundred Pipers* and *Wha'll be King but Charlie?* Although she traveled widely and spent her final years in Perthshire, she owned an Edinburgh house, Caroline Cottage, in Duddingston. One of her most popular songs is *Caller Herrin'*, in which she imitates the cries of the Edinburgh fishwives.

> *Wha'll buy my caller herrin'?*
> *They're bonnie fish and halesome farin';*
> *Wha'll buy my caller herring*
> *New drawn frae the Forth?*

> *When ye were sleepin' on your pillows,*
> *Dreamed ye aught o' our puir fellows—*
> *Darkling as they faced the billows,*
> *A' to fill our woven willows?*

Craigmillar

Immediately to the south of Duddingston, outside the Park, lies what one of its most distinguished citizens has described as "one of the most soulless housing estates twentieth century Edinburgh has given its workers to live in." Taking its name from an ancient ruin of a castle, once a favored residence of Mary, Queen of Scots, Craigmillar is not one housing estate but several, being what the planners call an "Agglomerative Housing Scheme Problem". Craigmillar was built in a period of some thirty years between the 1930s and the 1960s. With a population of 25,000, it has the highest crime rate, the highest suicide rate and the highest incidence of venereal disease in Edinburgh. Since the 1980s, like council estates everywhere, it has had to live with a serious drug problem. Yet it also has something else: a sense of community and a resolute spirit that stubbornly refuses to accept the status of victim. It is such qualities that led to the creation of the Craigmillar People's Festival, an annual event that has succeeded not only in changing the cultural atmosphere of Craigmillar, but providing a model for similar communities to follow.

The story of how the Craigmillar Festival began is the stuff of which legends are made. In the summer of 1961, Helen Crummy, a local housewife, wishing to send her son to violin lessons, approached her local headmaster, who told her that such instruction was not part of the curriculum and that she would have to pay for a private teacher. Su Braden, who interviewed Helen Crummy fifteen years later, described the reaction of her subject as follows:

> *It seemed incredible. There in the big city, the International Festival was feeding a nightly diet of Mozart and Brahms to 'culture vultures' from all over the world, and yet in Craigmillar a small boy could not learn the violin! The Edinburgh Festival, it seemed, was being mounted on the backs of the neglected communities living in places like Craigmillar.*

This story has lost something in the telling. As Helen Crummy made clear in her own account of the incident (published in her book *Let the People Sing!*) the headmaster turned out to be more sympathetic than he had first appeared to be. His name was Angus Lyall, and it was during a meeting of the School Mothers' Club that he gave encouragement to the idea of a People's Festival.

> *Once mooted the reasons came fast and furious. A festival—*
> * *could be a shop window for the talent in the area!*
> * *could give our children a pride in their surroundings!*
> * *could help the community understand local history and help them put down roots!*
> * *could help to combat the bad image the press gave the area!*
>
> *All agreed that the press was only interested in crime or sensationalism in Craigmillar—never the positive side. And there were many — we all knew that. The churches, guilds, pensioners' associations, clubs and other organisations worked tirelessly for the community. But these activities never seemed to merit press or media coverage!*
>
> *"A Craigmillar Festival!" Angus Lyall said enthusiastically. "A great idea! I'll show you how to do it—not do it for you!"*
>
> *And he did just that!*

Helen Crummy is today regarded as the founder of the Craigmillar Festival and, indeed, she later received an MBE for the contribution she has made to the regeneration of the area. But she herself has always been quick to disclaim sole credit. Her book lists more than five hundred people whose efforts made the success of the Craigmillar People's Festival possible. Many of these were, inevitably, local political activists and one of these, Alice Henderson, who was involved with Helen Crummy from the beginning, explained the strategy to Su Braden in 1976.

> *In an area as deprived as Craigmillar, you very rarely had good turn-outs for political meetings. Very few people were interested; but what they were interested in was their children, especially when they went on stage. This gave us a captive audience. What we thought was that we could put on some kind of a wee play with a social message... None of us were drama-trained although we all had an interest in it... we did Old Time Musical Hall and plays in school halls, involving the children.*

Then we got audiences who liked these and asked for more. We did things at Christmas, summer and maybe Easter throughout the year. We were really community action people first and foremost. I started up the Planning Workshop and had advisers and experts from the fields of archi- tecture and planning. We got them to talk about what's wrong with planning in this area, why is it that people are living in such a poor environment, and we began to have an awareness of why the poor pay more and why people at the other side of town have two cars, big houses and even summer cottages as well.

Such questions are often raised in areas that suffer deprivation, but they are particularly acute in this context, for the simple reason that "the other side of town" is so visible. Writing of her childhood, Helen Crummy tells us of Sunday afternoons playing with her siblings in the King's Park (as it was then). In the years ahead, it must often have crossed her mind that Craigmillar, with all its problems, lay less than two miles away from one of the homes of the reigning monarch, the Palace of Holyrood House.

Holyrood Palace

The story of the founding of Holyrood is an excellent example of the way that history can be transmuted into myth. King David I, the legend goes, while hunting one day in the forest of Drumselch, became cut off from his companions and was attacked by a ferocious stag. Unseated from his horse, the King tried to seize the stag's antlers—and found himself, quite miraculously, holding a cross. On the appearance of this cross, the stag took fright and fled. The cross, it seems, quickly disappeared again, but the King's life had been saved and, in gratitude, he decided to build an abbey, to be dedicated to the cross (or rood) that had appeared to him that day.

The historical account, of course, tells quite a different story. When King David's mother, Queen Margaret, fled to Scotland in 1066 to escape the invading Normans, she had in her possession a holy relic known as the "Black Rood", a fragment of the true cross, contained in a cruciform casket. When David succeeded to the throne in 1122, he built the abbey in memory of his mother's devotion to this relic. While this is a rather more credible explanation for the origin of the name, it is no less unsatisfactory in that it presents us with more questions than answers.

What, for instance, became of the relic? It has been assumed that Edward I, during the early years of the Wars of Independence, stole the Black Rood at the same time as he stole the Stone of Scone. Yet if that was truly the case—and if the relic were genuine—one would have assumed that it would have been preserved in the same manner. The fact that this did not happen would appear to suggest that Edward never had possession of the Black Rood in the first place. It is just possible, one supposes, that the relic survives, buried in the foundations of the abbey.

Indeed, the strongest argument for the authenticity of the "Black Rood" story lies in the fact that the legend of the stag is clearly an invention, which may have been intended to cover up King David's genuine reasons for founding the abbey. In any event, whatever the truth of the matter, Holyrood Abbey flourished as a community of Augustinian canons for over four hundred years and its final demise came about as a result of its value as a prize for invading English armies. In the 1540s, it was sacked twice within five years, once by the Earl of Hertford in 1544 and again by the Earl of Somerset in 1547, and never really recovered its position as a religious settlement. Today little remains of the Abbey, apart from a few ruins in the grounds of the Palace.

Holyrood Palace began life as the Hospitium or guest house of the abbey. As such, James IV found it a much more comfortable residence than draughty old Edinburgh Castle. By the time of his marriage to Margaret Tudor in 1503, he had transformed the building into a royal palace that was to be at the center of power in Scotland for the next hundred years.

Although its popularity with tourists is not nearly so great as that of the Castle, some of the older parts of the Palace are open to the public. These include the largest apartment in the Palace, the Picture Gallery—where Bonnie Prince Charlie held balls and levées during his short tenure of the Palace in 1745—the Chapel Royal and, of course, the apartments of Mary, Queen of Scots, a suite of four rooms, comprising Audience Chamber, Bedroom, Dressing-room and Supper Room, whose furnishings and fittings have been kept in the style of the

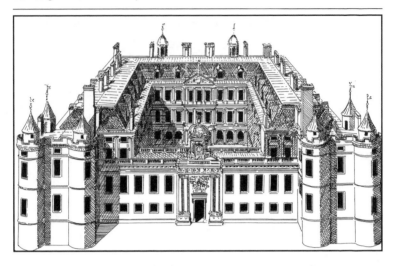

sixteenth century. Beneath these apartments, in Mary's time, were similar rooms used by the queen's husband, Lord Darnley.

Royal Murder

On the evening of March 9, 1560, the queen's apartments witnessed one of the most frightful murders in Scottish history. Queen Mary was holding a small supper party, attended by only a few friends and confidants, including her secretary, David Riccio. As the meal was being served, the guests were surprised by the abrupt appearance of first Lord Darnley and then his loyal follower, Patrick, Lord Ruthven, who wore a steel helmet and was heavily armed. Lady Antonia Fraser, in her biography of Mary, describes what happened next.

> *'Let it please your Majesty,' said Ruthven, 'that yonder man David come forth of your privy-chamber where he hath been overlong.' Mary replied with astonishment that Riccio was there at her own royal wish, and asked Ruthven whether he had taken leave of his senses. To this Ruthven merely answered that Riccio had offended against the queen's honour. On hearing these words, the queen turned quickly and angrily to her husband, realizing the Judas-like quality of his visit. She asked him if this was his doing. Darnley gave an embarrassed reply. Ruthven, by his own account, launched into a long and rambling denunciation of Mary's*

relations with Riccio, reproaching her for her favour to him, and for her banishment of the Protestant lords. Riccio had shrunk back into the large window at the end of the little room, but when Ruthven made a lunge towards him Mary's attendants, who seem to have been stunned into inaction, at last made some sort of protest. 'Lay not hands on me, for I will not be handled,' cried Ruthven, with his hand on his dagger: this was the signal for his followers, Andrew Ker of Fawdonside, Patrick Bellenden, George Douglas, Thomas Scott and Henry Yair, to rush into the room, also from the privy staircase. In the ensuing confusion the table was knocked over and Lady Argyll was just able to save the last candle from being extinguished by snatching it up as it fell (although presumably the flickering light from the large fireplace still filled the little room). While Riccio clung to the queen's skirts, Ker and Bellenden produced pistols, and others wielded daggers. Finally the fingers of the little Italian were wrenched out of the queen's skirts, and he was dragged, screaming and kicking, out of the supper-room, across the bed-room through the presence-chamber to the head of the stairs. His pathetic voice could be heard calling as he went 'Justizia, justizia! Sauvez ma vie, madame, sauvez ma vie!'

Here he was done to death by dagger-wounds variously estimated at between fifty-three and sixty: a savage butchery for a small body.

The spot where Riccio finally died is now commemorated with a small brass tablet.

The motive for his murder has never been fully established. Riccio, whose talents as a musician had won him the queen's favor, had consequently won the enmity of Lord Darnley, leading one to suspect that revenge for Riccio played some part in Darnley's own murder—described in Chapter Three—which took place seven years later. There must surely, however, have been a greater motive than simple jealousy. Riccio was not a man of action and could easily have been assassinated in secret. It certainly did not require the services of no fewer than six, heavily armed men. There is something singularly ritualistic about this crime, which was deliberately planned to take place in the presence of the queen.

The murder of Riccio and everything else to do with Mary continues to fascinate visitors, making the royal apartments the most popular part of the Palace. Indeed, the memory of this unfortunate queen permeates the Palace so completely that, unless one has an interest in her tragic reign, there is not a great deal of sightseeing to be done.

Lying directly behind the Palace, the Parade Ground has a long history as the location of troop reviews and civic gatherings of all kinds. In 1832, for instance, some 60,000 people gathered here to listen to the details of the Parliamentary Reform Bill. In more recent times, it was the site of the Scottish Miners' Gala Day picnic, an event that has sadly been discontinued with the disappearance of the Scottish mining industry. Nowadays, the most crowded event to be held on the Parade Ground is Fringe Sunday, which usually takes place at the end of the first week of the Edinburgh Festival. This is always a popular and joyous occasion, used by Fringe performers as a showcase for their particular productions, offering excerpts from their shows to attract custom.

The Palace's official function today remains that of a royal residence and it is perhaps for this reason that it has so little to offer to tourists. Unlike the Castle, many of the historical artifacts that are associated with it have been transferred elsewhere. For instance, just outside the Palace gate is a little lodge, known as Queen Mary's Bath, where according to tradition, the queen regularly maintained her famous beauty by bathing in white wine. Another tradition tells us, however, that it was through this house that the murderers of Riccio made their escape, a story that seems to have been confirmed by a discovery that was made in 1789. In that year, during repairs to the roof, a rather ornate dagger was found in the house. While this is presumed to be one of the weapons that was used in the murder, it is held today in the Museum of Antiquities in Queen Street and not in the Palace.

Exiles and Debtors
The Comte d'Artois, later to become the last Bourbon king of France, Charles X, is perhaps the Palace's most intriguing occupant. At the time of the French Revolution in 1789, d'Artois fled into exile and, after some years wandering around the courts of Europe, was finally given refuge by the British government, who permitted him to take up

residence at Holyrood. In December 1795 his entourage arrived at Leith, to be joined a few weeks later by the remaining members of his circle of dependents, including his mistress, Louise de Polastron.

For the most part, the exiled king and his party lived quietly and privately at Holyrood, seldom venturing beyond the boundaries of the Palace. It was not, though, an uncomfortable life. One of the royal entourage, the Comte de Vaudreuil, in a letter to his father in February 1796, declared that "the Scottish nobility is full of kindness, hospitality and good manners, and parties, balls and concerts are not wanting but it is better to keep a certain distance, following the example of our august Prince. We are in bed every night before midnight and we feel the better for it."

It was an exile that was to last almost nineteen years, ending only with the restoration of the French monarchy and the Comte's accession as Charles X, but even then Edinburgh was not to see the last of him. In 1830, after sixteen years of inept and repressive government, Charles X was forced to abdicate and immediately applied to the British government for aid. When this request was granted, Charles returned to Holyrood. According to one story, as he disembarked at Newhaven, one of the fishwives seized him by the hand and declared that she was happy "to see ye again among decent folk"!

The placing of d'Artois in Holyrood seems most appropriate when one considers that, prior to his arrival in Scotland, the future king had accumulated a rather heavy burden of debt. Although the abbey was in ruins and had long since ceased to perform any ecclesiastical function, it still retained the privilege of sanctuary. While this was not extended to serious criminals—murderers, for instance, could not benefit from it—the privilege was respected in the case of debtors.

In those days, a ritual known as "Letters of Horning and Caption" preceded imprisonment for debt. Three blasts on a horn by the Messenger-at-Arms would declare the recalcitrant debtor an outlaw and this would be followed by the serving of Letters of Caption, which were, in effect, an arrest warrant. In the precincts of Holyrood Abbey, an area known as the Girth, these Letters of Caption could not be served, nor could they be served anywhere in Edinburgh during the twenty-four hours of the Sabbath. This loophole led to the creation of a community of debtors, governed by an official called the Bailie, who administered the government of the Holyrood Sanctuary and with whom it was necessary to register before admittance. For a fee of two guineas, the debtor could enjoy complete freedom within the precincts of the Sanctuary. These precincts were clearly marked. At the east end of the Canongate, a white line was painted on the pavement, marking the boundary. On one side of the line, the debtor was safe; on the other, he could be arrested on any day except Sunday.

Sir Walter Scott describes this community in some detail, in his introduction to the first series of *Chronicles of the Canongate*, from the point of view of his character, Mr. Croftangry. A rather different writer, meanwhile, was to become a frequent visitor to the Sanctuary. In November 1833, Thomas de Quincey paid the first of what would be many visits to the Abbey Girth. At that time he was renting Caroline Cottage, Lady Nairne's house in Duddingston, where he lived with his wife and family. De Quincey's most recent biographer, Grevel Lindop, provides us with the following portrait of his subject at this time:

In 1834 De Quincey was forty-nine years old. Slow and, in some ways, reluctant though he had been to gain maturity, he could no longer avoid seeing that his youth was gone. His childhood friends had disappeared, his brothers and sisters were mostly dead. His mother was a distant, reproachful shadow. He had scarcely seen his second home, the Lake District, for five years, and with the cottage at Grasmere about to pass from his tenancy his last foothold there would soon be gone. His health was ruined; his great works on philosophy and mathematics would never be written; he had a wife and seven children whom he could barely support. He had no leisure for scholarship, no prospect before him but hack-authorship. He would never give up opium.

De Quincey seems to have been constitutionally incapable of avoiding debt. During his frequent sojourns in the Sanctuary, he roomed with a certain Miss Miller and before too long had run up a substantial bill with his landlady. As a result he was sued in the Bailie's court in 1834 and came very close to what would have been the greatest humiliation of all, that of being jailed for debt *within* the Holyrood Sanctuary!

In 1880 a law was passed abolishing immediate imprisonment for debt, as a result of which the privilege of sanctuary came to an end.

Nowadays, the district is associated with two institutions of a quite different character. The first of these is Moray House College of Education, which lies on the south side of the Canongate. Built in 1628, this was originally a mansion belonging to the Dowager Countess of Home, who left it to her daughter, the Countess of Moray. Like many Edinburgh buildings, it has a long and colorful history. Charles I often used it on his visits to Edinburgh and Oliver Cromwell made it his Edinburgh headquarters in 1648. There is also a tradition, unconfirmed by any historical evidence, that it was here—in a summerhouse in the garden—that the Treaty of Union of 1707 was signed. Today it houses Scotland's leading establishment for the training of schoolteachers.

The original Moray House is one of the last of the Old Town mansions, used by Oliver Cromwell as his residence while in Edinburgh. In appearance, it is not dissimilar to Old College. Standing nearby, however, on a site formerly occupied by the College gymnasium, a part of the college is housed in a building that would not look out of place in a sixties council estate.

The Scottish Parliament

Directly opposite the main gates of Holyrood is a building site where, at the time of writing, the new Scottish Parliament building is taking shape. Designed by the Catalan architect Enric Miralles (1955-2000) and originally due to be completed by autumn 2002, this building has been at the center of much controversy, mainly because of the escalation of its cost (from £45 million to over £200 million). The design concept has also come in for a deal of criticism. Miralles obviously thought in terms of the site, rather than a single building, and his plan envisages a group of buildings—likened, somewhat unkindly, by some, to a series of upturned fishing boats—rather than a single structure. While there still seems to be some doubt about its final completion date, it is assumed that it will be occupied by the Scottish Parliament by 2004. Its location in Holyrood, meanwhile, constitutes something of an irony.

As will be recalled from Chapter Five, everyone expected in 1997 that the new parliament would be based in the Old Royal High School on Calton Hill. When Donald Dewar, architect of the devolutionary

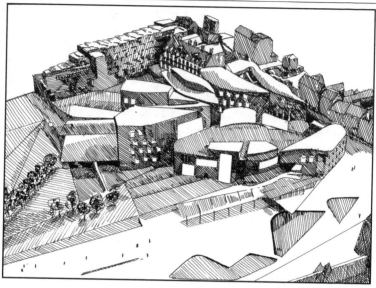

settlement, rejected this location, he did so on the grounds that it would give encouragement to nationalist opinion. Ever since the failed initiative of 1979, when a referendum that required approval from 40 percent of the electorate failed to meet its target, campaigners for a Scottish Parliament had regarded the Old High School as the legislature's natural home. Yet every Scottish nationalist worth his salt must surely know that power, albeit absent for four centuries, had once resided in Holyrood. It seems odd that Mr. Dewar, a man who possessed a wide-ranging knowledge of Scotland and a strong sense of history, appears to have been unaware of this in choosing the Holyrood site.

The announcement that the Parliament building was to be sited at Holyrood led to an immediate increase in office development in the area, which is now crowded with new buildings. Undoubtedly the most handsome of these is the new home of one of Edinburgh's most august institutions, *The Scotsman* newspaper. *The Scotsman* moved its offices from North Bridge—where it had been established for more than a century—to a charming new building that is reminiscent of the Museum of Scotland (see Chapter Three) and seems to have found its natural home at the foot of Arthur's Seat. Likewise, the BBC, after nearly eighty years in Queen Street, has since made a similar move.

Edinburgh's millennium project, "Our Dynamic Earth", offering a multi-media experience that charts the evolution of the planet, is sited nearby in a marquee-like structure, sometimes disparagingly known as "Scotland's Dome". Since it opened in 1999, this facility has received more than a million visitors. These are conducted in groups through eleven galleries in a tour that lasts approximately ninety minutes, employing the latest in interactive technology to communicate a sense of the various sights, sounds, temperatures and sensations to be found on earth. As one would expect, there is a strong commitment to education here. Schools groups are encouraged and there is a special "soft bone" area for the under-tens.

Some kind of agitation for the return of Scotland's parliament had been going on for more than a century, ever since 1886, when the Scottish Home Rule Association was formed. The story of this movement, and the many groups that contributed to its progress, is altogether too complex to be discussed adequately here, but there are a number of features of the movement that are worth pointing out. First, although the Scottish Home Rule movement has, from time to time, been identified with one political party or another, it always sought to transcend party politics—and, furthermore, was always at its best when it succeeded in doing so. For instance, in the negotiations that took place in the Constitutional Convention immediately preceding the creation of the parliament, every attempt was made by the participating politicians to reach an accommodation with their opponents. This was an important element in securing the approval of the Scottish people in the referendum of September 1997.

Moreover, the most prominent leaders of the movement, while naturally holding political views of one kind or another, have never been professional politicians. Roland Muirhead, who revived the Scottish Home Rule Association after the First World War, was a businessman who owned a tannery in the west of Scotland. John MacCormack, leader of the Scottish Covenant in the 1940s and 1950s, was a lawyer. Kenyon Wright, Chairman of the Constitutional Convention in the 1980s and 1990s, was, and remains, a minister of religion. The movement has always eschewed violence and, with the occasional exception (the theft of the Stone of Scone in 1952, for instance) any kind of extra-political activity. There may be one or two fanatics around—it would certainly be naïve to think otherwise—but, by and large, even the most extreme Scottish nationalists are content to pursue their aims by the use of constitutional mechanisms. In future, one of these mechanisms will be the Scottish Parliament.

The Scottish Parliament that was first elected in 1999, currently sitting, as mentioned earlier, in the Assembly Hall on The Mound, is composed of 129 MSPs (Members of the Scottish Parliament), elected by what is, for the United Kingdom, a novel electoral system. Seventy-three seats are directly elected, while the remainder takes the form of appointments, made from a list system that assigns seats on the basis of each party's share of the overall ballot. This system is designed to ensure that every Scottish interest group is represented within the Parliament.

Even so, the Scottish Parliament falls some way short of being a true national legislature. It has far fewer powers than many people, particularly in England, appear to imagine. It has no responsibility, for instance, for Scotland's economy, defense or foreign affairs, all of which remain under the control of Westminster. Indeed, even those powers that Holyrood does possess are somewhat circumscribed. Not surprisingly, therefore, many people in Scotland have expressed frustration with the Parliament, claiming that it has disappointed expectations.

Nevertheless, its very existence does have one important effect as far as the city of Edinburgh is concerned. For almost three hundred years, the city's status of national capital has been justified by little more than a strong sense of history and Scottish identity. The presence of the Scottish Office, the Supreme Court, even the General Assembly of the Church of Scotland, have not, in this respect, made up for the absence of a national legislature. The Parliament adds, as it were, the last piece in the jigsaw, with considerable implications for the cultural life of the city.

CHAPTER TEN

Open Horizons: Multicultural Edinburgh

"In more peaceful times, expansion of trade abroad brought new people to the city. Merchants, traders and craftsmen came from France, Germany, Denmark, the Low Countries, the Baltic and the Mediterranean. The Act of Union in 1707 brought Scotland into closer contact with the Colonies and resulted in the great wealth for some Edinburgh merchants, many of whom had black servants.

During the 18th century, Highlanders, displaced from the land, started to move to Edinburgh. Throughout the 19th century and continuing into the 20th, the other main groups to settle were Irish, Italians and Jews from Russia, Iceland and the Baltic States.

People were recruited during the Second World War to work in industry and. after the War a great number of settlers arrived from all over Europe. In the following years people from Commonwealth countries such as Hong Kong, the Indian sub-continent, areas of Africa and the West Indies came to fill gaps in the labour market."

Edinburgh City Council, *Peoples of Edinburgh*, 1997

The capital of Scotland is a truly multicultural city, of which by no means all of the citizens are Scots. During the 1980s two Edinburgh-based researchers, Tim Edensor and Mij Kelly, in the course of an oral history project, conducted no fewer than seventy interviews with Edinburgh residents who had arrived in the city from every part of the world. Some of these interviews were published in 1989 under the title *Moving Worlds* and reveal an astonishingly wide number of ethnic communities. People found themselves in the city for a variety of reasons; some came to study, a great many to find work, others to join partners who were already here, and not a few to escape political persecution. There are, of course, gaps in this diversity; surprisingly few Edinburgh citizens, for instance, are of Caribbean origin, but, all in all, it would be fair to say that every nationality in the world is represented in the city. And with the establishment of a facility for asylum-seekers about to be built near Turnhouse Airport, the ethnic mix of Edinburgh's population will inevitably become richer

Edinburgh has always maintained links with other countries. In the days when Scotland was an independent kingdom, it was of course the natural location for foreign embassies and, even today, there is a substantial diplomatic community, with approximately thirty countries maintaining consulates in the city. Possibly the most prominent of those, and certainly the best known, is the French consulate, since friendly relations between Scotland and France have a very long history. The Franco-Scottish concord, usually known as the "Auld Alliance", was initiated almost a millennium ago, when William I of Scotland entered into a formal league with Louis VII of France in 1168.

Politically, of course, this alliance may not always have been completely happy, but the cultural ties have, if anything, strengthened over the centuries. This is particularly noticeable in Scottish terms for food and drink, many of which have an obviously French derivation. Scottish housewives, for instance, will often use words such as *ashet* (serving dish), *pan* (bread) and *gigot* (leg of lamb). At school, children are taught Scottish country dancing, which has little to do with rural customs but derives its name from the French *contre-danse*. In addition to this, all the movements and steps have French names—*à la main, pas-de-bas, poussette*, etc.

In Edinburgh, the French connection is given expression by the activities of the French Institute. This is a meeting place for all who are interested in French culture, organizing public exhibitions, talks, lectures, film shows etc. In this, it works closely with the Franco-Scottish Society of Scotland, an independent charitable organization founded in Edinburgh more than a hundred years ago, in 1895, to foster contacts between the French and Scots. This society now has another seven branches throughout Scotland and acts as a focus for individuals and groups who wish to keep in touch with French culture, language, attitudes and current affairs.

Italian Roots

The French Institute is located in Randolph Crescent near the West End. The Italian Institute, situated in the Southside, carries out a similar program of events on behalf of Italian culture. Yet there is a subtle difference in the case of Edinburgh's relationship with Italy, in that the contact takes place at a more personal level. The city may be full of Francophiles but there is no discernible community of French origin in Edinburgh. On the other hand, such a community of Italians has been established since the eighteenth century, increasing through the nineteenth century as more people arrived from Italy. By 1875, it became possible for stars of the Italian stage—Tommaso Salvini and Adelaide Ristori—to bring their entire companies to Edinburgh in order to present seasons of Shakespeare in Italian translation.

Many Edinburgh Italians can trace their roots back to the province of Frosinone, particularly to the small town of Picinisco, in southern Italy. The first to arrive were craft workers, employed during the building of the New Town because of their specialist skills that were simply not available in Scotland. Even today, it is possible to see the handiwork of these early immigrants in the décor of Edinburgh homes. In the Southside, for instance, ornate cornices fashioned by Italian plasterers still decorate many flats.

These craft workers prospered, prompting many of their relatives and fellow-countrymen to follow them to Scotland. But not all of these new arrivals were craftsmen, and many were obliged to use their imagination in order to make a living. Some of them set up as street traders, selling, among other things, ice cream. During the nineteenth century, the Italian "Hokey-Pokey" man was a familiar sight in Edinburgh streets, selling ice cream from his barrow. Others were more creative, particularly the *figurinni*, who sold small glass figures of their own making. There were also a number of street musicians and it was to be in the field of music that the first substantial Italian cultural contribution was made.

On January 14, 1793, Natali Corri opened a new concert room at the head of Leith Walk. Charles Dibdin, in his *Annals of the Edinburgh Stage*, gives the following account of the enterprise and its founder.

Corri was a wonderfully enterprising man, besides being an excellent musician, but from unexplained causes he never came successfully out of his many ventures. Before the opening of the new rooms Corri seems to have been in some sort of partnership with another resident musician of the name of Urbani, who now, however, started a violent opposition to Corri, by giving a series of subscription concerts in the Assembly Hall, along with card and dancing assemblies. He engaged Yaniewitz, from Liverpool, as his leader, Lolli as principal violoncello, and Miss Waters as vocalist; and, in order to hurt Corri as much as possible gave the first of his concerts on the same evening as the opening of the new rooms. Corri spared himself no trouble to make his venture popular, and probably the novelty of the thing may, for a while, have drawn a sufficient number of people about the place to make it pay him.

Corri's concert room remained in business for the next twenty years; as we shall see, it was the venue for the evening concerts of the 1815 Music Festival, and must have been sustained by a substantial Italian element in the Edinburgh audience.

Although the venue no longer exists, the Italian presence remains. There are a number of Italian restaurants at the head of Leith Walk, and directly across the road from where Corri used to hold his concerts is the most celebrated of all Edinburgh Italian institutions, Valvona and Crolla. To describe this shop, founded by Alfonso Valvona and Emilio Crolla in 1925, as a provision store, while certainly accurate, seems somehow insufficient. Through its combination of the "West End" values of an Edinburgh quality grocer and its wide range of ingredients of Italian cuisine, Valvona and Crolla has won a legendary reputation in the food world. Indeed, even to walk across the threshold of the shop is to enjoy a gastronomic experience.

It is in the field of catering, of course, that the Italian influence on Edinburgh culture has been at its strongest, not only in terms of ice-cream parlors, fish and chip shops and the plethora of excellent Italian restaurants, but also in the everyday eating habits of Edinburgh citizens. This effect has been replicated in the field of the arts, where a quite definite Italo-Scottish consciousness has emerged.

The chief exponent of this cultural fusion is Professor Richard Demarco, a veritable force of nature in the Scottish arts world. Art critic Paul Overy, writing of Demarco in the *New Edinburgh Review* in the spring of 1979, declared that "undoubtedly his Italo-Scottish ancestry is the motor that propels him" and went on to draw the following profile.

Demarco was born in Leith in 1930. He studied painting at Edinburgh College of Art in the late forties and early fifties. He still produces very competent topographical drawings, which sell well, but which are surprisingly traditional compared to most of the work he has promoted over the last decade.

He taught art in schools for fifteen years before becoming one of the founders of the Traverse Theatre along with, among others, Jim Haynes (who later ran the London Arts Lab). Demarco started the small gallery in the Traverse and then set up a separate gallery, the Richard Demarco Gallery in Melville Crescent in 1967 where it remained until the mid-seventies. After a short period when he worked from an office in Great King Street, renting outside space for exhibitions, the Demarco Gallery moved to Monteith House in the High Street.

At first Demarco exhibited mainly Scottish and English artists, but increasingly began to show artists from abroad, searching out those areas then scorned by the British cultural establishment, not only countries on the other side of the Iron Curtain—Poland, Romania and Yugoslavia— but also Austria and Germany. For the 1970 Festival Demarco put on the most important show of contemporary West German art to have been seen in Britain (from Düsseldorf) at the Edinburgh College of Art.

By the mid-seventies the kind of work he was promoting and encouraging was more in the nature of process, performance or participation so that it no longer fitted into the concept of an art gallery. Joseph Beuys who had first shown and performed in the Düsseldorf exhibition was brought over by Demarco for several subsequent festivals. Demarco presented the extraordinary Cricot2 Theatre of Tadeusz Kantor from Kracow three times in Edinburgh and the third year also promoted Kantor at Riverside Studios in London. (Demarco was awarded a Gold Medal by the Polish Government for services to Polish culture, which he sees as an example of the recognition he feels he has never received in Scotland.)

Demarco's life and career can be seen as a prime example of a recurring theme that can be discerned in the activities of all the immigrant communities. Although usually concerned to maintain and develop their own particular cultures, the immigrants very quickly acquire an Edinburgh identity.

Jewish Edinburgh

In some instances, this happens quite naturally, while in others vigorous community leadership plays an important part. Edinburgh's Jewish community, for instance, was aided in this respect by the efforts of Rabbi Salis Daiches who, from 1919 until his death in 1945, acted as the unofficial leader of all Scottish Jews.

The Edinburgh Jewish community began to come into being during the nineteenth century, as a result of immigration from Eastern Europe. At one time, there was a quite definite Jewish quarter in the Old Town, known as the "Happy Land", and, like the Italians, these first immigrants worked as street traders, later branching out as traveling salesman, who journeyed into the countryside to sell goods from door to door. When Rabbi Daiches arrived in 1919, he found that there were two Jewish synagogues, one in the Old Town and the other in the Southside. In time, he would succeed in bringing both congregations together in one synagogue in Salisbury Road, Newington.

He was a man who believed in bringing people together. Seeing a correspondence between Scottish Presbyterianism and Orthodox Judaism, he sought to build on this affinity and taught his children to respect the beliefs of their neighbors. One of his sons, David, after an equally distinguished career as scholar, essayist and literary critic, returned to Edinburgh in 1977 and is currently the Honorary President of the Saltire Society. In his autobiographical memoir, *Two Worlds* (1956), he explains the nature of the Rabbi's appeal to Scots and Jews alike.

My father enjoyed his role as a public figure and played it superbly. In his letters to the press, his voice rang with the authority and the dignity of an official spokesman of his people, and similarly at public meetings in Edinburgh and throughout Scotland—at Masonic Lodges, the

Dunfermline Business Men's Club, the League of Nations Union, Burns Clubs—he would present with eloquence and passion the Jewish view of the subject under discussion. He had not been long in Edinburgh before he became known as one of the city's most distinguished public speakers, who could be counted on to make forceful oratorical contributions to any humanitarian or liberal cause. Of course he spoke too at Zionist meetings and at Jewish fund-raising occasions of all kinds, and looking back I seem to see an endless round of such occasions, but I think it was the speeches he made as a representative Jewish spokesman before non-Jewish and mixed audiences that gave him most satisfaction. For that, in his view, was an important part of the function of the modern Orthodox Jewish rabbi—to speak up for his people with dignity and equality before his fellow citizens.

David's brother, Lionel, had an equally distinguished career, becoming one of the most eloquent advocates ever to be heard at the Scottish Bar. One of Lionel's most celebrated cases took place in 1953, when he defended a Romanian Jew called Pinchis Haimovici, who had been posing as a Belgian aristocrat named Paul Dijon and who had been charged with illegally entering the country without a passport. Lionel's services were retained by Dijon's future wife, the Edinburgh jeweler and antique dealer, Esther Henry.

Esther Henry (1883-1963) was one of the most colorful characters that Edinburgh has ever known. Born in Newcastle-upon-Tyne at the end of the nineteenth century, she had set out as a teenager to make her fortune in the Scottish capital. She was a woman of great strength of character, well known for her somewhat eccentric appearance—she habitually dressed in dungarees and wore her long hair in a topknot—and her decidedly earthy manner of speaking. She owned an antique shop called The Luckenbooth, situated in premises next door to John Knox House, and counted among her customers King George V and Queen Mary, with whom she struck up a personal friendship.

At the time that Esther first met Pinchis Haimovici, she was seventy years of age and her future husband was approximately twenty years younger. (He had entered the UK on December 22, 1952 at Newcastle. This, of course, was Esther's hometown and presumably it had been some contact there that had redirected Haimovici to

Edinburgh.) When he turned up on Esther's doorstep on December 31, claiming to be a Belgian antiques dealer called Paul Dijon, Esther took an immediate shine to him. "I took one look at the bugger," she told Lionel Daiches later, "and that was it. I fell in love with him." She was not, on the other hand, taken in by the assumed identity. "Darlin', that's a fucking lie," she told him when he claimed to be a Belgian, "You're a bloody Jew like me."

She lost no time in helping him. That very night, she took him to see her friend Willie Merrilees, who had, by this time, risen to the rank of Chief Constable, and, as a result of this meeting, Haimovici—or Dijon, as we must now call him—voluntarily surrendered to Scottish justice. Three months later, after a hearing before the Sheriff Court, Dijon was released, only to be immediately re-arrested on the orders of the Home Secretary, on the grounds that he was an undesirable alien who ought to be deported. It was at this point that Esther engaged Lionel Daiches.

Lionel's defense of Dijon was grounded in the common law of Scotland. If his client was deported to Romania, he argued, he would be tortured and put to death on arrival. Since Dijon had refused to sign a declaration in support of the Communist regime, the Romanian government regarded him as a supporter of "Anglo-American imperialism". The man, it followed, was a fugitive from political persecution, who ought to be given asylum.

This argument proved successful, Dijon was released and, on April 27, 1953, he married Esther in a ceremony that became front-page news. It seems to have been a successful marriage and lasted for ten years before ending in tragedy on January 17, 1963, when an airliner crashed at São Paulo in Brazil and both Esther and "Prince Paul", as she liked to call him, were listed among the dead. They had been returning home from a lengthy holiday that they regarded as a belated honeymoon.

Esther Henry was greatly mourned. A woman of spontaneous generosity, ever ready to come to the aid of poor families when they were in particular need, she was always very popular in the Old Town. In addition to these acts of charity, which she always insisted must be kept as secret as possible, she had a brief, somewhat bizarre, flirtation with municipal politics. In 1936 she was elected to the council to represent one of the Canongate wards, having campaigned under the banner of Protestant Action!

Esther's support for the Protestant leader John Cormack seems particularly baffling when one considers that she had a number of Catholic friends. Perhaps she had been persuaded, as was the case with many other people at that time, by the power of Cormack's oratory. A more credible explanation is perhaps simply that Esther had an ambition to be a local politician and Protestant Action offered her the best hope of success. As far as religion was concerned, she never displayed any degree of anti-Catholic bias and was always proud to call herself a Jew.

Edinburgh Mela: Asian Influence

Religion, of course, is one of the chief means by which immigrants can best preserve their identity in a strange land. Many of the people who arrived in Edinburgh after the Second World War professed religions that had previously been unknown in the city. There are now at least two mosques in the city—one in the Southside, the other in Annandale Street, off Leith Walk—and a number of Hindu, Buddhist and Sikh temples. As well as these various faiths, many of the settlers are, of course, Christian and their presence in Edinburgh has helped to invigorate city congregations.

The emergence of an Edinburgh Asian community has had a double-handed effect on the culture of the local community. On the one hand, Asians have introduced the Scots to experiences that they would previously considered exotic. At the same time, the strong sense of identity that Asians consistently display has led native Scots to take a more detailed look at their own culture. These effects are most apparent in the field of catering. The successful establishment of so many Indian and Chinese restaurants in the city has led to Edinburgh people acquiring a definite taste for these types of cuisine. One of the most successful of all Edinburgh Asian entrepreneurs is Mrs. Shaheen Unis, who arrived from Pakistan in 1968. From premises in Dalry Road, Mrs. Unis supplies samosas, pakoras and nan bread, not only to Indian restaurants but also to retail outlets throughout the city. The popularity of such cooking has persuaded Scottish chefs to re-visit their own recipes, with the result that the Edinburgh Yellow Pages now lists more than three pages of Scottish restaurants, most of which practice a Franco-Scottish style of cuisine which is centuries old.

In the field of the arts, the traffic appears to have gone in the opposite direction. In 1995 the Indian, Pakistani and Bengali associations established the Edinburgh Mela, a weekend-long festival of Asian arts which takes place every August and has clearly been influenced by the success of the Edinburgh Festival Fringe. Pilrig Park, lying halfway between Edinburgh and Leith, is the venue for the event, accommodating three stages, a small cinema and enough space for an extensive bazaar. In 2002 a record crowd in excess of 30,000 from Edinburgh, Aberdeen, Dundee, Glasgow, Manchester, Bradford and beyond visited the Pilrig Park site. Among the artists appearing were the boys of the Gotipua Acrobatic Dance Troupe from Orissa, India, and there was a host of other musicians, dancers and artists from Scotland, Ireland and the Asian sub-continent to provide entertainment, color and atmosphere. The main Sunday night concert at the Usher Hall was a Bollywood Song and Dance spectacular, featuring top playback singers Sukhwinder Singh and Sunidhi Chauhan. Shafqat Ali Khan and Bollywood musicians and dancers treated the packed audience to an exciting, fast-paced performance of style and glamour.

Mela is a Sanskrit word meaning "family gathering". The Edinburgh Mela, although inspired by Asians, is certainly not exclusive and, in fact, exhibits an international awareness. In this respect, the host community is not forgotten and one of the highlights of the weekend took place on the Saturday evening, when there was a concert that paid tribute of one of Edinburgh's finest citizens, the recently deceased Hamish Henderson.

Hamish Scott Henderson was born in Blairgowrie in 1919. Although he was always somewhat reticent about his family background, this must have been fairly prosperous because he received a typically middle-class education at Blairgowrie High School, Dulwich College, London, and Cambridge University, where he took a degree in Modern Languages. During the Second World War, he served with distinction as an intelligence officer with the 51st Highland Division in Egypt, Libya, Tunisia and Sicily, where he fought at the side of the Italian partisans. This experience led to his most substantial book of verse, *Elegies for the Dead in Cyrenaica*, which won the Somerset Maugham Award in 1949. After the war, he worked for the Workers' Education Association for some years before being appointed to the staff of the School of Scottish Studies at Edinburgh University in 1952, a post he held until his retirement in 1988, when he was created an Honorary Fellow of the School. This post, which Hamish would often describe as "God's own job", enabled him to make a full-time commitment to the folk song movement, as singer, songwriter, collector, propagandist and organizer.

Hamish was always a very enthusiastic internationalist. Perhaps the most famous and most regularly performed of his many songs is *Freedom Come All Ye*, an anthem of international solidarity which he dedicated to Nelson Mandela, who was something of a hero as far as Hamish was concerned. Yet his enthusiasm extended to his own culture, too. In 1951 the American folklorist, Alan Lomax, arrived in Scotland as part of a collecting tour he was undertaking on behalf of Columbia Records, who were planning a series of albums on the folk songs of the world. With Hamish as his guide and assistant, he spent a very productive summer recording traditional singers. The recordings that they made, including the entire program of a ceilidh that was held at the end of People's Festival Week that year became the first deposits in the archives of the School of Scottish Studies.

The Edinburgh Mela concert was held in much the same spirit. One of the highlights of the evening was a new version of *Freedom Come All Ye*, performed by 45 musicians (led by Colin Blakey) on bagpipes and drums, samba drums, dhol drums, keyboards and brass section, with vocals by Fife Asian chorus Sangeet Mala and folk singer Sheena Wellington.

Winter Festival

This kind of occasion is typical of Edinburgh. Sometimes it seems as if the city's capital status carries with it a certain responsibility to be that much more open to international contacts. Whether or not this is truly the case, there is little doubt that Edinburgh is always at its best when exhibiting an international profile. Perhaps this is why people from all over the world flock to the city to celebrate the arrival of every New Year.

The celebration of the last night of the year, known as Hogmanay (the term is of unknown origin but probably has a French derivation) is the most important of all Scottish traditions. At one time it was celebrated in place of Christmas as the traditional end-of-year feast and, as a matter of fact, it is only within the last couple of generations that this has changed. The most common practice associated with the celebrations is first footing, a description of which is given by Alan Bruford in *A Companion to Scottish Culture* (1981).

This was done by men, especially younger men, and in this case the tradition has been carried on: perhaps women and children do less first-footing because of the association of the custom with drink, but it is also generally considered lucky for the real first foot, the first person to cross the threshold in the New Year, to be a man preferably one with dark hair. First-footers nowadays bring a bottle, sometimes food and a lump of coal or something black: this seems to be new, but peats are mentioned among first-foot gifts in earlier times.

Traditional guising at New Year normally involves singing as well as collecting food for consumption on the spot or later. This might happen either on Hogmanay or New Year's Day, and in some places has survived apart from first-footing as a children's custom. A popular rhyme to chant was:

> *Rise up, guidwife, and shak yir feathers:*
> *Dinna think that we are beggars:*
> *We're only bairnies come to play:*
> *Rise up and gie's oor Hogmanay.*

This clearly indicates the public aspect of the tradition, which is celebrated all over Scotland, with each town and village having its own time-honored spot for the revelers to gather. In Edinburgh, as noted in Chapter Three, the celebrations were long held at the Tron Kirk in the High Street. This meeting place seemed to lose its appeal after 1952, when the Tron ceased to be operational as a church, and for most of the next three decades the celebration of Hogmanay became a private matter, confined to people's homes. But sometime in the 1980s crowds began to gather once more at the Tron, in such numbers that in the interests of public safety the Council decided to put the celebration on a more organized footing. By this time, the practice of holding a public event at the end of the Festival had already become established and this was used as a model. A major incentive was undoubtedly the approach of the Millennium, and throughout the 1990s the event grew so popular that nowadays people are expected to buy tickets to attend. In 2002 some 300,000 tickets were issued, making this the largest street party in Europe and attracting visitors from all over the continent and beyond.

The Winter Festival, of which the New Year celebrations are the high point, differs from the summer Arts Festival in being both more public and less demanding on the audience. It begins at the end of November with the Christmas Light Night ceremony in East Princes Street Gardens, in which the city's festive lights, including the Christmas tree on the Mound (an annual gift from Norway) are switched on. The following Sunday, the first Sunday in December, Santa Claus leads a Grand Fantastical Christmas Parade, consisting of a number of specially designed floats, accompanied by brass bands and street performers, along Princes Street and up Lothian Road as far as Festival Square, where it comes to a triumphant conclusion. This inaugurates a series of events that run until the end of the holiday season.

Much of the activity takes place in East Princes Street Gardens, where an outdoor ice-rink, Winter Wonderland, is established and the Edinburgh Wheel, the UK's tallest Ferris wheel, gives visitors a particularly thrilling and vertiginous view of Edinburgh's city center. Farmers from Germany hold a traditional German market, serving a wide range of produce, together with mulled wine and festive snacks. In 2002 the Winter Festival acquired two additional markets: a Christmas farmers' market in Castle Terrace offering traditional

Scottish produce, and, on Castle Street, a continental market with 35 producers from across Europe. At all these events, the organizers accept and exchange Euros.

Although arts events are included, these are far from elitist in their appeal; they mostly take the form of pop concerts held in the Ross Bandstand, and the whole emphasis is on civic celebration. At the stroke of midnight on the last day of the year, the entire city center is illuminated by a spectacular firework display, initiating one of the largest street parties in Europe.

It is at this moment that the people of Edinburgh, whatever their origins, are aware that they are living in one of the most good-natured and stimulating cities to be found anywhere on the planet.

CHAPTER ELEVEN

"A Great and Ancient City": The Edinburgh Festival

"England has been starved of international art and artists for five years; thus I thought of an international festival of orchestral music, great soloists, drama, ballet—and opera—Glyndebourne Opera! Where could such a festival be held? Near London, I thought, it would have to be... Cambridge or Oxford... but I could not get anybody interested."
Rudolf Bing, Edinburgh Festival Programme, *1971*

There is a legend that the Edinburgh International Festival of Music and Drama began at a tram-stop in Princes Street in 1939. Rudolf Bing, so the story goes, was on his way back to his hotel after the performance of a touring production of *The Beggar's Opera* by the Glyndebourne Opera at the King's Theatre. Waiting for his tram, he looked up to see the ramparts of the Castle bathed in moonlight and was immediately reminded of Salzburg. "The idea of a Festival," Robert Ponsonby, one of Bing's successors as Festival Director, later remarked, "was born at that moment."

This is a nice story—and it might even contain some truth. Yet the Edinburgh Festival was *not* born as the result of a sentimental whim, nor had Bing's motives for creating it, in the first instance at least, anything to do with the city of Edinburgh, moonshine on the Castle ramparts notwithstanding. The ground for the Festival was actually prepared during the years of the Second World War. Edinburgh had the almost unique good fortune to escape large-scale bombing, and during this time a large influx of visiting soldiers and refugees from all over Europe found a native population that was warm in its welcome and considerate in its attendance to their needs. Organizations such as the WVS Allied Information Bureau in Princes Street did much valuable work in this respect, providing translations, organizing dances and other social events, putting relatives in touch with each other and promoting classes in everything from typing to map-reading.

Edwin Muir: Early Days

As far as the cultural requirements of the visitors were concerned, the British Council became heavily involved. H. Harvey Wood, the Council's Scottish Representative, had established a number of "friendly houses" throughout the city, meeting places where soldiers and refugees could gather with their compatriots. There was a Polish house, a French house, a Czechoslovak house and, later, an American house. In 1942 Wood hired the Scottish poet Edwin Muir to arrange the evening programs at each of these houses, an experience that Muir later described in his autobiography, *The Story and the Fable* (1987).

> *I still remember my first day in the Edinburgh office. As I had to know all the people I would be dealing with, Harvey Wood had arranged for a number of them to come, and the day passed in a continuous sequence of introductions and discussions. During the past years my wife and I had seen only a few people; now in a day I met more of them than I had done in a twelvemonth; and when I returned to my lodgings in the evening I went up to my room and did not stir from it again for fear of meeting someone else. But I soon got used to talking to many people; my new work was interesting; and I felt at last that I was doing something useful, like everybody else. Under the inspiration of Harvey Wood, the work of the Council in Edinburgh was universally admired at that time and it had attached to it the intelligence of the city, old and young, so that Edinburgh enjoyed an excess of life and enterprise. This made my own work easy. I drafted programmes for the foreign houses, arranged concerts, and wrote scripts, and was out for three or four evenings a week to see that everything was going as it should. Lecturers were willing to talk to our audiences in the friendly houses; Sir Herbert Grierson, though old now and lame, gave a great deal of his time to them; and when we wrote to London, T. S. Eliot and Stephen Spender and John Betjeman and Hugh Kingsmill and many others willingly came.*

> *All sorts of things were discussed in the friendly atmosphere of the houses: the war, the future of Europe, on which our hopes were beginning to fix themselves, the habits and traditions of different lands. The terrible memories, which the refugees brought with them, became more distant and bearable as they fell into the mould of a story, often repeated.*

Muir's conviction that he was "doing something useful" was confirmed by Harvey Wood himself, who later paid the following tribute to Muir.

> *With the minimum of apparent effort, in the intervals between the smoking of enormous numbers of cigarettes, Edwin made cultural history in Edinburgh. He brought to the Polish House, the Czechoslovak House, the French House and the American Centre, in an unending stream, poets, musicians, critics, painters and sculptors, novelists, architects of all nationalities and of uniform distinction. He sat in his room in Melville Street, in a blue haze of cigarette smoke, running his nicotine-stained fingers through his hair and spinning a web in which he entrapped almost every notable creative artist in Britain at that time.*

The sculptor, Hew Lorimer, later joined Wood and Muir. These three constituted a formidable team that ensured that the cultural programs arranged in Edinburgh would be the most ambitious to take place anywhere in the United Kingdom.

One of the first and most influential of their projects was a quite magnificent exhibition which took place in the National Gallery of Scotland in May 1941. A notice that appeared in *The Scotsman* at the time gives little indication of how significant this event was to turn out to be.

> *Its doors open today to the public who are invited to see an exhibition of works by the artists of our Allies. There are eight Allied countries represented, Poland making the chief contribution; the contributors also include artists, mainly soldier artists, from Belgium, Czechoslovakia. France, Greece, Yugoslavia, the Netherlands and Norway.*
>
> *The exhibition has been arranged by the British Council, a body of which exists to enable foreigners to acquire knowledge of the life and*

thought of the British people. A great many allied foreigners are at present gaining such knowledge at first hand, and the British Council have taken this opportunity to know something of the artistic activities of those who are temporarily with us.

One of the reasons why the Polish contribution was singled out for mention lies in the fact that the Polish army had decided that any artists serving in its ranks should be released from military duty in order to concentrate on art. This led to the inclusion of the work of some of Poland's leading artists, with names such as Feliks Topolski and Józef Natanson appearing in the catalogue. To accompany the exhibition, the British Council also arranged for lunch-time recitals of contemporary European music to be given, and these would continue throughout the war and beyond.

The lady who was most responsible for the continued success of these recitals was another colleague of Harvey Wood's, Miss Tertia Liebenthal MBE. Miss Liebenthal, the daughter of a Russian grain importer, was born in Edinburgh in 1890 at 34 Regent Terrace and never lived anywhere else. Her recitals, which became something of a civic institution, were notable for their presentation of twentieth-century music and for the opportunity they presented to new artists. Kathleen Ferrier, for instance, made her Edinburgh debut at one of Miss Liebenthal's recitals. The National Gallery recitals continued until Miss Liebenthal's death in 1970. As a matter of fact, this great lady collapsed and died at the penultimate concert of the series, shortly after announcing the program for the 700th concert, which was to feature two of her oldest friends, Peter Pears and Benjamin Britten.

"A Splendid Assemblage"

Such activities constitute the true roots of the Edinburgh Festival. They were not, however, the *only* roots, for the idea of a festival was anything but new. Indeed, the first Edinburgh Music Festival had been held in the city more than a century earlier, in 1815. Even before that, moreover, there was a season of concerts, which were given annually in St. Cecilia's Hall in the Cowgate. In 1847, while compiling his *Traditions*, Robert Chambers collected the memories of an old gentleman who had regularly attended these concerts decades earlier:

The vocal department of our concerts consisted chiefly of the songs of Handel, Arne, Gluck, Sarti, Jornelli, Guglielmi, Paisiello, Scottish songs, &c.; and every year, generally, we had an oratorio of Handel performed, with the assistance of a principal bass and a tenor singer, and a few chorus-singers from the English cathedrals; together with some Edinburgh amateurs, who cultivated that sacred and sublime music; Signor and Signora Domenico Corri, the latter our prima donna, *singing most of the principal songs, or most interesting portions of the music. On such occasions the hall was always crowded to excess by a splendid assemblage, including all the beauty and fashion of our city. A supper to the directors and their friends at Fortune's Tavern generally followed the oratorio, where the names of the chief beauties who had graced the hall were honoured by their healths being drunk.*

Before concluding this brief memoir of St Cecilia's Hall Concerts, I shall mention the chief performers who gave attractions to them. These were Signor and Signora Domenico Corri, from Rome; he with a falsetto voice, which he managed with much skill and taste; the signora with a fine, full-toned, flexible soprano voice. Tenducci, though not one of the band, nor resident among us, made his appearance occasionally when he came to visit the Hopetoun family, his liberal and steady patrons; and while he remained he generally gave some concerts at the hall, which made quite a sensation among the musicals. I considered it a jubilee year whenever Tenducci arrived, as no singer I ever heard sang with more expressive simplicity, or was more efficient, whether he sang the classical songs of Metastasio, or those of Arne's Artaxerxes, or the simple melodies of Scotland. To the latter he gave such intensity of interest by his impassioned manner, and by his clear enunciation of the words, as equally surprised and delighted us. I never can forget the pathos and touching effect of his Gilderoy, Lochaber no more, The Braes of Ballenden, I'll never leave thee, Roslin Castle, &c. *these, with the* Verdi prati *of Handel,* Fair Aurora *from Arne's Artaxerxes, and Gluck's* Che faro, *were above all praise. Miss Poole, Mr. Smeaton, Mr. Gilson, and Mr. Urbani were also for a time singers at the hall—chiefly of English and Scottish songs.*

But I should be unpardonable if I omitted to mention the most accomplished violin-player I ever heard, Paganini only excepted—I mean Giornovicki, who possessed in a most extraordinary degree the various requisites of his beautiful art: execution peculiarly brilliant, and finely articulated as possible; a tone of the richest and most exquisite quality; expression of the utmost delicacy, grace, and tenderness; and an animation that commanded your most intense and eager attention.

These concerts seem to have been discontinued after the opening of the Assembly Rooms in George Street in 1786, where, according to Chambers' anonymous correspondent "a pretty good subscription concert" was soon established. The idea of a music festival, therefore, must have seemed a very promising one in 1815.

As it turned out, this Festival was a comparatively modest affair, consisting of three morning concerts of sacred music and three evening orchestral concerts. There was an orchestra of sixty-two musicians, led by Felix Yaniewicz (a Polish violinist who was an Edinburgh resident) and conducted by Charles Ashley of London. The principal singers were Madame Marconi, Mrs. Salmon and Messrs. Braham, Smith, Swift and Rolle, and among the instrumentalists were Mr. Lindley (cello), Signor Dragonetti (bass) and Signor Corri (piano). A choir of 58 specially selected voices included local singers as well as choristers from Lancashire, Carlisle and London. It was at this festival that the cellist and composer, J. G. Schetky made his last professional appearance, coming out of retirement, at the age of seventy-eight, to play in the opening concert in Parliament House.

The first part of this concert was devoted to the music of Handel, opening with the Overture to *Esther*, while the second part consisted of an abridged performance of Haydn's oratorio *The Creation*. Handel's *Messiah* was given on November 2, and the final morning concert took place on November 4 with music by Boyce and Handel, concluding with the Coronation Anthem *Zadok the Priest*. The evening concerts on October 31 and November 1 and 3 took place in Corri's Concert Room in Broughton Street, at the top of Leith Walk. These were devoted mainly to the "modern" composers and included symphonies by Haydn, Beethoven and Mozart as well as vocal and instrumental solos.

Over 9,000 tickets were sold for these concerts and the festival made a profit of £1,500, which was immediately handed over to a number of charities. Edinburgh sought to replicate this success four years later in 1819, when the second Edinburgh Music Festival began with a concert in the Theatre Royal on the evening of Tuesday October 19. This was followed by a morning concert of works by Handel and Mozart on the 20th, a performance of *The Messiah* on the 21st, and the festival ended on the Saturday morning with a selection of pieces followed by Beethoven's *The Mount of Olives*, all in Parliament House.

Further evening concerts were given in the theater on the Wednesday and Friday when one of the works performed was a scena, *The Last Words of Marmion*, by Dr. Clarke to words by Walter Scott. For these concerts, the leader of the orchestra was, once again, Mr. Yaniewicz and the conductor throughout was Sir George Smart. Like the first festival, the 1819 event was a great success. According to the *Edinburgh Evening Courant*, a total of 8,526 people attended the concerts, yielding a profit of £1,232.10s. for a number of charities.

The next festival was held in 1824 when, in addition to the concerts, there was a grand Festival Ball with music by the Military Band of the Royal Dragoons. There was also a pageant, celebrating the Royal Society of St. Crispin, and featuring trumpeters, heralds, King Crispin himself, a Highland chieftain and an Indian prince. Although figures are not available, this too appears to have been a triumph, which raised a considerable sum for charity.

Unfortunately, this could not be said of the festival of 1843, which was presented in the Assembly Rooms in George Street. Despite receiving the patronage of Queen Victoria and Prince Albert, the event did not succeed in recouping its costs. Although this loss was comparatively small—just £60—it does seem to have been enough to discourage future initiatives. It would be nearly thirty years before another festival took place, and that would be restricted to a single event. In 1871, to celebrate the centenary of the birth of Sir Walter Scott, the prominent Scottish singer David Kennedy performed songs to texts by Scott at a concert in the Corn Exchange.

"Spiritual Refreshment"

Apart from those events, music has always flourished in Edinburgh. In 1909, when the great Italian tenor, Enrico Caruso, arrived to sing at the University's McEwan Hall, he was escorted from the station by a pipe band. It seems that Caruso was so delighted by this reception that he seriously considered appearing at the concert in full Highland dress.

As mentioned earlier, the concerts of Professor Donald Tovey at the Reid School of Music generated an interest in serious music that extended well beyond the bounds of the University. Interest in the visual arts has been maintained through the work of the Royal Scottish Academy and the work of distinguished practitioners from Ramsay through Raeburn to Cadell. Even theater—regarded by many as the Cinderella of the Scottish Arts—has a good record in Edinburgh, due mainly to the work of individuals such as William Murray and Robert Wyndham. As a matter of fact, the leading theatrical enterprise in Britain in the 1940s, Howard & Wyndham Ltd., founded by Wyndham's son, Fred, still had its head office at the Royal Lyceum, in Edinburgh.

All of these conditions would eventually combine to persuade Rudolf Bing that Edinburgh was the place where his vision of a post-war Festival would be realized. Initially, of course, as the quotation at the head of this chapter indicates, he did not have the city in mind, believing that the location would have to be nearer London. Then, in 1944, he outlined his ideas at a lunch in London's Hanover Square to a group of British Council officials, which included Harvey Wood. "Greatly daring," Wood later wrote, "but not without confidence, I recommended Edinburgh."

Bing, no doubt recalling his experience at the tram-stop in 1939, responded positively to this suggestion, and Wood, on his return to Edinburgh, began to sound out some support. Almost immediately, he received the enthusiastic backing of luminaries like the Countess of Rosebery, Professor Sydney Newman of Edinburgh University and Murray Watson, editor of *The Scotsman*. But his most important supporter proved to be the man to whom he submitted the proposal: Sir John Falconer, Lord Provost of Edinburgh. The Provost, in an article for the Festival program of 1951, recorded his initial reactions.

I thought it was a good idea, but the strange thing was, I didn't think about lots of concerts and plays and exhibitions. I thought about something else.

I thought of our poor, tortured world, lying in ruins after all the pain and misunderstanding of so many bitter years. And I thought of Edinburgh and how fortunate we'd been—almost alone among the capitals of Europe—in escaping the devastation. Surely we could provide some spiritual refreshment, surely this city could become a common meeting-place for all the peoples of the world?

Despite such support, the very first Edinburgh Festival seemed—and indeed *was*—a huge gamble. The immediate post-war period was a time of political uncertainty and economic austerity, and the whole enterprise might have ended in fiasco. Instead, something of a miracle took place, as described by Eric Linklater at the time.

In all its history Edinburgh had had no experience of such an undertaking, and the gloom that had rewarded our astonishing victory in a long and unnecessary war was aggravated by local scepticism about the native ability to house so vast and glittering an enterprise. But the faith of Falconer, Bing and Harvey Wood persisted against immediate doubt and general apathy, and into Edinburgh came the Glyndebourne Opera Company to present The Marriage of Figaro *and Verdi's* Macbeth; *the Vienna State Orchestra under Bruno Walter to let Beethoven speak for glory; Louis Jouvet from Paris to bring Giraudoux and Molière into the alliance; and also from France l'Orchestre des Concerts Colonne under Paul Paray. The Halle and the Scottish Orchestras arrived; the Old Vic and the Sadler's Wells Ballet; Kathleen Ferrier to sing Mahler's* Das Lied von der Erde, *and Schnabel, Szigeti, Primrose and Fournier to play chamber music by Schubert and Brahms.*

Triumph was the consequence of their advent; and darkness shivered and retreated. It was a triumph of courage, of faith in a vision; a triumph of elegance over drab submission to the penalties of emerging victorious from a modern war. The music critic of The Scotsman *was so moved as to write, in his review of a concert by the French orchestra:*

'Let us salute Paul Paray and his players, and in saluting them take up afresh the battle against all slovenly and spiritless things.'

That, clearly enunciated, was a battle cry for elegance which, if it had been heard and followed, would have saved us the spleen of much modern writing, painting and dramatic experiment. It was too demanding a battle-cry, but a natural response to M. Paray who, when he conducted his orchestra in the British national anthem, that so often sounds as if it were a lamentation for the pains of authority, made it clamour like a reveille bidding all good men to wake and bare their swords for a crusading monarch—and in the flash and inspiration of the fiddle-bows, imagined blades reflected the sunshine. Week after week the real, the visible sun, poured down its light on the town, and elegance in a hundred ways informed its life.

More than fifty festivals later, Sir John's vision is still in place. Indeed, one might reasonably claim that the idea of creating "a common meeting-place for all the peoples of the world" is what ensures the survival of the event. The Festival's official title, the Edinburgh *International* Festival of Music and Drama, is all too often forgotten.

At the same time, it is clear that the establishment of the Festival led, more or less immediately, to a new vitality on the Scottish arts scene. In 1955, for instance, the Edinburgh composer Thea Musgrave had her first success when the Saltire Singers performed her *Cantata for a Summer's Day* in the Freemason's Hall in George Street. Four years later, another Scottish composer, Iain Hamilton, celebrated the bicentenary of Robert Burns in the Usher Hall with *Sinfonia for Two Orchestras*. Despite the title of the piece, only one orchestra appears to have been involved, the recently renamed Scottish National Orchestra (it had previously been known as the Scottish Orchestra) conducted by Alexander Gibson, whose achievements over the next decade were, in the words of George Bruce, "of such importance to music in Britain as to warrant the term 'historic'." Perhaps the most solid of these achievements was Gibson's creation, in 1963, of the Glasgow-based Scottish Opera.

Another national company, Scottish Ballet, was also created as a direct result of the Festival. In 1961 an English choreographer called Elizabeth West brought her dance company to the Empire Theatre—

now the Festival Theatre—on the South Bridge. Many of the dancers in that company, then known as Western Theatre Ballet, had received their training in Scotland from teachers such as Marjorie Middleton in Edinburgh and Margaret Morris in Glasgow, and after the death of Elizabeth West, the company became known as Scottish Ballet.

Cinema, too, has received greater attention because of the Festival. The establishment of the Film Festival has not only acted as a focus for Scottish film enthusiasts, but has actually promoted a serious engagement with film within the wider intellectual community. This is not simply a matter of screening movies, but involves staging conferences and discussions, and publishing papers. A typical event took place in August 1982 under the title of *Scotch Reels*. John Caughie, one of the organizers, recalled its significance in a 1990 essay.

> *At the simplest, and most readily appropriate level, "Scotch Reels" identified a set of relatively consistent discourses which informed the representation of Scottishness, defining the images of Scotland which could slip comfortably into the national imaginary as familiar identities, and into the national and international image markets as tradable symbolic goods. These representations reproduced and, in cinema particularly, often refreshed the identities by which we are invited to recognize our difference and our status as a great wee nation. Unfortunately in the case of Scotland, it was argued, they were almost entirely regressive, launching their appeal from a vanished or vanishing past. It is perhaps a measure of their simplicity, but also of their seductive explanatory power, that the governing discourses can be identified quite schematically: "tartanry", "kailyard", "Clydeside".*

The Festival's most sensational and longest-lasting impact, however, was made in the field of theater, its creation having somewhat fortuitously coincided with a revival in theatrical activity in Scotland. Due to the work of dramatists such as Wilson Barret in Edinburgh (and Aberdeen), James Bridie in Glasgow, A. R. Whatmore in Dundee and Marjorie Dence and David Stuart in Perth, a modern Scottish theater movement was beginning to come into being. For the first time in almost a century, it became possible for Scottish actors and writers to make their living exclusively in Scotland and, as a result, a new, distinctively Scottish, theatrical voice began to be heard. At the second Festival in 1948, this voice was heard in all its full-throated splendor in a modern version of an old Scottish classic, Sir David Lyndsay's *Ane Satyr of the Thrie Estaitis*.

This ancient work is an allegorical morality play. The old Scottish parliament was known as "the Estates", encompassing the Spirituality, the Temporal and the Merchants. Lyndsay's satire is therefore a critique of the state of Scotland. In 1979 the English critic Peter Happe, described the play in an essay that accompanied a publication of the text.

In the first part of his play the King is shown to be at fault, falling into sensual temptation, and failing to reform the abuses of the clergy whose main object was self-advancement. One can see here two traditional ideas. One is the unity of society with its constituents working together in a balance, an idea which is perhaps a descendant from Plato's Republic. The other is the criticism of Church abuses, and here we find him working over similar material to Chaucer and Langland. It is interesting that the figure of the Pardoner is so important in his analysis. In the second part of the play the King's personal fate is much less important, and Lindsay switches attention to the state itself, outlining what is really a programme of reform. Again the techniques of the morality are present: temptation by crafty and successful vices, an elaborate structure of clowning and intrigue by the court vices who are skilled in the art of flattery and lies, and the intervention of the virtues who quickly expose the villains and give the opportunity for a more healthy society. Lindsay also finds room for passages of folly which are not strictly related to the main action but echo the comedy and irreverence we have noted in the folk-elements of the morality plays.

This play had not been seen in Edinburgh—or indeed anywhere else—since 1554, when it was presented on the recently constructed Greenside play field on the northern slope of Calton Hill, very close to where the present Playhouse Theatre stands today. The acting text obviously needed to be brought up to date for modern audiences and, since the original had taken some nine hours to play, the script had to be adapted to a manageable size. The Edinburgh playwright, Robert

Kemp, who was also Chairman of the Gateway Theatre, carried out this work. The most appropriate connection of all lay in the fact that the producer, Tyrone Guthrie, was the great-grandson of the Disruption leader Dr. Thomas Guthrie, whose efforts in the 1840s had led to the construction of the Assembly Hall, where the play was presented. As Martin Cooper, drama critic of the *Daily Herald,* commented:

> *Everyone is comparing the Satire with Reinhardt's production of Every-*
> *man at Salzburg and there is little doubt it will become a permanent*
> *feature of each year's Festival. But whereas Everyman is a foreign impor-*
> *tation the Satire is bone-Scottish—forthright, violent and (forgive me my*
> *kind Scottish hosts) monstrously one-sided as good satire must be.*

The Fringe

Guthrie's innovative production of the *Thrie Estaitis* gave theater in Scotland an enormous boost, as did the foundation of another Festival institution that came into being very quickly. The Edinburgh Festival Fringe is one of the greatest gatherings of theatrical artists to be found anywhere in the world and has given its name to a distinctive style of theater, yet, strangely, its origins can be traced directly to a certain absence of tact on the part of the Festival's first director.

Rudolf Bing does not appear to have been a very diplomatic man. At one of the first meetings of the Festival Committee, he made the quite impolitic suggestion that the Festival should be launched with a High Mass in St. Giles! Someone, probably H. Harvey Wood, had to take him aside and explain why this suggestion was so inappropriate in Presbyterian Edinburgh, but this did not prevent him from making another *faux pas,* which was to have a rather more salutary consequence. In one of the first public speeches he made concerning the Festival, Bing rather gave the impression that what was planned was an elitist affair. International artistes, he said, would be performing for international audiences, i.e. visitors. As far as the people of Edinburgh were concerned, their role would be restricted to that of hosts, driving taxis, serving food, or providing accommodation. Not unreasonably, a number of people took exception to any such idea, and this led, in 1951, to the creation of the Edinburgh People's Festival.

This Festival, which was, in fact, initially sponsored by the Labour Party, was at first as much a political as an artistic initiative. The theater companies that took part in it—Clyde Unity and Theatre Workshop—certainly took an openly and unashamedly left-wing stance, arguing that culture and politics were not divisible. But the People's Festival also set a precedent in that it demonstrated quite clearly that it was possible to take part in the Edinburgh Festival without actually being invited to do so. As a direct result of this initiative, the Festival Fringe was born.

The importance of the Fringe to the Edinburgh Festival cannot possibly be underestimated. It is the Fringe that creates the atmosphere in which the Festival thrives, the Fringe that ensures that the essential vitality of the Festival is not dissipated, the Fringe which has embedded the very idea of Festival in the consciousness of the Edinburgh public.

In addition to all this, the Fringe is always great fun, not only for its audience, but for its participants and even for its critics. In his book about the Fringe, *City of a Thousand Worlds*, one of the Fringe's most experienced reviewers, Owen Dudley Edwards illustrates this with many amusing anecdotes, such as the following, which involves Owen's wife, Bonnie. Bonnie is also a reviewer (they have been reviewing Fringe shows for *The Scotsman* since 1974) and on the occasion in question had just been to see the Cambridge Mummers perform a play about the poets Rimbaud and Verlaine, a production she had disliked intensely.

> *Bonnie and I would talk about the day's shows when we met at home, usually after midnight, and might supply one another with some errant reference needed for the ultimate verdicts we were preparing for early morning delivery to* The Scotsman. *The lunchtime after one such exchange I found myself in the YWCA looking at a Cambridge Mummers'* Prometheus Bound, *in translation from Aeschylus. It failed to set me on fire, but it was not bad. My departure was stopped in its tracks by the President of the Mummers, no less. He asked me my opinion. True to the practice of my great chief, I produced my customary formula, namely meaningless response rather than curt refusal.*

'Interesting,' I said, as nasally as possible. His gaze continued importunate, so I thought for a moment, swallowed, and pronounced: 'Interesting.'

'That's very interesting,' he said, infringing my copyright courteously. 'Yesterday we had a different show at this time, and the lady from The Scotsman *said it was interesting.'*

That sounded like one of the more indelicate Donald McGill postcards. Well, The Scotsman *had many ladies, and the self-exculpatory participle was, as Mr President had just shown, nobody's monopoly.*

'And when will your review appear?' On this I could speak with some generous freedom. 'God alone knows,' I said piously. 'At the moment there are seventy-five reviews in the pipeline awaiting appearance.'

'So it could be some days,' he said, 'and some days before the lady's review is printed also.'

'What was that show?' I asked, uninterested but feeling the need of some courtesy before I got out. He told me.

'That was no lady,' I said, 'that was my wife.'

In 2002 the number of individual companies taking part in the Fringe was only slightly less than 1,400, not counting the large number of buskers, acrobats, jugglers and street musicians who are to be seen performing in the Royal Mile throughout the Festival period. A glance at the program will reveal an astonishing mixture of the traditional and the innovative, the tried and trusted and the downright adventurous. There are plays, exhibitions, concerts, events—mostly workshops concerned of various forms of artistic activity—musicals, dance shows and, somewhat optimistically given the fact that the Scottish school term begins before the opening of the Festival, a fair sprinkling of children's shows.

There are also some shows that defy categorization, such as the very popular Lady Boys of Bangkok. This transvestite cabaret takes place in a marquee and has become established over the past few years in the Meadows.

One element that has recently grown considerably is stand-up comedy, probably due to the institution of the Perrier Comedy Awards in 1985. (These awards might be described as the Oscars of Edinburgh Comedy. Every comic would love to win one, even though they all seek to deny the Perrier's importance.) Comedy events now account for almost a quarter of Fringe listings, leading some observers to fear that the day cannot be far off when this form of cheap and easy theater will predominate. Even as things are, the Fringe acts as a showcase for emerging comedy talent and a number of Fringe venues—the Assembly Rooms, the University's Pleasance Theatre and the most serious casualty of the 2002 Cowgate fire, the Gilded Balloon—have become thoroughly commercialized in this respect.

Yet the true importance of the Fringe lies in the scope it gives to serious drama, not simply in terms of emerging talent, but also with regard to the many fine plays that mainstream theater tends to ignore. Brian Friel's *Dancing at Lughnasa*, Harold Pinter's *The Dumb Waiter* and Arthur Miller's *After the Fall* were all given all-too-rare outings at the 2002 Festival Fringe. At the other end of the scale, there is a great deal of dross, with the occasional jewel waiting to be discovered underneath it. In this respect, we should try to gain some perspective on the event and try not to be too censorious.

Every year, the Fringe seems to increase in size, with hundreds of companies presenting thousands of shows. Most Fringe performers are young and adventurous and, although many will find at least a degree of success, many more are certain to be disappointed.

It is not generally understood, particularly among the local population, what an expensive business setting up a Fringe production can be. Quite apart from the usual costs of production—set, costumes etc.—Fringe companies are faced by a number of expenses specific to Edinburgh. Renting venues is far more expensive than it is anywhere else, and indeed dearer than it would be in Edinburgh at any other time of the year—and there are many hidden costs. In order to be included in the Fringe program, for instance, companies have to obtain membership of the Fringe Society, currently costing approximately £400. Accommodation, too, can be difficult. One of the most persistent legends of the Festival tells how many Edinburgh citizens, irritated by the influx of visitors, flee the city for the months of August and September, renting out their houses to Fringe performers. This is one legend that is actually true, although it omits to mention how much profit is made out of the practice. Sleeping on a Marchmont floor during the Festival can cost as much as the best hotel accommodation at other times of the year.

In spite of such difficulties, the Fringe continues to grow, with more and more (mostly) young people arriving in the city to perform in theirs shows. Edinburgh potentially offers a large and appreciative audience; in 2001 the Fringe sold just under 900,000 tickets, more in three weeks than the combined sales of both Edinburgh football clubs for the entire season, but this is certainly not guaranteed. Among the hundreds of Fringe companies who arrive at the start of the Festival, a large proportion close down after a few performances. This is due partly to the sheer size of the event—it is no longer possible, as it was at the beginning, for everyone to see everything—and partly to the fact that festival-goers have become more discriminating with the passing of the years. The Fringe is therefore self-regulating and any argument against the size of the event rather misses the point.

Yet such arguments continue to be made, usually by people who are opposed to the whole idea of the Festival in the first place. For all its success, the sad fact is that the Edinburgh Festival has never lacked enemies. In 1947, for instance, before a single Festival event had taken place, Sir Thomas Beecham, the famously irascible conductor of the Royal Philharmonic Orchestra, made a speech in which he told the people of Scotland that they would be "damn fools" if they allowed a Festival to go ahead in Edinburgh, and predicted a "complete fiasco" if it did.

Scottish Rivalry

This prediction was, of course, triumphantly confounded but it seems rather significant that Sir Thomas did not make these remarks in Edinburgh but during a visit to Glasgow, a city which has cast envious eyes on the Festival since the very beginning. Rivalry between Edinburgh and Glasgow is of very long standing, perhaps inevitably so. Glasgow, after all, is Scotland's largest city and must naturally resent so much prestige, power and influence residing in its eastern neighbor. As Glasgow's leading cultural commentator, Jack House, was to remark rather wistfully in 1976, "I just wish Glasgow had thought of it first."

A short examination of Glasgow's attitude to the Edinburgh Festival will immediately reveal one of the most important truths, concerning not just the Festival but the nature of the city of Edinburgh itself. Several times over the last fifty years, Glasgow has attempted to set up a similar annual event. One thinks of the Commonwealth Festival in the 1970s, Clydefair International in the 1980s and Mayfest in the 1990s. All of these have resulted, after only a couple of year's operation, in ignominious failure. Even the yearlong festival, which took place during Glasgow's designation as European City of Culture in 1990, was, despite all the money poured into it, no more than a qualified success. Laying all inter-city rivalry to one side, one is obliged to ask why Glasgow, with its greater size, its greater population, with all its famous wit and energy, cannot succeed in creating a festival to match that of Edinburgh.

Why, in other words, has Edinburgh succeeded where Glasgow has failed?

The answer has to do with the nature of the city of Edinburgh, its history, its geography, its sense of tradition, the spirit of its people, in short its whole personality. Lord Harewood, Director of the Festival from 1961 until 1965, perhaps expressed this best in an article he wrote for the Festival *Souvenir Programme* in 1971.

> *Edinburgh is the perfect city in which to hold a festival, partly because it is of exactly the right size to provide an impressive frame and yet not to swamp a programme with its everyday activities, partly because it is a marvellous place in its own right. Scotsmen are used to making up their minds and disinclined to accept other people's valuation, and this independence applied to their festival as to anything else. While I respect the independent spirit I used sometimes to wish that people quoted in the press, would sometimes say they liked the festival they found in their midst rather than dilating on the inconveniences it caused them. Nonetheless, it would be inappropriate to omit to say how that every time I drove from the airport to start one of the dozens of visits I made to the city for meetings, my first glimpse of the Castle, whatever the weather, whatever my mood, never failed to produce that lifting of the spirit which is commonly associated with love.*

After the first Festival in 1947, the novelist E. M. Forster put the matter a little more succinctly. He concluded an article for the *Sunday*

Times with the remark: "I have no space left to enlarge on the friendliness and hospitality with which the visitor to Edinburgh is greeted. The atmosphere is perfect. One has the sense of a great and ancient city, which cares about the arts."

That judgment seems to sum up the whole matter.

Further Reading

Bold, Alan, *Scotland, a Literary Guide*. London: Routledge, 1989.

Braden, Su, *Artists and People*. London: Routledge, Kegan and Paul, 1978.

Brown, Rev. Thomas, *Annals of the Disruption*. Edinburgh: MacNiven & Wallace, 1893.

Bruce, George, *Festival in the North*. London: Robert Hale & Company, 1975.

Campbell, Donald, *A Brighter Sunshine*. Edinburgh: Polygon Books, 1983.

Campbell, Donald, *Playing for Scotland*. Edinburgh: Mercat Press, 1996.

Cant, Malcolm, *Marchmont, Sciennes and the Grange*. Edinburgh: Malcolm Cant Publications, 2001.

Chambers, Robert, *Traditions of Edinburgh*. Edinburgh: W. & R. Chambers, 1824.

Cockburn, Lord, *Memorials of His Time*. Edinburgh: T. N. Foulis, 1910.

Evans, Hilary and Mary, *John Kay of Edinburgh*. Edinburgh: Paul Harris, 1980.

Edwards O. D. and Richardson G. (editors), *Edinburgh—A Literary Anthology*. Edinburgh: Canongate, 1983.

Fraser, Antonia, *Mary, Queen of Scots*. London: Weidenfield & Nicolson, 1969.

Gallagher, Tom, *Edinburgh Divided*. Edinburgh: Polygon Books, 1987.

Glen, Duncan, *Makar's Walk*. Edinburgh: The Scottish Poetry Library, 1990.

Guthrie, Rev. Thomas, *Autobiography*. Edinburgh: William Isbister, 1873.

Henderson, Jan-Andrew, *The Town Below the Ground*. Edinburgh: Mainstream Publishing, 1999.

Knox, John *The History of the Reformation*. Edinburgh: Saltire Classic, 1957.

Lindop, Grevel, *The Opium Eater*. Oxford: Oxford University Press, 1981.

Lochead, Marion, *Edinburgh Lore and Legend*. London: Robert Hale, 1986.

MacGregor, Alasdair Alpin, *The Golden Lamp*. London: Methuen, 1964.

McKean, Charles, *Edinburgh: Portrait of a City*. London: Century, 1991.

Mackenzie, Agnes Mure, *The Kingdom of Scotland*. Edinburgh: W. & R. Chambers, 1940.

Maclaren, Moray, *The Capital of Scotland*. Edinburgh: Douglas & Foulis, 1950.

McLaren, J. Wilson, *Edinburgh Memories and Some Worthies*. Edinburgh: W. & R. Chambers, 1926.

Massie, Allan, *Edinburgh*. London: Sinclair-Stevenson, 1994.

Muir, Edwin, *An Autobiography*. London: The Hogarth Press, 1987.

North, Christopher (ed. J. H. Alexander) *The Tavern Sages*. Aberdeen: Association of Scottish Literary Studies, 1992.

Royle, Trevor, *Precipitous City*. Edinburgh: Mainstream, 1980.

Sleman, Francis, *Flesh and Bones: The Life, Passions and Legacies of John Napier*. Edinburgh: Napier Polytechnic, 1989.

Sillar, Eleanor, *Edinburgh's Child*. Edinburgh: Oliver & Boyd, 1961.

Smith, Charles J., *Historic South Edinburgh*. Edinburgh: Charles Skilton, 1978.

Stevenson, Robert Louis, *Edinburgh: Picturesque Notes*. London: Eveleigh, Nash & Grayson, 1900.

Youngson, A. J., *The Making of Classical Edinburgh*. Edinburgh: Edinburgh University Press, 1970.

Ten of the Best Edinburgh Novels

The Heart of Midlothian, Sir Walter Scott (1818)
Regarded by many as Scott's finest book, this is a superb evocation of Edinburgh's Old Town during its golden age. Simultaneously a study of a particular urban milieu and a critique of a society in which "the truth is dead", it features some of Scott's most vibrant and colorful characters.

Marriage, Susan Ferrier (1818)

This is the novel that earned for its author the title of "Scotland's Jane Austen". The story, set in Edinburgh and the surrounding countryside, is unremarkable, the novel's main strength lying in Ferrier's satirical humor. This is seen at its most effective in the portrait of an ancient and eccentric Edinburgh matron, Mrs. McShake.

St. Ives, Robert Louis Stevenson (1897)

An adventure story, in which the hero is a prisoner in Edinburgh Castle during the Napoleonic period, this is one of the few Stevenson novels to have an Edinburgh setting. Although unfinished at the time of the author's death, several attempts have been made to write an ending. The most successful of these is by Jenni Calder (Richard Drew Publishing, 1990).

The Drinking Well, Neil Gunn (1947)

Iain Cattanach, a Highland exile, comes to Edinburgh to serve an apprenticeship in a law office. The landscape of the city is used to underline his disillusion and his determination to return north to work on his father's sheep farm. There are some excellent Edinburgh scenes; the commercial life of the New Town, lodgings in the Southside, and one marvellous passage depicts the Royal Mile at midnight.

The Prime of Miss Jean Brodie, Muriel Spark (1962)

The novel for which Muriel Spark will always be remembered. A charismatic schoolteacher finds herself in trouble when she introduces her radical teaching methods in a school for "well-bred" girls. Miss Brodie, for all her idiosyncrasies, is totally believable, as is the setting, which provides a vivid picture of Edinburgh in the 1930s.

Three Novellas, John Herdman (1987)

Herdman is perhaps unique among Scottish writers in that he combines a wicked sense of humor with an extremely skillful prose style. These three stories examine the pretensions of the

Edinburgh middle-class with an engaging wit that is absolutely devastating.

Knots & Crosses, Ian Rankin (1987)

This is the first of the highly successful Inspector Rebus series. According to its author, it was not initially intended to be a crime thriller, but was rather an attempt to update *The Strange Case of Dr. Jekyll and Mr. Hyde*. The entirely authentic Edinburgh locations were used because, as a former student at the University and a resident of Marchmont, this was the environment he knew best.

The Other McCoy, Brian McCabe (1990)

One of the funniest novels to appear in Scotland for many years. While waiting for his big break—a five-minute spot on television's *Hogmanay Show*—a stand-up comic struggles to survive the Edinburgh winter.

Trainspotting, Irvine Welsh (1993)

No list of Edinburgh novels would be complete without Irvine Welsh's powerful treatment of the drugs scene. The story of a group of friends and their adventures with heroin is actually a rites-of-passage novel, surging with a raw energy that the author only occasionally manages to keep under control.

The Bone Yard, Paul Johnson (1998)

This is a nightmarish view of Edinburgh, set in the not-too-distant future. Johnson very cleverly uses the technique of the crime novel to express what is essentially a political viewpoint. The case is convincingly argued, although the author rather under-estimates the ability of the Edinburgh ethos to defy the ravages of history.

Index of Literary & Historical Names

Index of Places and Landmarks